W9-AUI-826

American Responses to the Holocaust

INTERAMERICANA
INTER-AMERICAN LITERARY HISTORY AND CULTURE
HISTORIA LITERARIA INTERAMERICANA Y SUS CONTEXTOS CULTURALES
HISTOIRE LITTERAIRE ET CULTURE INTERAMERICAINES

VOLUME 12

Notes on the quality assurance and
peer review of this publication:

Prior to publication, the quality of
the works published in this series
is reviewed by external referees
appointed by the editorship.

Hans Krabbendam / Derek Rubin (eds.)

American Responses to the Holocaust

Transatlantic Perspectives

Bibliographic Information published by the Deutsche Nationalbibliothek
The Deutsche Nationalbibliothek lists this publication in
the Deutsche Nationalbibliografie; detailed bibliographic
data is available in the internet at http://dnb.d-nb.de.

Library of Congress Cataloging-in-Publication Data
Names: Krabbendam, Hans, 1964- editor. | Rubin, Derek, 1954- editor.
Title: American responses to the Holocaust : transatlantic perspectives /
Hans Krabbendam, Derek Rubin (eds.).
Description: New York : Peter Lang, [2017] | Series: Interamericana ; Vol. 12
| Includes bibliographical references and index.
Identifiers: LCCN 2017006402 | ISBN 9783631719664
Subjects: LCSH: Holocaust, Jewish (1939-1945)—Foreign public opinion,
American. | Public opinion—United States. | Public opinion—United
States. | Jews—United States—Politics and government—20th century. |
Holocaust, Jewish (1939-1945) —Influence.
Classification: LCC D804.45.U55 A487 2017 | DDC 940.53/18—dc23 LC record
available at https://lccn.loc.gov/2017006402

Cover image:
The American flag flying at half-mast in Buchenwald.
United States Holocaust Memorial Museum, courtesy of Robert Pettit.

Printed by CPI books GmbH, Leck.

ISSN 1618-419X
ISBN 978-3-631-71966-4 (Print)
E-ISBN 978-3-631-72005-9 (E-PDF)
E-ISBN 978-3-631-72006-6 (EPUB)
E-ISBN 978-3-631-72007-3 (MOBI)
DOI 10.3726/b10961

© Peter Lang GmbH
Internationaler Verlag der Wissenschaften
Frankfurt am Main 2017
All rights reserved.
Peter Lang Edition is an Imprint of Peter Lang GmbH.

Peter Lang – Frankfurt am Main · Bern · Bruxelles · New York ·
Oxford · Warszawa · Wien

This publication has been peer reviewed.

www.peterlang.com

Table of Contents

Hans Krabbendam and Derek Rubin

Transatlantic Perspectives on American Responses to the Holocaust: An Introduction

The Holocaust figures large in American memory. The number of museums and research centers is growing and the Holocaust functions as a point of reference in debates about domestic issues, slavery and native Americans. Also outside the United States the American perspective circulates when new films, such as *Son of Saul* (2015) are released and new museums, such as the National Holocaust Memorial and Museum in the Netherlands are opening. Increasingly the trend of differentiation and multiplication of perspectives on the Holocaust are accepted. Researchers have acknowledged the use of the Holocaust as an instrument to serve political or economic goals, but also the opportunity to seriously examine universal human rights.[1] In Europe the Holocaust was framed as a symbol of evil that the European Community now has overcome. This may sound a bit too optimistic and celebratory, but reminds us that the Holocaust serves as a serious mode of reflection on the foundations needed to protect humanity. These two issues, the particular and the universal and the tension between the two is visible in the essays in this volume. They cover the dynamics of responses to the Holocaust from both sides of the Atlantic in which American and European perspectives interact, from the earliest moment on, when the first glimpses of the terror became public.

---

1   Peter Novick, *The Holocaust in American Life* (Boston: Houghton Mifflin, 1999); Peter Novick, *The Holocaust and Collective Memory: The American Experience* (London: Bloomsbury, 2001); Alan Mintz, *Popular Culture and the Shaping of Holocaust Memory in America* (Seattle: University of Washington Press, 2001); Hilene Flanzbaum, "The Americanization of the Holocaust," in Hilene Flanzbaum, ed., *The Americanization of the Holocaust* (Baltimore: Johns Hopkins University Press, 1999); Edward T. Linenthal, *Preserving Memory: The Struggle to Create America's Holocaust Museum* (New York: Viking Press, 1995); Lawrence Baron, "The Holocaust and American Public Memory, 1945–1960," *Holocaust and Genocide Studies* 17.1 (2003): 62–88; Alvin H. Rosenfeld, "The Americanization of the Holocaust," *Commentary* 99. 6 (June 1995): 35–40; Daniel Levy and Natan Sznaider, *The Holocaust and Memory in the Global Age* (Philadelphia: Temple University Press, 2006); Martin L. Davies and Claus-Christian W. Szejnmann, eds., *How the Holocaust Looks Now: International Perspectives* (New York: Palgrave, 2006), xxiii.

All essays revolve around American responses. When Hilene Flanzbaum complained in 1999 about the "Americanization of the Holocaust" he meant something different from similar European complaints. Europeans used the term to reject sensationalist exploitation of the Holocaust, ascribed to the dominance of American products of popular culture. Flanzbaum had an inside view. He deplored the lack of solid knowledge about the Holocaust in America, the replacement of real knowledge by sanitized versions of the horrors and the downplaying of the Jewish factor in these representations. In a way this was inevitable since the Holocaust was experienced indirectly and mediation had to take place. Flanzbaum described that the American Jewish community had the means and the motives to commemorate and inform, and had to stay distinct against pressures of adaptation to the public ways of media. These factors, the strong interest, the strong means of mediation propelled a heated debate. Though these debates delayed the completion of monuments and museums, they deepened reflection on Holocaust memory.

Peter Novick deplored this strong presence of the Holocaust in American consciousness, because it revealed a pathology in American society: it defined the Jews as victims, and curtailed a mature understanding of the Holocaust. The uniqueness of the Holocaust was broadened to have a universalist implication in support of other victims. For Jews in America the memory of the Holocaust combined a particular and a universal feature: it gave them a separate identity in the country and connected them with global moral issues. While Americans might find this acceptable because it suited their own needs, voices of rejection have become more critical of commercial popularization and commodification, moving towards trivialization. In the first 15 years after the end of World War II the return of soldiers, the arrival of victims, and the Eichmann trial a wave of articles and books cast the survivor in the role of the hero.

Other voices are less pessimistic, in 1990, Michael Berenbaum argued that Americanization of the Holocaust connects the history of the Holocaust to American debates "about pluralism, tolerance, democracy, and human rights that America tells about itself."[2] Behind these debates about mediation lies the concern that these acts and products normalize the horrendous event. This concern subjects each new contribution to a moral inspection, and is suspicious of the automatism that each victim going public becomes a celebrity. Connecting the Holocaust to other phenomena risks stripping the language of meaning.

---

2   Michael Berenbaum, *After Tragedy and Triumph: Modern Jewish Thought and the American Experience* (Cambridge: Cambridge University Press, 1990), 20.

As the Holocaust grew into an omnipresent event in American culture, it also became a subject of American studies, both as a window on internal trends and as a topic to which outsiders responded. The present collection makes this kind of debate the core of its investigation by putting what has traditionally been the focus of Jewish Studies and Holocaust studies in a new American studies perspective. This perspective emphasizes a comparative approach that looks at the similarities and differences between responses in Europe and the United States, and the transatlantic interaction. When Americans responded to information on the early signs of the Holocaust, they were dependent on European sources; they received official and informal responses, some were confirmed, others were contradicted; some were ignored, others provoked a response. This book follows the chronology of this transatlantic exchange, which begins with the debate whether or not the American authorities turned a cold shoulder to European Jews. This alleged abandonment of the Jews in Europe created a contrast with the post-war attention for the Holocaust victims.

Jeffrey Demsky revisits the opposition to Nazi Anti-Semitism and the Holocaust in America. He claims that historians writing about this theme have often felt reluctant to introduce fresh theories, methods, and data, which blocked the view on a countermovement of voices criticizing Nazi atrocities, which was much stronger than assumed. The evidence of domestic anti-Semitism and xenophobia built up to an image of American similarity to Europe's lack of defiance to the Nazi threat, narrowing the gap between Europe and America, as both were guilty of avoiding responsibility. Demsky turns away from an exclusive concentration on executive decisions and public opinion, and includes legislative initiatives. His essay is a plea to look for counter examples to American isolationism/nativism; and they can be found. While unsuccessful in turning the tide for Jews seeking asylum, the Dickstein committee did succeed in putting Nazi propaganda on the table. Later the Federal Information Office spread information brochures on Anti-Semitism and atrocities. Exposing Nazi bigotry and contrasting it with American liberty served to build support for the war and encouraged a broader concern for human rights.

Closely related to this issue, and even more laden with moral indignation, is the Allies governments' failure to stop the Holocaust by military interventions in 1944. Jan Láníček enters this debate with a detailed analysis of the reception and publication of the most extensive report on the Holocaust which escaped Jews brought to the allies in 1944. These stories were the very first eyewitness reports on the situation in Auschwitz-Birkenau. Láníček places the response of the US and the UK governments in a broader perspective. Their primary concern was to achieve a military victory, which they saw as the only way to liberate the Nazi victims, and they would not spare military equipment for humanitarian intervention. Some historians have suggested a causal link between popular anti-Semitism and failing policies. Without suggesting this direct link Láníček shows that the authorities took into account public opinion that did not favor the Jews, and were hesitant about concentrating too exclusively on the fate of the Jews, which might reduce broad support for the war. Moreover, they were careful of accepting these atrocity reports too easily and they were concerned for the safety of their POWs. Both transatlantic allied partners shared these concerns that delayed the release of the eyewitness report, until it hit the American press when the camps were approached by Russian troops.

The theme of speaking or keeping silent continued after the war. Hasia Diner challenges the widespread myth that survivors who came to America did not want to share their experiences. Diner richly documents her claim that survivors were not passive recipients of American benefactors, but actively shared their survival stories and participated in small-scale memorials. In the 1980s, oral history projects and other organized initiatives to document the Holocaust were started and the 1960s baby boom generation challenged the first generation of survivors, feeding the idea that the previous generation had remained passive. But in fact, the new generation belonged to established American Jewish organizations or created new programs, acting in public to call attention to other displaced persons and to demand compensation or restitution of lost possessions. Also the new generation demonstrated its frontal opposition to expressions of anti-Semitism in the US in the 1960s, challenging the common Jewish American approach of restraint.

Simultaneously, American Jewish organizations focused their attention on Europe in order to give humanitarian assistance to Jewish communities, as Laura Hobson Faure explains in her essay on France. American Jewry was in a process towards full integration in American society and benefited from the increased empathy after the Shoah. Philanthropy often bridged the gap between different Jewish factions, by cooperating in the United Jewish Appeal and the Joint Distribution Committee for fundraising and distribution. However, ideological and class divisions still permeated in the "Jewish Marshall plan". After about a decade the organizations realized that they needed to cooperate. This helped build consensus and led to cooperation and centralization, without erasing all characteristics of the original organizations. This transatlantic endeavor reflected the prosperity of American Jews, their efficiency and skills in social programming, which they applied in France and which brought them closer together at home.

The same process of cooperation is visible in the World Jewish Congress (WJC), which contemporaries and researchers alike have taken as a purely Zionist project ran by Americans, but which in fact embraced a global agenda and promoted the return of Jewish refugees to their home countries, as Zohar Segev argues. By actively supporting the restoration of Jewish communities in the European diaspora, American Jews justified their own choice of remaining in the US, next to the Zionist ideal of resettling in Palestine. American Jewish support for European Jews created a clear role for American Jews that broke the potential monopoly of the state of Israel as the sole guardian of Jewish rights. The status of the WJC was in fact recognized by the UN. Ironically, the efforts of its humanitarian action strengthened American Jewry more than Jewish life in post-Holocaust Europe, which had suffered more than the WJC could restore. The transatlantic relation was crucial, but its main effect was strengthening the worldwide unity of the Jewish community.

David Frey and Viktoria Sukovata's essays elaborate on the dire situation of Jews in Eastern Europe. Frey describes how, less than a decade after the Holocaust, a series of large-scale expropriations and evictions of the heavily Jewish Budapest middle-class in 1951 proved that the human rights provisions in the Hungarian constitution were hard to maintain. These clauses were a result of the peace treaties after World War II, but were violated after the Communist take-over. The American Legation in Budapest and the State Department set up a program to collect evidence of human rights violations in Hungary, Romania, and Bulgaria. Frey argues that this legal evidence from hundreds of Hungarians, who were re-settled by virtually the same methods as the Nazi's had used, stirred a debate that was the opposite of a "Holocaust silence" in the early postwar period. Eventually even the highest levels of the Hungarian government entered the debate, claiming that the evicted were class enemies who also threatened the future of the Jews.

On the other side of the Atlantic the US used these stories to show that the postwar oppression in Communist regimes paralleled the Nazi regime. But in America there were also similarities as US officials protested against Hungarian deportations, but could not do anything to prevent them or help the victims. History seemed to repeat itself, except that this time the refugees went to Israel. This explosion of anti-Semitic feelings in Hungary politicized Holocaust memory by establishing a link with global human rights issues.

On a larger geographical level, Viktoria Sukovata explains why the US and the USSR were worlds apart in defining the nature of the Holocaust. America joined the war late, did not fight on its own soil, and suffered relatively few casualties. Its experience of the Holocaust was largely based on the stories of survivors who immigrated to start new lives. In the American perspective, therefore, the Jews were at the center of the Nazi horrors. The Red Army, on the other hand, liberated its own territory littered with concentration camps; and the war losses were enormous, both in the number of soldiers and in civilians. Moreover, the fate of the Soviet Prisoners of War was almost as gloomy as that of Jews in ghettos, and Slavic civilians who were hiding Jews, shared their fate on discovery.

Soviet reporters were the first to record and expose the atrocities, and initially the shock of the fate of Jews penetrated into mainstream culture. In the course of the 50s and 70s, however, further dissemination was suppressed, because it might hurt the Soviet state. The official view focussed on the victory of the Soviet Army which had conquered the Nazis who would have used the Slavic population as 'slaves'. Focussing specifically on the Jewish experience would have hurt the 'international solidarity' in the Soviet empire. Cold War distrust preserved and strengthened the difference in perspective. Political change, the end of the Cold War, brought the specific Judeo centric and the broad perspective of the Holocaust together.[3] These changes show how current pressures shaped the interpretation of the Holocaust. This was also visible in the artistic domain.

Emiliano Perra analyses the Italian debates on "the Americanization of the Holocaust". He stipulates that the political situation in the country in which miniseries and films are shown, determines whether they are severely criticized for being Americanized. In Cold War Italy the Communist Party was especially wary of the American emphasis on individual stories and emotionalism. The lack of political analysis in the miniseries *Holocaust*, for instance, might lead to comparisons between the Third Reich and the Soviet model of totalitarianism. Fifteen years later, *Schindler's List*, generated very little debate, since the political situation had relaxed. The Italian film *Life is Beautiful* stimulated heated debate, partly because of its use of comedy, and partly because criticizing the film was a way of attacking the contemporary Italian government. The miniseries *Perlasca*, on the other hand, emphasized national qualities and appealed to a broad political spectrum; therefore its American features triggered little discussion. In each case the transatlantic political relations were a defining factor on Americanization of the Holocaust in the sense of trivialization.

Dana Rufolo discusses four theater plays about the Holocaust, two by American and two by Austrian playwrights. The American dramas use the Holocaust to

---

3   Against the individual experience that was highly appreciated in the US and the SU put
     a collective one. See also, Linda Jacobs Altman, *The Forgotten Victims of the Holocaust*
     (Berkeley Heights, NJ: Enslow, 2003).

comment on American values—Tony Kushner's *A Bright Room called Day*—or invite the audience to identify with the altruism or intelligence of the characters, rather than with the Holocaust experience—Arthur Miller's *Incident at Vichy*.

The two Austrian plays deal with the country's own war heritage. For decades there was silence on Austrian participation in Anti-Semitic Nazism, but since the 80s, "voices of Austrian conscience" can be heard and seen on stage. One of the reasons why the Austrian public is now prepared to be critical of its own heritage, is because the plays do not only portray characters who behave despicably, but also altruistic characters who therefore appear to be redemptive. The characters in *Heldenplatz* are so burdened by the past, that they are killed by it; *Jedem das Seine* presents the audience with a musical that is rehearsed by Jewish captives together with their Austrian captors. By presenting this communal effort, and by suggesting that all the characters die in a fire beyond their controleven though in reality the captors may well have been co-responsible for this firet—he play stresses the common Austrian identity of all the characters, thus mitigating the feeling of guilt.

Comparing these plays leads to the impression that between America and Europe there is a great divide: direct experience of Holocaust and the national consciousness of collective guilt. For Americans the Holocaust has not been a direct assault on their faith in humanity, rather America is exempt from this taint of insane emotions; therefore the American plays focus on moral dilemmas or contemporary issues. The Austrian plays constitute an acknowledgement that their society is capable of racism, and of turning upon its own members, even if this acknowledgement is softened by the presence of redemptive characters in the plays. A play that Rufolo mentions for comparison—*Broken Glass* by Arthur Miller—is the strongest example of the transatlantic perspective, as it shows the effect of the Holocaust on American Jewry.

The final essay explores the transition from individual experience to collective memory mediated by the mass media. Małgorzata Pakier returns to 1953 when the broadcast of Hanna Kohner's story was the first instance of televising the Holocaust experience. The narrative celebrated triumph over tragedy, as it was a story of a survivor, including a romance and a happy ending. Its significance was only appreciated decades later. It became part of the imaginative project of one person whose shared memories created a publicly accessible artefact of a traumatic experience. These public representations created a communal cultural memory that in turn influenced the personal memories and narratives of the survivors, leading Hanna to describe herself as a victim in her memoires thirty years later, a role she had resisted in the TV show. Comparable with the psychological process in which children adopt their parents memories, through a filter of their own experiences and framework, later generations formed their memory of the Holocaust through a mixture of the personal narratives of the survivors and the public cultural form the media has cast these in.

Following the chronology of transatlantic responses to the Holocaust, we can conclude that there was no transatlantic silence during World War II, although native Anti-Semitism and other concerns delayed and downplayed the distribution of information. Neither did Jewish organizations or the American government restrain their responses to the Holocaust during the first decades after the war. The aid to the direct victims of the Holocaust, the so-called "Jewish Marshall plan" intended to rebuild the Jewish communities in Europe, but in effect united and strengthened American Jewry itself, and created a worldwide Jewish community, which provided an alternative to Zionism.

The perspective in Eastern Europe was different from Western Europe. Though during the war the news about the Shoah spread in Eastern Europe, soon after the liberation new waves Anti-Semitism caused repeatedly new outburst of repression, while the new political constellation of Soviet-dominated states battled against special attention to the Jewish victims out of fear for comparisons of totalitarian methods and for disturbing the solidarity among its international population. Americans felt as handtied as during the war.

After the war the modern mass media spread the American perspective through cultural expressions. Its production of films and television series generalized the uniqueness of the Holocaust into stories of individual moral choices or of human rights issues. In time these mass media cultural "translations" may shape personal and historical memories. Yet, transatlantic differences will remain visible as the older genre of theater plays, which elicited a tighter bond with audiences, shows. American plays often shared the characteristics of films, while European plays attempted to come to terms with feelings of guilt over the war past. In conclusion, these essays show that the dynamics of the transatlantic responses to the Holocaust and to each other contribute to a richer repertoire of reflection and the continued relevance of this attention for today.

Jeffrey Demsky

Going Public In Support: Reconsidering American Public Discourse About Nazi Anti-Semitism and the Holocaust

Abstract: *This essay revisits the alleged lack of American opposition to Nazi Anti-Semitism and the disclosure of the Holocaust. Historians have often felt reluctant to introduce fresh theories, methods, and data. This attitude blocked the view on a countermovement of voices criticizing Nazi atrocities, which was much stronger than assumed.*

Introduction

In the late 1960s and early 1970s scholars began publishing studies critical of the United States' response to Nazi anti-Semitism and the Holocaust.[1] Their findings, that government officials could have, and should have, taken a more forceful stand against Nazi prejudice has become an integral part of the country's collective memory. Institutions of remembrance from Washington D.C. to California teach students that while the Nazis and their collaborators bear guilt for having implemented a racially-motivated program of murder, Americans also share moral responsibility for having been so-called bystanders to the genocide.[2] The wider significance of this finding is that moral indignation, focused on what more

---

1   Saul Friedman, *No Haven for the Oppressed: United States Policy toward Jewish Refugees, 1938–1945* (Detroit, MI: Wayne State Press, 1973), 328; Henry Feingold, *The Politics of Rescue The Roosevelt Administration and the Holocaust, 1938–1945* (New Brunswick, NJ: Rutgers University Press, 1970), 15; David Wyman, *Paper Walls: America and the Refugee Crisis, 1938–41* (Amherst, MA: University of Massachusetts Press, 1968), 10–14; Arthur Morse, *While Six Million Died: A Chronicle of American Apathy* (New York: Random House, 1968), 38–42.

2   Theodore Hamerow, *Why We Watched: Europe, America, and the Holocaust* (New York: W.W. Norton, 2008); 389; Steven Baum, *The Psychology of Genocide: Perpetrators, Bystanders, and Rescuers* (New York: Cambridge University Press, 2008), 124; David Cesarani, "Mad Dogs and Englishmen: Toward a Taxonomy of Rescuers in a 'Bystander' Country-Britain 1933–45," in David Cesarani and Paul A. Levine, eds., *Bystanders to the Holocaust: A Re-evaluation* (Portland, OR: Frank Cass, 2002), 28–56; Raul Hilberg, *Perpetrators, Victims and Bystanders: The Jewish Catastrophe, 1933–1945* (New York: Asher, 1992), 253; Deborah Lipstadt, "Witness to the Persecution: The Allies and the Holocaust," *Modern Judaism* 3 (1983): 323.

might have been done, sometimes trumps historical inquiry about the steps that were taken to help.

The so-called American abandonment of the Jews reflects a deeper truth.[3] Following World War I, a legacy of diplomatic isolationism gripped the US. In 1924, Congress passed by a wide margin, and President Calvin Coolidge signed into law, legislation establishing a quota system limiting immigration into the US.[4] These were the "paper walls" that enabled bureaucrats to restrict undesirable visa applicants. The National Origins Act affected a wide range of potential immigrants—Southern, Central, and Eastern Europeans—and completely banned Asians. While Jews were not singled out for proscription, concerns about their continued migration played a role in the new regulations' appearance. The law's co-sponsor, Albert Johnson (R-WA), spoke directly to this issue. Citing data from an American consuls' report, he shared with his colleagues apprehensions that several hundred thousands "Polish subjects of the Hebrew race…were anxious to emigrate to America immediately."[5] Owing to the period's prevalent nativist mindsets, one that held European Jews were most likely Bolshevists hoping to radicalize the US, such reports took on increased importance.

Such xenophobic attitudes persisted into the subsequent decade. During the 1930s, the combination of the Great Depression and the memory of World War I losses pushed American public opinion and policy toward isolationism. While isolationism and nativism were not identical, the two mentalities shared a belief that the US should steer clear of all things foreign. Americans faced their own challenges. Particularly this was true in a decade where the citizens' recorded unemployment rates hovered between fifteen and twenty five percent.[6] Beginning in 1935 and continuing until 1939, Congress passed a series of Neutrality Acts to prevent Americans' entanglement in overseas disputes. Though oriented toward

---

3 Alexander Groth, *Accomplices: Churchill, Roosevelt, and the Holocaust* (New York: Peter Lang, 2011), 1; Frank Brecher, "David Wyman and the Historiography of America's Response to the Holocaust: Counter-Considerations," *Holocaust and Genocide Studies* 5 (1990): 423; David Wyman, *The Abandonment of the Jews: America and the Holocaust, 1942–1945* (New York: Pantheon, 1984), 340; Herbert Druks, *The Failure to Rescue* (New York: Speller, 1977), 98.

4 Jeffrey Demsky, "Immigration and the Nazi Era," in Patrick Hayes, ed., *The Making of Modern Immigration: An Encyclopedia of Ideas* vol. 1 (Santa Barbara: ABC CLIO, 2012), 372.

5 As quoted in Mae Ngai, *Impossible Subjects: Illegal Aliens and the Making Of Modern America* (Princeton, NJ: Princeton University Press, 2004), 19–20.

6 Ira Katznelson, *Fear Itself: The New Deal and the Origins Of Our Time* (New York: Liveright Publishing Corporation, 2013), 244.

trade rather than immigration issues, the laws bolstered earlier nativist legislation, establishing an extra layer of insularity that ensured more than just an ocean
helped separate America from Europe.[7]

Added to this is a somewhat more disturbing explanation for Americans' dis-
interest in Nazi goings on, and specifically their intensified persecution of Jews.
Just as some Ku Klux Klan leaders had successfully unpacked anti-Semitic messages during the twenties, domestic voices again stoked these impulses during the
thirties. William Dudley Pelley was an unabashed bigot who believed that Jews
should be removed from Christian societies. Shortly after Hitler's rise to power,
he founded the so-called Silver Shirts Legion, a nationwide organization with
fifteen thousand members at its peak strength.[8] Father Charles Coughlin, the
popular radio priest, also peddled sermons that employed anti-Semitic rationales
to explain national suffering.[9] Domestic mistrust of Jews, and admiration for
Nazism, achieved its most conspicuous form in February 1939, when more than
twenty thousand German sympathizers convened in New York City to honor "true
patriot" white gentiles. Speakers at this session dazzled the crowd with orations
favorably comparing Adolf Hitler to George Washington.[10] Such events may not
have matched the sway known to hooded Klansmen marching on the Capitol
fifteen years before, but they indicate that pockets of domestic intolerance for
Jews and other non-Protestant minorities continued to exist.

It was from this churning of nativist, isolationist, and anti-Semitic mindsets
that the "angry days" of the early 1940s took their form.[11] America First Committee spokesman Charles Lindbergh personified this conflation. His September
1941 Des Moines speech about "war agitators" reinforced fears of a foreign Jewish
cabal seeking to undermine Christian American values, in this sense expressed
through isolationist preferences.[12] Such statements not only betrayed Lindbergh's

---

7   C. Paul Vincent, "The Voyage of the St. Louis Revisited," *Holocaust and Genocide Studies*
    25 (2011): 252–253; Steven Wall, "Neutrality and Responsibility," *Journal of Philosophy*
    98 (2001): 390; Guerra Everett, "The Neutrality Act of 1939," *Annals of the American
    Academy of Political and Social Science* 211 (1940): 95.

8   Leo Ribuffo, *The Old Christian Right: The Protestant Far Right from the Great Depression
    to the Cold War* (Philadelphia, PA: Temple University Press, 1983), 64.

9   Alan Brinkley, *Voices of Protest: Huey Long, Father Coughlin, and the Great Depression*
    (New York: Knopf, 1982), 266.

10 Francis MacDonnell, *Insidious Foes: The Axis Fifth Column and the American Home
    Front* (New York: Oxford University Press, 1995), 45.

11 Lynne Olson, *Those Angry Days: Roosevelt, Lindbergh, and America's Fight Over World
    War II, 1939–1941* (New York: Random House, 2013), 364.

12 Ibid., 390.

conclusions about a so-called Jewish monolith, but they also encapsulated the types of domestic rationales that scholars would later point to when forming their arguments about the American "abandonment." Although Lindbergh and his supporters articulated a minority position, one that quickly dissipated following US entry into World War II, residue of their out-of-hand rejections to support foreign Jews rendered problematic later calls for American involvement in combating the Nazis' program of murder.

Since these arguments first appeared, scholars who specialize in American reactions to Nazi anti-Semitism have uncovered examples of this indifference toward Jewish well being among government officials,[13] social commentators,[14] and ordinary citizens.[15] Even the authors of those studies that assert the United States could not have done more to combat Nazi anti-Semitism and the Holocaust, nevertheless acknowledge the damaging prevalence of American bigotry.[16] Such a preponderance of evidence has had a powerful effect on scholars' thinking. It not only influences the way professors teach the chronology, it also shapes their thinking when forming new inquiries. The primary result of this dominant narrative, perhaps unwittingly, is that researchers who specialize in American reactions to the Holocaust are reluctant to introduce fresh theories, methods, and data. In the absence of such innovations the debate remains conspicuously stagnant.

Such tendencies though powerful, are not, however, intractable. This essay offers a history that does not begin with the premise that Americans abandoned

---

13   Michael Marrus, *The Unwanted: European Refugees From the First World War Through the Cold War* (Philadelphia, PA: Temple University Press, 2002), 284; Joseph Bendersky, *The Jewish Threat: Anti-Semitic Politics of the US Army* (New York: Basic Books, 2000), 14; Richard Breitman, *Official Secrets: What the Nazis Planned, What the British and Americans Knew* (New York: Hill and Wang, 1998), 182.

14   S. T. Joshi, *Mencken's America* (Athens, OH: Ohio University Press, 2004), 145; Matthew Bruccoli, *Fitzgerald and Hemingway: A Dangerous Friendship* (London, UK: Andre Deutsch, 1994), 34.

15   Susan Welch, "American Opinion Toward Jews During the Nazi Era: Results from Quota Sample Polling During the 1930s and 1940s," *Social Science Quarterly* 95 (2014): 615–635; Victoria Saker Woeste, "Insecure Equality: Louis Marshall, Henry Ford, and the Problem of Defamatory Anti-Semitism, 1920–29," *Journal of American History* 91 (2004): 877–878.

16   Robert Rosen, *Saving the Jews: FDR and the Holocaust* (New York: Thunder's Mouth, 2006), 39, 115; Peter Novick, *The Holocaust in American Life* (New York: Houghton Mifflin, 1999), 51, 256; William Rubenstein, *The Myth of Rescue: Why the Democracies Could Not Have Done More to Save the Jews from the Nazis* (New York: Routledge, 1997), 36.

European Jewry. My approach is not an apologia. Rather, this study engages and complements the ongoing intellectual movement away from the "abandonment" perspective.[17] Scholars now present evidence of Christian Americans' concern for European Jews,[18] a humanitarian sentiment some trace directly to the Oval Office.[19] Not surprisingly, this revisionism does not convince those who continue to believe that Christian American antipathies scuttled rescue initiative, and that Franklin Roosevelt allegedly shared these biases.[20] Although important, these sorts of questions rest outside of my research focus. In terms of methodological innovation, debates about which figures were, or were not, prejudiced add little new perspective. Instead, the innovation I am recommending relates primarily to new source selection, which may in turn provide a more contextualized understanding of policies as imperfect as the times during which they were made.

Specifically, I would like to push inquiries beyond executive branch renditions. Focusing on the executive branch is common to nearly every published study on the topic.[21] This approach is reasonable since the US Constitution assigns primary

---

17 Joseph Bendersky, "Dissension in the Face of the Holocaust: The 1941 American Debate Over Anti-Semitism," *Holocaust and Genocide Studies* 24 (2010): 93; Sarah Pinnock, "Atrocity and Ambiguity: Recent Developments in Christian Holocaust Responses," *Journal of the American Academy of Religion* 75 (2007): 514; Tony Kushner, "'Pissing in the Wind?' The Search for Nuance in the Study of Holocaust 'Bystanders,'" in Cesarani and Levine, eds., *Bystanders*, 61.

18 Susan Elisabeth Subak, *Rescue and Flight: American Relief Workers Who Defied the Nazis* (Lincoln, NE: University of Nebraska Press, 2010), 3; Caitlin Carenen, "The American Christian Palestine Committee, the Holocaust, and Mainstream Protestant Zionism, 1938–1948," *Holocaust and Genocide Studies* 24 (2010): 273–296; Carla Mc Clafferty, *In Defiance of Hitler: The Secret Mission of Varion Fry* (New York: Farrar Straus Giroux, 2008), 14; James G. McDonald, Richard Breitman, Barbara McDonald Stewart, Severin Hochberg, *Advocate For the Doomed* (Bloomington, IN: Indiana University Press, 2007), 3.

19 Edward Shapiro, "FDR and the Holocaust," Review of Rafael Medoff, *FDR and the Holocaust: A Breach of Faith*, in *Society* 51 (2014): 302–306, here 303; Richard Breitman and Alan Lichtman, *FDR and the Jews* (Cambridge, MA: The Belknap Press of Harvard University Press, 2013), 59, 116; Gulie Ne'eman Arad, *America, Its Jews, and the Rise of Nazism* (Bloomington, IN: Indiana University Press, 2000), 129.

20 Rafael Medoff, "American Responses to the Holocaust, New Research, New Controversies," *American Jewish History* 100 (2016): 385; For contrary charges, that Roosevelt was a closeted-Jew, see Glen Jeansonne, *Gerald L. K. Smith: Minister of Hate* (New Haven, CT: Yale University Press, 1988), 80.

21 For example, Robert Shogun, *Prelude To Catastrophe: FDR's Jews and the Menace of Nazism* (Chicago, IL: Ivan R. Dee, 2010); 139; Melissa Jane Taylor, "Bureaucratic Response

responsibility for the handling of foreign affairs issues to the executive and its bureaucracy, and in this regard, the State Department holds particular sway. Nevertheless, scholars' over-reliance on executive branch archives sows a circular methodology in which their conclusions are predetermined by sourcing. Widening the locus of inquiry can lessen this tendency. The American government is a shared-powers system. While each component of the executive-legislative-judicial triad retains specific areas of responsibility, officials in each branch exercise so-called checks on their governing partners. This practice facilitates institutional communication, and allows those officials outside the direct policy making body to signal their concerns and preferences.[22]

With regard to the question of American responses to the Holocaust, welcoming legislative voices into the conversation will inject fresh air into a debate that has become one-dimensional and flat. The US Congress possesses significant foreign policy powers. During the thirties and forties, members used floor statements to raise awareness levels on the issue of Nazi anti-Semitism. They offered resolutions recommending new policies. Congressmen held committee hearings, subpoened witnesses, and issued reports explaining why Nazi anti-Semitism threatened all Americans. Lawmakers, or *representatives*, are required to perform oversight on behalf of their constituents' concerns. They are perhaps the governmental officials most sensitive to public attitudes due to the electoral pressures associated with their short tenures.

The *Congressional Record*—a verbatim listing of all lawmakers' utterances— houses a wealth of data regarding officials' reactions to Nazi anti-Semitism. To date, it is largely unexamined. While there is some existing published work about the role of Congress in the discussion of European Jews, the authors of these studies mainly exist to demonstrate that lawmakers joined their inter-branch

to Human Tragedy: American Consuls and the Jewish Plight in Vienna, 1938–1941," *Holocaust and Genocide Studies* 21 (2007): 243–267; Richard Breitman et al., *U.S. Intelligence and the Nazis* (Cambridge, UK: Cambridge University Press, 2005), 4–5; Monty Noam Penkower, *The Jews Were Expendable: Free World Diplomacy And The Holocaust* (Urbana, IL: University of Illinois Press, 1983).

22 James Thurber, "An Introduction to Presidential-Congressional Rivalry," in Thurber, ed., *Rivals for Power: Presidential-Congressional Relations* (Lantham, MD: Rowman and Littlefield, 2013), 1–26; Charles O. Jones, *Separate But Equal Branches: Congress and the Presidency* (New York: Chatham House, 1999), 67; Louis Fisher, *The Politics of Shared Power: Congress and the Executive* 4th ed. (College Station, TX: Texas A&M University Press, 1998), 213.

colleagues in *ignoring* European Jewish suffering.[23] I would like to consider this data more thoroughly. Within weeks of Hitler becoming Germany's chancellor, a robust congressional discourse emerged. Some lawmakers denounced Nazi hostility to democratic values. Others specifically condemned their anti-Semitism. At times, these strains overlapped and it is not possible to identify what motivated a person's outrage. These discursive expressions of defiance, however, shared one recurring theme: Americans must combat—not placate—bigotry both overseas and at home.[24]

Such arguments may have belied a deeper purpose. After all Americans, too, have a heritage of ethno-racial hostilities. Jim Crowism and Nazism were not the same things.[25] But by going public in support of persecuted German minorities, pluralist-minded lawmakers could signal their preferences on a range of related issues. Words matter. Language cannot be undone. Skeptics might characterize this activity as boosterism, or rhetoric. However, if enough verbiage exists, and the embedded rationales persist over time, I submit that they constitute a compelling conversation that requires later generations to take notice. Statements discrediting Hitlerism are not significant because they helped save lives, or changed the course of history. Rather, the language is worthy of our attention because it contradicts the canons of the academic debate that has set the contours for Holocaust memorialization.

Once we free ourselves of a vision of the 1930s as a period of pervasive, unchecked hostility toward minorities, and move beyond studying government

---

23 Robert Beir, *Roosevelt and the Holocaust: A Rooseveltian Examines the Policies and Remembers the Times* (New York: Barricade Books, 2006), 72, 259; Katznelson, *Fear*, 21, 39; Edward Shapiro, "The Approach of War: Congressional Isolationism and Anti-Semitism," *American Jewish History* 74 (1984): 49, 55; Sarah Peck, "The Campaign for an American Response to the Nazi Holocaust," *Journal of Contemporary History* 15 (1980): 368.

24 Cheryl Jorgensen-Earp, *Discourse and Defiance Under Nazi Occupation: Guernsey, Channel Islands, 1940–1945* (East Lansing, MI: Michigan State University Press, 2013), 6; Tom Lawson, "Shaping the Holocaust: The Influence of Christian Discourse on Perceptions of the European Jewish Tragedy," *Holocaust and Genocide Studies* 21 (2007): 404–420; Theodore Blumoff, "The Holocaust and Public Discourse," *Journal of Law and Religion* 11 (1994–95): 595.

25 Dan J. Puckett, "Reporting on the Holocaust: The View from Jim Crow Alabama," *Holocaust and Genocide Studies* 25 (2011): 219–251; J.P.H. Grill and Robert Jenkins, "The Nazis and the American South in the 1930s: A Mirror Image?" *Journal of Southern History* 58 (1992): 668–671; Leland Bell, "The Failure of Nazism in America: The German American *Bund*, 1936–1941," *Political Science Quarterly* 85 (1970): 585–599.

officials who displayed personal and professional biases, we learn new stories. Moving beyond traditional ideas about executive branch failures allows us to consider the ways in which speaking up for Jews reflected the period's creedal attitudes, and signaled what would become a wider social effort to marginalize prejudice.[26] Rather than exclusively noting the activities of those who persistently held negative sentiments toward ethnic, racial, and religious minorities, we should explore the tension between the two different historical reconstructions. We already know much about those Americans that turned away their faces; we need to learn more about those who saw in their repudiation of Nazi anti-Semitism an opportunity to uphold values that the nations' founders and inheritors claimed to cherish.

Congress Begins a Public Discourse Condemning Nazi Anti-Semitism

It is true that State Department diplomats,[27] Immigration and Naturalization Service bureaucrats,[28] and even some White House officials displayed profound indifference to reports of Nazi anti-Semitism.[29] This finding, however, does not encompass every mindset across the entire US government. Pockets of concern for Jews appeared in the legislature soon after the Nazi regime emerged.[30] While it is important not to overstate the significance of these voices, they were present throughout the thirties and forties, and may have influenced

---

26 Christine Knauer, *Let Us Fight as Free Men: Black Soldiers and Civil Rights* (Philadelphia, PA: University of Pennsylvania Press, 2014), 4; Stephen Whitfield, "The Theme of Indivisibility in the Post-War Struggle Against Prejudice In the United States," *Patterns of Prejudice* 48 (2014): 235; William Ross, "The Role of Religion in the Defeat of the 1937 Court-Packing Plan," *Journal of Law and Religion* 23 (2007–08): 643; Robert Fleegler, "Theodore Bilbo and the Decline of Public Racism, 1938–1947," *Journal of Mississippi History* 68 (2006): 1–3.

27 Max Paul Friedman, "The US State Department and the Failure to Rescue: New Evidence on the Missed Opportunity at Bergen-Belsen," *Holocaust and Genocide Studies* 19 (2005): 26–50.

28 Richard Breitman and Alan Kraut, *American Refugee Policy and European Jewry, 1933–1945* (Bloomington, IN: Indiana University Press, 1987), 136.

29 Rafael Medoff, *FDR and the Holocaust: A Breach of Faith* (Washington, DC: David S. Wyman Institute for Holocaust Studies, 2013), 6.

30 Rafael Medoff identifies a "small but vocal group." See *Blowing the Whistle On Genocide: Josiah E. Dubois, Jr., And The Struggle For A US Response To The Holocaust* (West Lafayette, IN: Purdue University, 2009), 6.

President Roosevelt's eventual decision to create a War Refugee Board to manage American relief efforts.[31]

The exact number of legislators involved is difficult to quantify. The *Congressional Record* indexes the categories "Jews" and "Germany" yet it contains no floor statements under the category of "Jews"—in fact, no such category existed—during the Seventy-second Congress (1931–32). By 1933–34, however, as Adolf Hitler gained power, there were nearly fifty remarks or resolutions in which Judaism was addressed. In 1935, nearly forty more instances were recorded. Lawmakers that stirred on this issue represented differing regions, religions, and political parties. A theme connecting their remarks was that Hitlerism—and its hallmark anti-Semitism—was un-American. Since the House of Representatives provides the most credible record of open debate in the United States, these utterances may be said to have captured a nascent American discourse on the threat. Rather than turning away it would seem, once Adolf Hitler had seized power in Germany, some members of Congress quickly recognized a potential danger and shared their concern with their colleagues.

One such person was New York Representative Joe Gavagan, a Catholic and a Democrat. Outraged by the Nazi scapegoating of Jews, he took to the House floor in March 1933 to publicly record his disgust. "Once again humanity is aroused from its lethargy by the persecution of a member race of the human family," he declared. "Is there a more appropriate legislative body in the world than the House of Representatives to send forth an appeal against this injustice and iniquity?"[32] Apparently Gavagan's remarks struck a chord. A few days later, William Sirovich, a Jewish Democrat representing New York City, addressed the House for ten minutes. In his remarks, Sirovich blasted the "foul, iniquitous, and brutal treatment of the nationals of Jewish extraction by the cowardly, sadistic, paranoid madman in modern Germany, Adolf Hitler."[33] Lawmakers from other districts joined the discussion with Sirovich. What followed was an exchange in which statements initially tailored to condemn Nazi intolerance evolved into a discussion of American bigotry against Jews. Thomas Blanton, a Presbyterian Democrat representing the 17th District in Texas was explicit, complaining about the "unreasonable, foolish and cruel persecutions of the Jews right here in the nation's capital." Why should we, he asked, "tolerate without protest Jewish persecution here in Washington?"[34]

---

31 Ariel Hurwitz, "The Struggle Over the Creation of the War Refugee Board," *Holocaust and Genocide Studies* 6 (1991): 17–31.

32 Joe Gavagan, *Congressional Record*, H 73, 1st sess. (22 March 1933): 771–777.

33 William Sirovich, *Congressional Record*, H 73, 1st sess. (27 March 1933): 884.

34 Thomas Blanton to Sirovich, *Congressional Record*, H 73, 1st sess. (27 March 1933): 886.

Emanuel Celler, a Democratic representative from New York, certainly agreed. In remarks he delivered in April 1933, the Jewish American lawmaker depicted the Nazis in a negative light. "Hitler may not be murdering the Jews, but he is killing them economically and starving them into submission." He warned, "There are repercussions far beyond Germany's borders as anti-Semitism is rearing its foul head in other countries."[35] As a Jewish American lawmaker, it might seem obvious for him to address this issue. But not all Jews serving in Congress did the same. Like Celler, Sol Bloom represented a New York district with many Jewish voters. However, Bloom was unable to believe that the "warm-hearted German people he had known" would support Adolf Hitler.[36] Even after learning about Nazi concentration camps and genocide, Bloom did not join his colleagues in their campaign for a vigorous American response. Such a position confounded his contemporaries[37] and it continues to vex those who study him.[38] Looked at another way, Bloom's silence amplifies the principled nature of those who did take a stand. Irrespective of their creed, the elected officials who spoke up bore witness to Nazi racism's broader threat to humankind, and they used their offices to thwart its spread in the US.

Protestant Republican Edith Nourse Rogers from Massachusetts first spoke out in mid-1933. "Mr. Speaker," she began, "I take the floor to protest the brutal and unwarranted treatment of the nationals of Jewish extraction in Germany by Adolf Hitler. Our forefathers fled from religious oppression to New England. We from that section especially sympathize with any persecuted race. Jews are being subjected to unwarranted treatment in Germany today."[39] Pennsylvanian Method-ist Jesse Swick similarly lamented, "The cause of liberty, freedom and justice, three of the most important parts of modern civilization has received its most recent

---

35 Emanuel Celler, *Congressional Record,* H 73, 1st sess. (20 April 1933): 2019.

36 Sol Bloom, *The Autobiography of Sol Bloom* (New York: G.P. Putnam's Sons, 1948), 227.

37 In a postwar interview, after Bloom's death, Emanuel Celler characterized Sol Bloom as "a weakling…he didn't help." As quoted in David S. Wyman and Rafael Medoff, *A Race against Death: Peter Bergson, America and the Holocaust* (New York: Free Press, 2002), 144–145.

38 Jeffrey Demsky, "Reconsidering Sol Bloom: The Challenges of Jewish American Ac-commodation During the Second World War," paper presented to the Western Jewish Studies Association Annual Conference, University of British Columbia, Vancouver, Canada, 14 May 2015.

39 Edith Nourse Rogers, *Congressional Record,* H 73, 1st sess. (26 April 1933): 3289. In 1939, Rogers co-sponsored unsuccessful legislation designed to permit German Jew-ish children safe haven in the US. See Susan Forbes Martin, *A Nation of Immigrants* (New York: Cambridge University Press, 2011), 152.

blow at the hands of Adolf Hitler and his subsequent persecution of the Jews." He declared, "Americans everywhere recognize the rights of human beings to worship God as they please."[40] Massachusetts' Catholic Democrat John McCormack echoed this declaration. "I have watched with increasing anxiety developments in Germany since Adolf Hitler assumed controlling power." Like dozens of others who spoke out during early 1933, McCormack expressed concern that the "ruthless agonizing of the Jews" in Nazi Germany reflected a general hostility to democratic principles such as "liberty, justice, and equality."[41] His words found common cause with William Connery, a Connecticut Catholic, who similarly reminded his colleagues that the Nazis were not "confining their brutality to just Catholics and Jews," but rather their actions were "a part of a larger pattern of religious oppression."[42]

When the second session of the Seventy-third Congress opened in January 1934, lawmakers renewed their warnings about the violence done to democratic freedoms by Nazi bigotry. By a wide majority,[43] the representatives voted to install a panel to investigate Nazi propaganda efforts in the United States and to look into citizens with Nazi ties in the US. The seven-member panel, chaired by John McCormack, was called the Special Committee on Un-American Activities Authorized to Investigate Nazi Propaganda and Certain Other Propaganda, and was widely known as the McCormack-Dickstein Committee. Its hearings convened dozens of times in several cities including Washington, D.C., Newark, New Jersey, Asheville, North Carolina, and New York City. This body would later become the infamous House Un-American Activities Committee, known for its so-called red baiting.[44]

In terms of promoting active policies to aid endangered Jews, the new committee had little impact. This does not, however, render its efforts insignificant, as much as it makes them more challenging to contextualize. The hearings occurred many years before the Nazis' war on Jews; it is methodologically challenging to assess their value in relation to later questions of American atrocity responses. While lawmakers' words did not carry with them policy weight, they demonstrated the existence of top-level officials' concerns for European Jewish welfare. In this light, legislators' inquiries from the early 1930s are revealing because they

---

40 Jesse Swick, *Congressional Record,* H 73, 1ˢᵗ sess. (22 May 1933): 3968.

41 John McCormack, *Congressional Record,* H 73, 1ˢᵗ sess. (9 June 1933): 5441.

42 William Connery, *Congressional Record,* H 74, 1ˢᵗ sess. (22 July 1935): 11569.

43 The vote was 168 to 31. See MacDonnell, *Insidious,* 41.

44 Walter Goodman, *The Committee: The Extraordinary Career of the House Committee on Un-American Activities* (New York: Farrar, Straus, Giroux, 1968), 10–26.

provide glimpses of American leaders starting to "envision" the Nazi threat.[45] As one expert has observed, "The menacing shadow of Hitlerism appeared…rumbles of un-American propaganda reached Dickstein's ears. It was rumored Hitler was stretching his iron hand across the sea…with governmental shears in hand, Dickstein [committee] set out to destroy the web of un-American propaganda spreading over the US."[46]

In May 1934, the commission investigated a group called the "Friends of New Germany." Led by a publicity-seeking demagogue named Heinz Spanknoebel, the "Friends" were a direct organ of Deputy Führer Rudolf Hess.[47] The group maintained affiliates in New York City and Chicago, and at its peak ranged in size from five to ten thousand members. Spanknoebel's ability to stoke bigoted sentiments, however, led to his hurried departure from the United States. When the committee's vice chairman, Samuel Dickstein, alerted Justice Department officials that Spanknoebel had failed to register as a paid foreign agent, deportation procedures commenced. Spanknoebel left the country clandestinely.[48]

While Spanknoebel returned to Germany, his "Friends" remained behind. In May 1934, the committee subpoenaed the group's new leader, Fritz Gissibl.[49] "Does your association see its discontent and anger against the Jew in general?" asked Chairman McCormack. Gissibl's response was somewhat ambiguous. He replied, "We are against those that were against the Germans." McCormack then

---

45 Benjamin Alpers, *Dictators, Democracy and American Public Culture: Envisioning the Totalitarian Enemy, 1920s-1950s* (Chapel Hill, NC: University of North Carolina Press, 2003), 17, 38.
46 As quoted in Alex Goodall, "Diverging Paths: Nazism, the National Civic Federation, and American Anticommunism, 1933–39," *Journal of Contemporary History* 44 (2009): 61.
47 Ibid., 57.
48 Sander Diamond, *The Nazi Movement in the United States, 1924–1941* (New Haven, CT: Yale University Press, 1974), 99–100, 113–119; Leland Bell, *In Hitler's Shadow: The Anatomy of American Nazism* (New York: Kennikat, 1973), 26–30; 46. Committee Vice Chairman Samuel Dickstein inquired with the State Department about Gissibl's immigration status. In the request for information, he attached for Secretary of State Cordell Hull's review a two-page memorandum containing redacted testimony in which Gissibl acknowledged that he received his orders directly from Adolf Hitler. See Dickstein to Cordell Hull, 5 December 1935, box 5/3. Samuel Dickstein Papers, 1923–44, American Jewish Archives, Cincinnati (hereafter: Dickstein Papers).
49 In 1936, the "Friends" changed their name to the "German-American *Bund.*" Gissibl played a leading role in selecting the new *Bund* leader, Fritz Julius Kuhn. See Diamond, *Movement,* 162, 217–18; Bell, *Shadow,* 55–58; Goodman, *Extraordinary,* 17.

responded, "Well you [and your associates] came over here and engaged in activities against the Jewish people." The witness replied, "I do not think it was that so much, Mr. Chairman, as it was to organize the Germans and unite them." Apparently Gissibl's explanation did not fool Chairman McCormack, who pointed out that the efforts of the Friends of New Germany "were directed only against the Jews."[50]

Walter Kappe, the editor in chief of the pro-Nazi *Deutsche Zeitung*, was another witness brought before the McCormack-Dickstein Committee. The *Zeitung* was an American-based paper geared toward German immigrants. In practice, it served as a domestic outlet for Nazi propaganda. Dickstein saw the *Zeitung* for what it was. "As a member of Congress I have tried to clear the air in this country," he proclaimed. "But you and your paper made unjustifiable attacks upon me as a Jew." Kappe retorted, "[O]nly as one that is fighting and saying things about Germany that are in my estimation untrue." Dickstein continued to press the witness, "If I said the Nazis have removed certain Jewish doctors, lawyers, and judges, that is not an untrue slander against Germany." In his reply, Kappe answered "No." "And if I said that Germany has put certain Jewish peoples into a concentration camp," continued Dickstein, "that was not lying about Germany was it?" Once again, the witness had to agree.[51]

In 1935, the claim that Nazi anti-Semitism threatened American values became an official part of the congressional narrative. Following seven months of investigations, the McCormack-Dickstein Committee issued its report, declaring that Adolf Hitler and his Nazi Party had "made every effort to disturb American citizens of German birth in this country ... and through the form of propaganda to have twenty million honest-to-goodness Americans subscribe to his racial philosophies."[52] This finding provided other social commentators, writers, journalists, and editors an official basis for their stories, which in turn focused additional negative attention on Hitlerism. Such overlaps may not have blunted the escalating Nazi violence. Rather, their historical significance rests in the snapshots they offer of American officials trying to untangle, and explain to the American public, the brutal nature of German fascism.

---

50 United States Congress, House, *Special Committee on Un-American Activities, Investigation of Nazi Propaganda Activities and Investigation of Certain Other Propaganda Activities* 73 (H) 2nd sess. (Washington, DC: Government Printing Office, 1934), 100–101.

51 Ibid., 154; Diamond, *Movement*, 87–90.

52 Samuel Dickstein, Congressional Record H 74, 1st sess. (25 July 1935): 11861. See also "US Finds Nazi Menace," *Pennsylvanian Weekly News*, 25 February 1934, box 16/6, Dickstein Papers.

Socio-Cultural Discourse in Opposition to Nazi Anti-Semitism

Members of Congress were not the only Americans publicly discussing the Nazi threat to the Western liberal tradition in general, and to Jewish welfare in particular. Indeed, during the 1930s, writers, journalists, and artists also spoke out. Notably, the themes that had first appeared in Congress reappeared in cultural discourse. Here again the issue is not how many victims they helped to rescue. Rather, I am focused on intention. Vocalizing support of a foreign minority, even in an atmosphere of heightened isolationism, indicates that some elected officials attached great value to defending their idea of Americanism.

In October 1930, almost three years before the Nazis assumed power, *Time* magazine devoted a full column to a story titled "Plate Glass Riots," which reported that German citizens, "stones in their pockets," had "shrewdly distributed themselves in front of Jewish-owned stores." "So adroit was the vandalism," the reader learned, that "there remained not one person to be arrested."[53] An additional Weimar-era article from the *New Republic* told of a "scandalous attack on Jewish students" that "constituted another link in the chain of fascist anti-Semitic activity."[54] Such reporting increased after January 1933. "Who Stands behind Hitler?" asked a headline in the *Nation*. Listing several of Hitler's goals, such as abjuring the Versailles Treaty and reviving the German economy, the article closed with the observation that the new leader "emphasized the anti-Jewish position."[55] In a *Time Magazine* article titled "Nazis Amuck," readers learned that German paramilitary soldiers had assaulted seven Jewish Americans traveling abroad. The story closed by reporting that the number of Jews attacked by followers of the new regime ran "into the hundreds."[56]

Some authors pushed the envelope further by linking German and American bigotry. Pulitzer Prize-winning poet laureate Archibald MacLeish was one well-known Protestant commentator who concluded that anti-Semitism was a potential wedge that bolstered the Nazis' "divide and conquer" strategy. While scholars have examined various aspects of his ninety-year life,[57] they have not

---

53 "Plate Glass Riots," *Time Magazine*, 27 October 1930, 22.
54 *New Republic*, 13 July 1932, 224.
55 "Who Stands behind Hitler?" *Nation*, 22 February 1933, 197.
56 "Nazis Amuck," *Time Magazine*, 13 March 1933, 15.
57 Robert Vanderlan, *Intellectuals Incorporated: Politics, Art, and Ideas Inside Henry Luce's Media Empire* (Philadelphia, PA: University of Pennsylvania Press, 2010), 7–10; Scott Donaldson, *Archibald MacLeish: An American Life* (New York: Houghton Mifflin, 1992), xiv; Bernard Drabeck, Helen Ellis, and Seymour Rudin, eds., *The Proceedings of the Archibald MacLeish Symposium, May 7–8, 1982* (Lanham, MD: University Press

explored MacLeish's role in binding an American defense of religious freedom to discussions of Nazi anti-Semitism. MacLeish had a national platform for sculpting public discourse. As an editor at *Fortune Magazine* he helped determine the periodical's content. He thought combating anti-Semitism was an issue worthy of column space.

In 1935, he penned a series of private memorandums to his publisher, Henry Luce Jr., recommending an investigation of anti-Jewish scapegoating. "There is anti-Semitic talk around the country," he observed. "The activities of Mr. Hitler in Germany have had their effect here." He informed his boss, "We would be well advised [to drag] the whole issue into the light of day for all to see."[58] The next year, Archibald MacLeish and other *Fortune Magazine* editors authored a book-length study called *Jews in America*. Its opening pages framed Nazi anti-Semitism as a collective danger. "The unbelievable record of Nazi barbarities," the manuscript begins, "concerns non-Jews as well as Jews."[59] Hammering away at the connection between anti-Semitism and social ruin, he asserted, "Any nation that permits a minority to live in fear is a nation which invites disaster."[60] MacLeish's narrative also conflated the terms anti-Semitic and anti-democratic, shining a light on the potential comfort that domestic expressions of bigotry lent Nazism. "Any man who loathes Fascism," he argued, "will fear anti-Semitism and also the various conditions which encourage it."[61] Published by prominent Protestant commentators, the missive helps repudiate the claim that Jews were a people entirely spurned in the US by its government and citizens.

Writers who took up this question did not only examine Nazi social intolerance in Germany. Some wove cautionary tales about America succumbing to a Nazi-style dictatorship. This broader message helped personalize the threat for non-Jews, who may have rested in the belief that they had nothing to fear. Sinclair Lewis's *It Can't Happen Here* (1935), for example, was a thinly veiled description of current events that described American paramilitary units and a popular

---

of America, 1988); R.H. Winnick, ed., *The Letters of Archibald MacLeish, 1907–1982* (Boston, MA: Houghton Mifflin, 1983); Warren Bush, ed., *The Dialogues of Archibald MacLeish and Mark Van Doren* (New York: Hutton, 1964).

58 "Luce," box 8, November 12, 1935, Archibald MacLeish Papers, 1907–81, Library of Congress, Washington DC (hereafter: MacLeish Papers)

59 Editors of *Fortune Magazine*, *Jews in America* (New York: Random House, 1936), 3.

60 Ibid., 9.

61 Ibid., 11.

radio priest who spewed bigotry.[62] The books' charismatic antagonist, Buzz Windrip, upon legally winning the US presidency, declares a state of emergency and amasses all federal powers. Dissenting legislators and judges face imprisonment as Windrip soon plunges the US into militaristic conquests. A political police force known as the "Minute Men" keeps domestic order and dissenters are murdered or sent to concentration camps, where they disappear forever.[63]

Such yarns may have stoked Americans' anxieties on various levels. Some experts see in Lewis's account an apologue about Huey Long. In 1935, as he was writing, the Louisiana "Kingfish," whose appeal rested largely on what one scholar has termed a "primitive" leftist rhetoric, steeped in promises of wealth redistribution, was emerging as a credible challenger to President Roosevelt.[64] The fact he was assassinated prior to the manuscripts' publication does not erase the perception that he had served as the plot's muse. Various literary devices also sustain this possibility. Both Long and the Windrip character credited their youthful experiences as rural medicine salesmen with honing their later skills at promoting political elixirs. Both proudly extolled the virtues of rustic cuisine and bolstered their populist credentials by embarrassing foreign dignitaries.[65] Perhaps the most disturbing similarity between the two figures came with their use of militiamen to further their political aims. While Windrip's "Minute Men" could be counted on

---

62 Sinclair Lewis, *It Can't Happen Here* (New York: Dramatists Play Service, 1936). Other works of fiction from the period also employed this leitmotif. In 1934, Rex Stout, a popular detective-story author, published *The President Vanishes*, describing a fascist conspiracy to capture the White House launched by Wall Street financiers, munitions makers, and a paramilitary group known as the "Gray Shirts." This plotline mirrored factual accounts from the period, notably General Smedley D. Butler's report to the McCormack-Dickstein committee. See Jules Archer, *The Plot to Seize the White House: The Shocking True Story of the Conspiracy to Overthrow FDR* (New York: Skyhorse Publishing, 2007), 139.

63 Lewis, *It Can't*, 57, 61, 64, 67, 69, 95, 104, 108, 114.

64 Nicholas Wapshott, *The Sphinx: Franklin Roosevelt, the Isolationists, and the Road to World War II* (New York: W.W. Norton, 2015), 36.

65 In 1930, then Governor Long received the German consul in New Orleans wearing silk pajamas and a pair of brightly colored blue slippers. While the diplomat took offense, news of the episode delighted Long's rural constituents. In Lewis's story, President Windrip affected a similar slight, and sowed similar populist rewards, by refusing to attend a dinner hosted by the Duke of York. See Garry Boulard, *Huey Long Invades New Orleans: The Siege of A City, 1934–36* (Gretna, LA: Pelican Publishers, 1998), 115–116.

to shoulder opposition out of the way, Long saw in the Louisiana National Guard a tool for projecting his authority.[66]

These "clever and unmistakable" overlaps have informed some authorities' conclusions that Lewis achieved the "most chilling and uncanny treatment" of Huey Long's imprimatur on American politics.[67] However, as is often the case with creative license, cultural consumers may take from identical artifacts differing interpretations. Lewis may have channeled any number of "New Deal Dissidents"—Pelley,[68] Coughlin,[69] "General" Art Smith,[70] or Gerald "L.K." Smith[71]—as he developed his prose. *It Can't Happen Here* is also a possible parable for external Nazi subversions, rather than a commentary on a grassroots movement. One writer remarked that Lewis's descriptions of concentration camps "parallel exactly similar descriptions of such institutions in Germany."[72] In Lewis's story, Hermann Göring and Joseph Goebbels "become" Lee Sarason, Windrip's chief lieutenant; Hitler's Storm Troopers "become" the Minute Men, Windrip's private army; and Hitler's *Mein Kampf* "becomes" *Zero Hour*, Windrip's campaign biography.[73] Viewed in this light, Lewis's purpose in writing his book may not necessarily have been to comment on domestic affairs, but rather to help readers recognize that what was happening in Europe could also be exported to America.

A non-Jewish member of the "Hollywood Anti-Nazi League,"[74] Sinclair Lewis was an unabashed Adolf Hitler critic. His partisan bent led some to characterize

---

66 Ibid., 116.

67 Ibid., 115.

68 For a discussion of Pelley as Windrip see Phillip Jenkins, *Hoods and Shirts: The Extreme Right In Pennsylvania, 1925–1950* (Chapel Hill, NC: University of North Carolina Press, 1997), 121.

69 Stephen Ortiz, "The "New Deal" for Veterans: The Economy Act, the Veterans of Foreign Wars, and the Origins of New Deal Dissent," *The Journal of Military History* 70 (2006): 418.

70 David Lobb, "Fascist Apocalypse: William Pelley and Millennial Extremism," *Journal of Millennial Studies* 2 (2000): 1.

71 Robert Rabin, "Federal Regulation in Historical Perspective," *Stanford Law Review* 38 (1986): 1248.

72 Keith Ronald Perry, *The Kingfish in Fiction: Huey P. Long and the Modern American Novel* (Baton Rouge, LA: Louisiana State University Press, 2004), 55.

73 Ibid.

74 Michael Birdwell, *Celluloid Soldiers: The Warner Bros. Campaign against Nazism* (New York: New York University Press, 1999), 25–30.

the story as "agitprop."[75] Nevertheless, the tale had broad resonance across the US. *It Can't Happen Here* reached fifth place on the 1936 nationwide best-seller list.[76] It was also performed in a theater version as part of the Works Progress Administration's Federal Theatre Project. During fall 1936, government-funded actors performed the tale over twenty-five times before audiences in such cities as New York, Boston, Chicago, San Francisco, Cleveland, Miami, and Seattle. The poster for the Detroit performance is particularly illustrative for discussions of the story's interior message. The artwork featured a soldier, sporting Hitler's distinctive moustache, wearing a black uniform adorned with the outline of what appears to be a German Eagle badge on his chest. With his bayonet affixed to his rifle, the figure cuts a menacing pose, set against an image of the continental US. Such tales of an exported Nazism subverting the US echoed earlier congressional findings. They represented another possible way for Americans to learn who Adolf Hitler was, and how his ideas might impact their lives.

As the thirties drew to a close, the theme of the Nazi danger persisted in American cultural discourse. The film, *Confessions of a Nazi Spy* (1939) is the period's most notable relic about combating Nazism. Warner Bros. released the film to highlight Nazi subterfuge.[77] This was risky as the leaders of other Hollywood studios were taking great care to appease the German regime.[78] German émigré Anatole Litvak directed the film and the famed Jewish actor Edward G. Robinson

---

75 For "agitprop," see Gary Gerstle, *The American Crucible: Race and Nation in the Twentieth Century* (Princeton: Princeton University Press, 2001), 164; Michael Denning, *The Cultural Front: The Laboring of American Culture in the Twentieth Century* (New York: Verso, 1996), 56–58; Clayton Koppes and Gregory Black, *Hollywood Goes to War* (New York: Free Press, 1987), 22; K.R.M. Short, "Hollywood Fights Anti-Semitism, 1940–1945," in Short, ed., *Film and Radio Propaganda in World War II* (Knoxville, TN: University of Tennessee Press, 1983), 151–152.

76 Alice Payne Hackett and James Henry Burke, *80 Years of Best Sellers, 1895–1975* (New York: Boker, 1977), 121.

77 For contemporary newspaper accounts, see "Witnesses Link Spy Plot to Reich," *New York Times*, 5 November 1938; "Four German Spies Are Sentenced," *New York Herald Tribune*, 3 December 1938.

78 Ben Urwand, *The Collaboration: Hollywood's Pact With Hitler* (Cambridge, MA: Belknap Press of Harvard University Press, 2013), 144; Thomas Doherty, *Hollywood and Hitler, 1933–1939* (New York: Columbia University Press, 2013), 291; Neal Gabler, *An Empire of Their Own: How the Jews Invented Hollywood* (New York: Crown Books, 1988), 338.

starred in it. Both men were members of the "Hollywood Anti-Nazi League" who saw in the film a vehicle for damaging Hitlerism.[79]

Confessions of a Nazi Spy stressed three basic points. First, Nazi Germany sought to destroy the United States by fomenting religious, racial, and class hatreds. Second, the Nazis maintained domestic-based propaganda organizations to help them achieve their goal. Lastly, Americans needed to awaken to the dangers posed by the Nazis.[80] *Confessions* trumpeted these claims through a "vigorous and often outrageous public relations campaign."[81] Local theater owners, for example, were encouraged to drum up interest by placing anonymous phone calls alerting citizens that "the Nazis were coming."[82] In Washington State, law enforcement officials investigated a handbill, ostensibly produced by the *Bund*, which warned citizens "if you see this film Hitler will take serious reprisals on you when he realizes his inevitable destiny over America!"[83]

Officials of the German government reacted to the movie with fervor. A diplomat stationed in Los Angeles issued oblique threats that *Confessions* might result in "difficulties" between the American and Nazi governments.[84] Likewise, the German charge d'affaires stationed in Washington D.C. complained bitterly to Secretary of State, Cordell Hull.[85] The German government refused to show the film, as did Ireland, Hungary, Switzerland, Holland and Norway. In the United States, however, *Confessions* earned positive reviews. A May 1939 *Variety* piece has proven prescient. After praising Warner Brothers for making a movie of great importance, the author closed the story by noting, "decades from now what's happening may be seen in perspective. And the historians will almost certainly take note of this daringly frank broadside from a picture company."[86]

As the thirties ended, Americans had fashioned both political and cultural discourses condemning Nazi anti-Semitism and related intolerance. Particular emphases sometimes differed, but public expressions of outrage became a means through which some citizens sought to fulfill the American promise and to strengthen the national character. Once the US entered World War II, federal information officers used the theme of battling bigotry as a frame for public

---

79 Birdwell, *Celluloid*, 70.
80 Koppes and Black, *Hollywood*, 28–29.
81 MacDonnell, *Insidious*, 63.
82 Ibid., 67.
83 As quoted in MacDonnell, *Insidious*, 67–68.
84 Koppes and Black, *Hollywood*, 27–29.
85 Birdwell, *Celluloid*, 76.
86 As quoted in MacDonnell, *Insidious*, 70.

discussions on America's war aims. These steps institutionalized the argument that Nazism was dangerous, anti-Jewish bigotry was abhorrent, and the two phenomena were inexorably linked.

Federal Information Officers Condemn Nazi Anti-Semitism and Genocide

Historians have discussed for some time how events such as the Great Depression and the Second World War forged a new American identity.[87] The many millions of immigrants and first-generation citizens who lived through these experiences emerged as bona fide "Americans."[88] This process was not wholly spontaneous. During the thirties and forties, the federal government took unprecedented action to promote ethnic variety in the socio-cultural mainstream. Organizations such as the Farm Security Administration, the Works Progress Administration, and the Office of War Information dedicated significant resources to raising levels of awareness about the many different types of people living in the US.[89]

Of course, Americans' struggles to promote ethno-racial tolerance predated this period. While African American males gained their full rights of citizenship following the US Civil War, their civic equality was often limited by social conventions. Asians in the US also faced persistent inequities. During the 1930s, these sentiments coalesced around a powerful boycott aimed at damaging Japanese silk producers.[90] The economic strategy to demean Japanese businesses soon took on

87 Deborah Dash Moore, *GI Jews: How World War II Changed A Generation* (Cambridge, MA: Belknap Press of Harvard University Press, 2004), 154; Kenneth Heineman, *A Catholic New Deal: Religion and Reform in Depression Pittsburgh* (University Park, PA: Pennsylvania State University Press, 1999), 43; Lizabeth Cohen, *Making a New Deal: Industrial Workers in Chicago, 1919-1939* (New York: Cambridge University Press, 1990), 54, 111, 125.

88 Neil Baldwin, *The American Revelation: Ten Ideals That Shaped Our Country from the Puritans to the Cold War* (New York: St. Martin's, 2005), 158; Andrea Most, *Making Americans: Jews and the Broadway Musical* (Cambridge, MA: Harvard University Press, 2004), 26–27; Barbara Savage, *Broadcasting Freedom: Radio, War and the Politics of Race, 1938- 1948* (Chapel Hill, NC: University of North Carolina Press, 1999), 60–61.

89 Nicholas Nathanson, *The Black Image in the New Deal: The Politics of FSA Photography* (Knoxville, TN: University of Tennessee Press, 1992), 4–9; Short, "Hollywood," 169; Monty Noam Penkower, *The Federal Writers' Project: A Study in the Government Patronage of the Arts* (Urbana, IL: University of Illinois Press, 1977), 26, 72.

90 Nathan Becker, "The Anti-Japanese Boycott in the United States," *Far Eastern Survey* 8 (1939): 51.

a social component as well. College students held "bonfire boycotts" featuring participants communally disrobing and setting their silk apparel aflame. Hollywood luminaries staged bawdy "strip tease" performances in which actresses' silk undergarments came to rest in a red-white-blue garbage pail.[91] Such activities indicated Americans' growing ill ease with Japanese people, a sentiment that later resulted in the creation and operation of wartime detention centers.

Nevertheless, there is also evidence from the period indicating minority citizens' ties to their primary reference groups loosened, in favor of growing assimilation. The spread of American popular culture and consumerism, industrial-class formation and organization, and the nationally unifying expressions of the fight against totalitarianism supported this process.[92] In 1938, a twenty-six-week-long nationally broadcast radio series, funded by the federal government, reset the domestic boundaries of ethnicity, religion, and race. *American All, Immigrant All*, presented richly detailed—and complimentary—portraits of the various new ethnicities and races now included within the designation "American." This sort of program represented a break from the period's nativist voices. Indeed, the series' creative visionary, a Quaker woman named Rachel Davis DuBois, specifically intended for the radio program to counterbalance what she characterized as Father Charles Coughlin's "yelling."[93] Her proposal caught the attention of federal education officials who saw it as a way to promote what was becoming a bourgeoning field of intercultural education.

This process accelerated once the nation entered World War II. Federal information officers reasoned that contrasting stories of Nazi intolerance with an exposition of American liberties would yield ideological gains.[94] Prior to June 1944, when the United States first landed troops in Western Europe, this type of intellectual battle had great significance. For example, at roughly the same time that State Department officials decided it was best to ignore the genocide,

91 Lawrence Glickman, *Buying Power: A History Of Consumer Activism in America* (Chicago: University of Chicago Press, 2009), 226, 241.

92 Ngai, *Impossible*, 4.

93 Savage, *Broadcasting*, 24.

94 Steven Casey, *Cautious Crusade: Franklin D. Roosevelt, American Public Opinion, and the War against Nazi Germany* (New York: Oxford University Press, 2001), 61; Clayton Laurie, *The Propaganda Warriors: America's Crusade against Nazi Germany* (Topeka, KS: University Press of Kansas, 1998); 210; Sydney Weinberg, "What to Tell America: The Writer's Quarrel in the Office of War Information," *Journal of American History* 55 (1968): 73–89; Cedric Larson, "The Domestic Picture Work of the Office of War Information," *Hollywood Quarterly* 3 (1948): 434–443.

information agencies' managers discussed publicizing the types of reports that contrasted Nazism with American liberty.

Archibald MacLeish, already involved in this conversation prior to World War II, became one of the information officers managing the effort. During 1941–42, he supervised the Office of Facts and Figures, an agency that coordinated governmental information on a range of issues, including Nazi activities.[95] He briefly was assistant director of the Office of War Information, and ended the war as Assistant Secretary of State for Public and Cultural Relations. As was the case during his time at *Fortune Magazine* before the war, the various posts he held in government helped him to shape public attitudes. This was indeed a pressing task. More than six months after the United States had entered the Second World War, 52 percent of the public admitted they did not have a clear idea what the war was about. "I can see why we are fighting the Japanese," one respondent told a Gallup pollster in August 1942, "but I cannot see why we are fighting the Germans…I suppose we are fighting for democracy."[96]

One way that MacLeish's agency attempted to raise public awareness about the war effort was through the publication of thematic brochures. His outfit paid specific attention to President Roosevelt's "Four Freedoms," and particularly the assurance that the US would fight to uphold the global right to unfettered worship.[97] In early 1942, his Office of Facts and Figures distributed 2.5 million copies of an illustrated, sixteen-page brochure entitled *Divide and Conquer: What Hitler Wants You To Think*.[98] This government publication outlined several reasons for Americans to fear Nazism. "Hitler hopes to destroy unity in America." Readers learned that, "Both physically and mentally, all his tricks are now being directed against us."[99] Squarely addressing the issue of German hostility to non-Protestant minorities, the government publication informed citizens that, "The Jews

---

95　Laurie, *Propaganda*, 64–65; R. Keith Kane, "The O.F.F.," *Public Opinion Quarterly* 6 (1942): 204–220.

96　As quoted in Richard Steele, "American Popular Opinion and the War against Germany: The Issue of Negotiated Peace, 1942," *Journal of American History* 65 (1978): 708.

97　Harvey Kaye, *The Fight For the Four Freedoms: What Made FDR and the Greatest Generation Truly Great* (New York: Simon & Schuster, 2014), 67, 72.

98　*Divide and Conquer: What Hitler Wants You To Think* (Washington, DC: US Government Printing Office, 1942). For printing and distribution data, see David Culbert, ed., *Information Control and Propaganda: Records of the Office of War Information*, Part I: "The Director's Central Files, 1942–1945," (Frederick, MD: University Publications of America, 1986), reel 8: 0049. Hereafter cited as *Records*, ed. Culbert, pt. 1.

99　MacLeish Papers, "O.W.I.," box 53.

in Warsaw have been packed into a ghetto." "Nazi guards," the text continued, "patrol an eight foot wall topped by broken glass and barbed wire."[100] Such prose mirrored the reports of persecutions, ghettos, and concentration camps that had dotted American public discourse throughout the 1930s.[101] In 1942, the main difference was that the US was now war with Germany, and under those conditions, readers might more fully trust the accuracy of a document coming out of the federal government.

In addition to noting anti-Jewish activities, *Divide and Conquer* highlighted Nazi persecution leveled against Christians. "Poland's Catholic Church," the narrative reads, "has been practically wiped out .... Six hundred thirty one churches, four hundred fifty four chapels, and two hundred fifty three convents have been destroyed or closed."[102] From the brochure, American readers learned the government's view that opposition to bigotry benefited the US. "We have seen how Hitler's strategy was to create internal distress in every nation he planned to attack." The pamphlet advised its citizens that, "Our job as Americans is one of individual awareness to avoid falling into Hitler's trap."[103]

Soon after *Divide and Conquer* appeared, President Roosevelt dissolved the Office of Facts and Figures and created a new agency called the Office of War Information. An expansive bureaucracy with offices in Washington D.C., London, New York, and San Francisco, the new organization provided a home to many so-called New Dealers.[104] In the opinion of its supporters, the Office of War Information played a vital role in expanding the public flow of knowledge.[105] Others, however, lamented its appearance. The American literary critic Edmund Wilson provided a stinging rebuke. Pointing to Archibald MacLeish and Robert Sherwood, the playwright and overseas direction for the Office of War Information Wilson exclaimed, "With MacLeish and Sherwood at the White House...their

---

100   Ibid.
101   Robert Abzug, *America Views the Holocaust, 1933–1945* (Boston, MA: Bedford/ St. Martin's, 1999), 16; "They're at it Again," *Commonweal*, 9 March 1934, 510; Stanley High, "The War on Religious Freedom," in Pierre van Passen and James Wise eds., *Nazism: An Assault on Civilization* (New York: Smith and Haas, 1934), 25–39.
102   MacLeish Papers, "O.W.I.," box 53.
103   Ibid.
104   Thomas Fleming, *The New Dealers' War: FDR and the War Within World War II* (New York: Basic Books, 2001), 201.
105   Gerd Horton, *Radio Goes to War: The Cultural Politics of Propaganda during World War Two* (Berkeley and Los Angeles, CA: University of California Press, 2002), 43–45.

awful collectivist cant makes me uneasy."[106] Wilson's analysis provides a snapshot of the larger contest: seizing upon reports of Nazi bigotry as a way to reconfigure Americans' thinking.

President Roosevelt empowered the Office of War Information to "coordinate an informed and intelligent understanding at home and abroad of the war effort, government policies, combat activities, and general war aims."[107] The agency continued the practice of the Office of Facts and Figures, using pluralist-themed brochures to explain American war aims. Some of the topics they examined included *War Jobs for Women* (1943), *Nazi War Against the Catholic Church* (1942), *Negroes and the War* (1943) and *Tale of A City* (1943). In July 1942, one month after the agency's founding, assistant director George Barnes authored an internal memorandum relevant to discussions of the American response to the Holocaust. "Is there any facility," the message began, "for checking the authenticity and accuracy of reported atrocities?" Citing a concern that "we shall certainly have an increasing number of inquiries," the document closed with the statement that "we should be prepared to answer them with some authority."[108]

Archibald MacLeish worked directly on the issue. Along with such men as Robert Kitner, an executive of the National Broadcasting Company, and political figures such as Milton Eisenhower, Adlai Stevenson, Nelson Rockefeller, and Assistant Secretary of War John McCloy, MacLeish chaired a group called the "Committee on War Information."[109] In May 1942, these men met to "develop a policy for the disclosure of atrocity information." They agreed that such releases should occur with "the specific purpose of giving the public an accurate idea of the enemy."[110] Attached to the meeting's agenda was an eight-page discussion of how best to present the evidence. "Photographs, movies, posters, speeches, governmental and eyewitness testimony" were listed as possible methods. "It would be wise to have a policy [on atrocities] ready," the group concluded. "If we do not prepare," members feared, "any number of unfortunate things may happen."[111]

---

106   Edmund Wilson, "Edmund Wilson on Writers and Writing," *New York Times Review of Books* 24 (17 March 1977).
107   For the full mandate, see United States Cong. Subcommittee of the Committee on Appropriations, *Hearings on the National War Agencies Appropriations Bill for 1944* 78 (H), 1st sess. (Washington, DC: Government Printing Office, 1943), 829.
108   *Records*, ed. Culbert, pt. 1, reel 12: 0754.
109   For the Committee of War Information, see "Subject File," "OWI," box 52, MacLeish Papers. See also Breitman and Kraut, *American*, 172.
110   "O.W.I.," box 52, MacLeish Papers.
111   Ibid.

It was important to highlight German noncombatant violence even prior to June 1944, when the United States first landed troops in Western Europe. Preparing public opinion against the kinds of repression America had mobilized to defeat played a significant role in war mobilization.

Some in the Office of War Information recognized that combating Nazi anti-Semitism, specifically, complemented this endeavor. "We should coldly and factually establish Hitler's plan to exterminate the Jews in Europe," officials in Robert Sherwood's overseas branch argued. "We should make a point in news and talks of telling people the fullest facts. Anti-Semitism has been a potent weapon of Nazi political warfare and the time has now come to use it against them."[112] Shortly thereafter, this rationale appeared in an agency brochure. Published in March 1943, *Tale of a City* was a twenty-three-page story that depicted through words, statistics, and illustrations the German tyranny ongoing in Warsaw, Poland. *Tale of a City* paid particular attention to the Jewish plight. At "eighty-three deaths per thousand men," Americans learned, the life expectancy for Jews living in the Warsaw Ghetto was "sixty percent less" than it was for occupants residing in other modern cities.[113] The brochure advised that in Poland, "which has been made the principal Nazi slaughterhouse," German authorities are now carrying into effect "Hitler's oft-repeated intention to exterminate the Jewish people in Europe."[114] The ghettos established by the Nazi invaders were "systematically emptying.... None of those taken away is ever heard from again. The able-bodied are worked to death in labor camps. The infirm are left to die of exposure or are deliberately massacred in mass execution."[115]

The publication was not a minor effort. At a distribution of just under 2 million copies, *Tale of a City* (1943) was the Office's second-largest domestic release. The brochure's publicity far exceeded that of numerous other works including *The Four Freedoms* (1942), *Battle Stations for All* (1943) and *Nazi War against the Catholic Church* (1942).[116] The story represented for Americans, tales of Nazi brutality that had earlier been reported in *Divide and Conquer*. For those in the US aware of Nazi anti-Semitism since the 1930s, *Tale of A City* represented a deepening of

---

112 As quoted in Jeffrey Demsky, "Four Freedoms, For All: American Information Agencies and the Effort to Publicize Nazi Crimes Against Humanity," *Revue LISA* 10 (2012): 119. http://lisa.revues.org/4869.

113 *Records*, ed. Culbert, pt. 1, reel 9: 0150.

114 Ibid., pt. 1, reel 9: 0160.

115 Ibid.

116 *Records*, ed. Culbert, pt. 1, reel 8: 0049. Distribution levels: *Four Freedoms*: 600,000; *Battle Stations*: 200,000; and *Nazi War against Catholic Church*: 250,000.

the government's oppositional discourse. It was a tangible example of officials taking seriously the need to teach Americans about Nazi social hatreds, tying the phenomenon to wider messages about what the nation had mobilized to defeat.

Tale of a City also garnered media attention. The *New York Times* discussed the brochure. Crediting the Office of War Information as its source, the *Times* piece began, "Warsaw is being subjected to a deliberate Nazi pattern of death, disease, starvation and the wholesale elimination of population."[117] In its closing section, the *Times* story reprinted President Roosevelt's December 1942 genocide acknowledgment, in which he condemned the Nazis'"bestial policy of cold-blooded extermination." While such efforts to raise awareness levels did not end the killings—and, it might also be observed that continued government inaction, even with a firm knowledge of the genocide, appears to bolster scholars' arguments about America turning away—my point is that the issue had piqued officials' concern. Irrespective of whether or not the US acted to blunt the killings, only months after the president first expressed his abhorrence, almost 2 million pieces of official literature trumpeted these sentiments to the nation and world.

The brochure drew encouraging responses from ordinary citizens. Stuart Perry of Adrian, Michigan wrote the Office of War Information on March 19, 1943. He stated that he was "perfectly delighted" with the publication. "The subject matter is exactly the kind that I want to see widely broadcast."[118] Another letter written by Dr. Douglas Hill at Duke University stated that, "You are to be congratulated on the excellence of your pamphlet *Tale of A City*."[119] Perhaps, the most compelling reaction came from an organization called "American Friends of Polish Democracy" that termed the *Tale of a City* a "wonderful contribution to the Polish-Allied cause."[120]

Tale of a City also attracted congressional attention. In an April 1943 letter to Massachusetts Senator Henry Cabot Lodge Jr., Director Davis explained what his agency saw as the importance of publicizing atrocity information. "All available evidence points to the fact that most Americans still have little accurate conception of what domination by the Nazis means." "*Tale of a City*," he informed the powerful lawmaker, "illustrates from a concrete example what happens under Nazi occupation." He closed his letter by relaying, "the pamphlet has been widely reprinted by a great many newspapers throughout the country."[121]

---

117 *New York Times*, "Tyranny," 14 February 1943.
118 *Records,* ed. Culbert, pt. 1, Perry to Davis 19 March 1943, reel 9: 0172.
119 Ibid., pt. 1, Hill to Davis, 28 April 1943, reel 9: 0182.
120 Ibid., pt. 1, Malinowski to Davis, 3 June 1943, reel 9: 0189.
121 Ibid., pt. 1, Davis to Lodge Jr., 2 April 1943, reel 9: 0178.

Such feedback demonstrates a continued broadening in the public discourse. The letters about *Tale* highlight Americans inferring the relationship between World War II and the fight against ethno-religious persecution. That this development came out in a government publication reflected the larger decision by the Office of War Information to disseminate war stories that went beyond military matters. This practice was not original. It was part of a ten-year campaign found in both governmental and socio-cultural discourse. The basic theme of these debates centered on Nazi bigotry—and, indeed all expressions of social intolerance—as being harmful to free societies.

Conclusion

The appearance of Nazism resulted in calamity for European Jews. And the fanning of religious hatred in Germany carried with it a potential to undermine the rights and security of Jewish people elsewhere, even in the United States. Following the outbreak of World War II, British authorities interned tens of thousands of immigrant Jews on the suspicion they may lend comfort to the enemy. Similar fears of subversion resulted in the US removing people of Japanese heritage from free society.[122] While the Japanese American and European Jewish relocations were vastly different, with only the latter instance denoting genocide, they are relatable in what they teach us about the limits of civic guarantees. Assurances of individual freedoms are not sacrosanct. Citizens may be stripped of their rights, if officials determine they might utilize those liberties to tear at the social fabric.[123]

This is what makes the breadth of Americans' discursive arguments in defense of European Jewry notable. As European Jews lost their civic security, an assortment of like-minded Americans coalesced into action. Using various media, they disputed Hitler's claims that Jews posed a peril to humankind, and observed that the most pressing danger to global peace was the fanning of racial and religious hatreds. While skeptics might recall the adage "talk is cheap," I have attempted to argue this view misses the mark. Far from "abandonment," this domestic discourse provides a thematic basis for devising a new intellectual framework. Although

---

122 For visual depictions of the Japanese detention centers, originally suppressed by the US government, see Dorothea Lange, Linda Gordon, and Gary Okihiro, *Impounded: Dorothea Lange and the Censored Images of Japanese American Internment* (New York: W.W. Norton, 2006).

123 Brian Masaru Hayashi, *Democratizing The Enemy: The Japanese American Internment* (Princeton, NJ: Princeton University Press, 2004), 34.

these words did not save many Jews, they foreshadowed a sea change in domestic attitudes toward Jews and other non-Protestant minorities.

The prevalent characterization of prewar American society as unwelcoming toward ethno-racial minorities, and the insistence that wartime State Department intransigence embodied the nations' response, has discouraged scholars from studying this evidence. However, for historians willing to reconsider these judgments, I submit that public discourse, other voices in the American government outside of just the State Department, including Congress and mid-level bureaucracies, offers glimpses of an American mindset that held anti-Semitism was objectionable, whether it occurred in Boston[124] or Berlin. Moving past the received canon[125] can demonstrate a layered American response, one in which decrying Nazi anti-Semitism enabled citizens to demonstrate their support for the period's more liberalizing impulses.[126] This existing drive received additional momentum during the early 1930s, as reports of Nazi cruelty began to appear. During World War II a subsequent movement emerged that aimed to help persecuted minorities, especially European Jews—to make sure they were not abandoned—and this movement's efforts would ultimately outstrip all those that had preceded it.

---

124 Stephen Norwood, "Marauding Youth and the Christian Front: Anti-Semitic Violence In Boston and New York During World War II," *American Jewish History* 91 (2003): 233–267.

125 Federico Finchelstein, "The Holocaust Canon: Rereading Raul Hilberg," *New German Critique* 96 (2005): 7.

126 Hasia Diner, *We Remember With Reverence and Love: American Jews and the Myth of Silence After the Holocaust, 1945–1962* (New York: New York University Press, 2009), 20; Carole Fink, *Defending the Rights of Others: The Great Powers, the Jews, and International Minority Protection, 1878–1938* (New York: Cambridge University Press, 2004), 56; Stuart Svonkin, *Jews Against Prejudice: American Jews and the Fight for Civil Liberties* (New York: Columbia University Press, 1999), 12; Walter Jackson, *Gunnar Myrdal and America's Conscience: Social Engineering and Radical Liberalism, 1938–1987* (Chapel Hill, NC: University of North Carolina Press, 1990), 1–9.

Jan Láníček

Allied Governments' Responses to Reports About the Nazi Extermination Campaign Against the Jews in 1944

Abstract: *Some historians have suggested a causal link between popular anti-Semitism and failing policies to protect the Jews from the Holoacaust. But the US and the UK governments hesitated because they feared it might reduce broad support for the war. The allied governments were careful of accepting the first reports about the Holocaust because they were concerned for the safety of their POWs.*

Contemporary historiography of the Holocaust is one of the most developed historiographies on any historical subject. For decades historians have discussed issues that pertain to the various aspects of the Nazi extermination campaign against the Jews, to Jewish responses to the genocide, *and* to the behaviour of so-called bystanders—actors who were not directly involved in the mass murder but were in a position to influence events. Since the 1960s, historians have increasingly challenged the prevailing silence about the Allied responses to the Nazi persecution of the Jews throughout the 1930s and 1940s. This sensitive issue of how the powerful Allies—the United States, Britain, and the Soviet Union—responded to the Nazi racial policies has polarised historians. Some historians have condemned the alleged Allies' indifference and passivity, while others have emphasised that the Allies did all that was within their power and thus they cannot be accused of "the abandonment of the Jews," to borrow David Wyman's phrase.[1] In 1997, William Rubinstein published his controversial study entitled *The Myth of Rescue*. He rejected the notion that the Allies might have saved a significant number of Jews from Nazi Europe and argued that historians should reconsider their predominantly accusatory narratives concerning the Allied responses.[2] In

---

1   For good surveys on the historiography of the Holocaust see: Tony Kushner, ""'Pissing in the Wind?" The Search for Nuance in the Study of Holocaust "Bystanders"," in David Cesarani and Paul A. Levine, eds., *Bystanders to the Holocaust: A Re-evaluation* (London: Frank Cass, 2002), 57–76; Tony Kushner, "Britain, the United States and the Holocaust: In Search of a Historiography," in Dan Stone, ed., *The Historiography of the Holocaust* (London: Palgrave, 2004), 253–275.

2   William D. Rubinstein, *The Myth of Rescue. Why the Democracies Could Not Have Saved More Jews from the Nazis* (London: Routledge, 1997); for another book that rejects

contrast, Theodore S. Hamerow recently concluded that anti-Semitism in the Allied countries should be blamed directly for the death of Jews during the war.[3] This polarization of opinion among historians mirrors the moods in the society at large which, in Tony Kushner's words, still demands easy explanations, and desires to create "saints and sinners" in the Holocaust.[4] As it appears, a debate between the two groups of historians gradually became almost impossible, with neither side being willing to listen to the arguments of the other. It is therefore important to revisit some of the fundamental issues shaping the Allies' responses and to provide an explanation for their behaviour in a broader context, and also in a comparative perspective, all the while searching for common features of the Allied response on both sides of the Atlantic.

In my essay I adopt the approach suggested by Michael Marrus who argues that we should try to comprehend the conduct of a bystander "by making a painstaking effort to enter into their minds and sensibilities."[5] Similarly, in line with Marrus' approach we need to understand that "there is great danger that the historian will apply to subjects the standards, value systems, and vantage point of the present, rather than those of the period being discussed," and that this is an attitude we should avoid.[6] In doing so, the essay offers an impartial view of the Allied response to the wartime genocide and places Allied responses within the context of their general policies during the global war they led against the Axis.

---

the criticism of the Allied policies see: Robert N. Rosen, *Saving the Jews: Franklin D. Roosevelt and the Holocaust* (New York: Basic Books, 2006). See the articles by Demsky and Sukovata in this volume.

3   Theodore S. Hamerow, *Why We Watched: Europe, America and the Holocaust* (New York: W. W. Norton, 2008). For other studies that present the accusatory perspective, see especially: Arthur D. Morse, *While Six Million Died: A Chronicle of American Apathy* (New York: Random House, 1968); Henry L. Feingold, *The Politics of Rescue: The Roosevelt Administration and the Holocaust* (New York: Holocaust Library, 1970); David S. Wyman, *Paper Walls: America and the Refugee Crisis 1938–1941* (Amherst, MA: The University of Massachusetts Press, 1968); David S. Wyman, *The Abandonment of the Jews: America and the Holocaust 1941–1945* (New York: Pantheon Books, 1984); Bernard Wasserstein, *Britain and the Jews of Europe, 1939–1945* (London: Institute of Jewish Affairs, 1979).

4   Tony Kushner, "Britain, America and the Holocaust: Past, Present and Future Historiographies," in Jan Láníček and James Jordan, eds., *Governments-in-Exile and the Jews during the Second World War* (London: Vallentine Mitchell, 2013), 54.

5   Michael R. Marrus, *The Holocaust in History* (London: Penguin Books, 1989), 157.

6   Ibid.

This essay centres on the information that was available in the west concerning the persecution of the Jews, and the ways divergent groups in the Allied countries, primarily governments and journalists, treated the incoming reports. Wartime responses of the Allied countries to the Holocaust of European Jews were first of all dependent on the incoming information about German policies in Europe. Reports about the Nazi persecution of the Jews were continually pouring in to the west and access to this information was relatively unrestricted from the time of the Nazi rise to power in 1933 until late 1941, when Germany declared war on the United States. American envoys remained in the embassies and consulates in Hitler's Germany and American journalists there were able to collect information about the deterioration of the Jewish position in Nazi held territories.[7] Their work was facilitated by the Nazis themselves. The German press proudly trumpeted to the world the achievements of the Third Reich in limiting the "malicious" Jewish influence in societies throughout Nazi-controlled Europe. The "de-Judification" (*Entjudung*) of European societies under the Nazis and the "ghettoization" of the Jews were publicly announced by Nazi propaganda as the only correct way to solve the Jewish problem in Europe. Yet this propagandist machinery deliberately remained silent about the systematic extermination of the Jews being carried out by Nazis and their collaborators beginning in the summer of 1941. In spite of the Nazis' efforts to conceal the crimes committed in the east and elsewhere, reports about the mass murder of the Jews frequently found their way to the west. Richard Breitman documents how Allied intelligence services intercepted and deciphered messages sent to Berlin by German troops in the east, describing the systematic killing of Jews.[8] Also Michael Fleming has proven that the British and Americans knew much more about the extermination camps in the east than historians have thought they did until recently.[9] Furthermore newspapers in neutral and Axis countries brought the extermination campaign in the east to the attention of the public. Also, on several occasions people who directly witnessed Nazi crimes prepared reports intended to reveal to the Allies the true meaning of the Nazi "New Order" in Europe. Among them, couriers of the underground movements and prisoners who escaped from the Nazi death camps played prominent roles.

---

7   Ami-Bat Zucker, *In Search of Refuge: Jews and US Consuls in Nazi Germany 1933–1941* (London: Vallentine Mitchell, 2001).

8   Richard Breitman, *Official Secrets: What the Nazis planned, what the British and Americans Knew* (New York: Hill and Wang, 1998).

9   Michael Fleming, *Auschwitz, the Allies and Censorship of the Holocaust*, (Cambridge, UK: Cambridge University Press, 2014). Compare to Martin Gilbert, *Auschwitz and the Allies* (London: Michael Joseph, 1981).

In light of the abundant, if fragmentary, information that was available about the genocide, the question arises as to how this was treated by decision-makers and journalists in the west. This essay documents a very problematic treatment of the incoming intelligence and identifies the main factors that shaped the Allied responses to the Holocaust or Shoah during the Second World War. I revisit this issue by analysing the Allies' treatment of one of the most detailed reports depicting life in Nazi concentration camps that ever reached the Allied countries, the so-called Auschwitz Protocols (the Auschwitz Reports, or Vrba-Wetzler Report). Using the American attitude as a paradigm, the essay concludes with a wider transatlantic comparison of other Allied countries' responses and provides a transatlantic perspective to the responses to the Holocaust.

On Sunday November 26, 1944, the War Refugee Board (WRB), the US governmental agency created by President Roosevelt in January 1944, and charged with responsibility for "the refugees" (the Jews were not explicitly mentioned), released a brochure entitled *German Extermination Camps – Auschwitz and Birkenau.*[10] It brought to the public's attention a full version of the Auschwitz Protocols–a report compiled from the eye witness accounts of five escapees from the Auschwitz death camp. Walter Rosenberg and Alfred Wetzler escaped from Auschwitz in April 1944 and Czeslaw Mordowitz and Arnošt Rosin in late May 1944. All four escapees reached Slovakia and with the help of the Slovak Jewish underground prepared extensive and comprehensive reports about the Auschwitz camp complex. These reports were later transmitted via several routes to Switzerland, the Vatican, and Hungary.[11] The escaped prisoners spent almost two years in Auschwitz and witnessed all the stages of the murderous process in that death factory. They estimated that around 1,765,000 Jews had been killed in the Auschwitz Camp complex between April 1942 and April 1944. The first summaries of the report were received in Washington in June and July, but the full version was not transmitted by the US embassy in Bern until mid-October 1944, more than three months after the full version was available in London.[12] The statements of the

10 Box 5 and 7, War Refugee Board (hereafter: WRB), Franklin Delano Roosevelt Presidential Library, Hyde Park, NY (hereafter: FDRPL).

11 For the full report see: David S. Wyman, ed., *America and the Holocaust: A Thirteen-Volume Set Documenting the Editor's Book The Abandonment of the Jews* (New York/London: Garland Publishing, 1990), Vol. 12, 1–64. Document no. 1. "German Extermination Camps – Auschwitz and Birkenau," November 1944.

12 Wyman argues that the "delay apparently resulted from the low priority the American legation in Bern gave to WRB matters." See Wyman, *Abandonment of the Jews*, 324. Martin Gilbert, *Auschwitz and the Allies* (London: Michael Joseph, 1981), 327. On

four escapees were further corroborated by another report by a Polish non-Jewish prisoner Jerzy Tabeau who escaped from Auschwitz in 1943 (*Report of a Polish Major*). Hence with the help of the escapees and European underground channels, this comprehensive depiction of Auschwitz finally reached the Allies. When the WRB, more than seven months after their escape, released the full version of their accounts, the American newspapers offered extensive coverage of the event. Eighty-three daily newspapers and magazines across the United States published articles informing the American public about the content of the Protocols.[13] Yet the report was released too late in the United States to have any impact on the situation in Auschwitz. Soon afterwards, when Soviet troops had already made their way deep into Polish territory, the Germans blew up the gas chambers and crematoria in Auschwitz and Birkenau in a desperate effort to cover up every trace of their crimes against humanity.

An analysis of the American responses to the Protocols needs to take into account that the reports came out at the final phase of the war, when the Allied armies in the east and west had reached the pre-war border of Germany and were preparing a final push into the heart of the Third Reich. The Allies had acknowledged earlier that they knew of the crimes committed by the Nazis against the civilian population. The St. James Declaration of January 13, 1942, signed by the governments-in-exile of occupied countries, condemned the brutal Nazi policies against the subjugated nations. Yet no distinction according to nationality, race, or religion had been made. Over the summer of 1942, Allied statesmen received specific reports, including the so-called Riegner telegram, revealing to the world the Nazi plans for the murder of four million Jews. In November 1942, a courier of the Polish underground, Jan Karski, arrived in London and described the horrific details of his visit to the Warsaw ghetto and one of the transit camps in the Lublin region, Izbica Lubielska, the antechamber to the death camp of Belzec.[14] As a consequence of receiving these reports and testimonies, on December 17, 1942, eleven governments of the United Nations, including the United States, Britain, and the Soviet Union, issued a declaration explicitly condemning the Nazi "bestial

the escape of the prisoners see Miroslav Kárný, "The Vrba and Wetzler Report," in Israel Gutman and Michael Berenbaum, eds., *Anatomy of the Auschwitz Death Camp* (Bloomington, IN: Indiana University Press, 1994), 553–567.

13 Report on Press and Public Reaction to War Refugee Board. Release of Accounts of Auschwitz and Birkenau, box 7, WRB, FDRPL.

14 For Karski's account of his visit in the Warsaw ghetto and in the transit camp, see: Jan Karski, *Story of a Secret State* (London: Hodder & Stoughton, 1945).

policy of cold-blooded extermination" against the Jews.[15] This declaration received the widest possible publicity in the Allied press. Yet because it did not promise any specific rescue or relief measures, apart from the threat of the post-war retribution, it fell short of the expectations expressed by activists in the Allied countries.

We could therefore suppose that once this "official secret" was publicly acknowledged, people in the west, including their governments, were aware of the Nazi genocidal policy and it became common knowledge. However, as Yehuda Bauer suggests, it is difficult to identify when "information" became "knowledge."[16] The information about the Nazi racial policies was widely available, but before somebody "knew" of the genocide, he had to go through several stages. Bauer has summarized them as follows: "first, the information had to be disseminated; then, it had to be believed; then, it had to be internalized, that is, some connection had to be established between the new reality and a possible course of action; finally, there came action, if and when action came." Only then was an individual able to fully comprehend the situation of the Jews in Europe.[17] Similarly, Victoria Barnett has argued that the information was widely available, but "[t]hroughout the World, the predominant reaction to reports from Europe was disbelief, indifference, passivity, and a sense of powerlessness."[18] Understanding whether the Allies and their leadership were able to comprehend the incoming information about the extermination of the Jews appears to be crucial for an analysis of the governments' responses to the ongoing genocide in occupied Europe. Nevertheless, we should also be aware that we are dealing with a genocide that occurred during a time of a total war. There were other factors that shaped the responses of governments to Nazi barbarities. Thus, we need to contextualise the Allied responses toward persecuted minorities within their efforts to win the war against Nazi Germany in the first place.

When the WRB published the report in November 1944, the New York Times on its front page concluded that this was the first detailed report gathered from eye-witnesses about the organized atrocities. This was not entirely accurate given that Allied governments had been receiving eye-witness reports since 1941, but the identity of the eye witnesses, and the fact that they wrote the reports were

15 Henry Feingold, "The Surprising Historic Roots of Holocaust Denial," in Debra R. Kaufman et al., eds., From the Protocols of the Elders of Zion to Holocaust Denial Trials: Challenging the Media, Law and the Academy (London: Vallentine Mitchell, 2007), 69.
16 Marrus, Holocaust in History, 158.
17 Ibid.
18 Victoria Barnett, Bystanders: Conscience and Complicity During the Holocaust (Westport, CT: Greenwood Press, 1999), 51.

rarely revealed to the general public. Referring to the WRB, the *New York Times* informed its readers that the US government had verified the content of the report, and that it represented "a true picture of the frightful happenings in these camps. [The WRB] is making the reports public .... in the firm conviction that they should be read and understood by all Americans."[19] American journalists were primarily concerned about spreading unverified information that might be considered wartime propaganda. The *Washington Post* noted scepticism in American society based on the experience of allegedly fabricated "atrocity stories" describing German crimes in occupied Belgium and France during World War I, a sentiment widely shared by decision-makers in Washington and London.[20] The 1944 articles in the mainstream American media secured widespread publicity for the escapees' reports. However, as we analyse the path to the final publishing of the reports, we can see a highly complex example of the Allies' responses to reports of the extermination campaign against the Jews. As such, it was symptomatic of the American responses to what we now call the Holocaust.

Shortly after receiving the full report, the officials in the WRB identified five ways to potentially utilise the Auschwitz Protocols. Aside from a proposal to bomb the camps, put forward in the report by the Slovak Jewish underground, the WRB mainly suggested using the report as propaganda.[21] Hence John Pehle, the Director of the WRB, provided the report first to the Congress and later, on November 26, 1944, to the American press and public. Interestingly, the American government was the only Allied government to release the full version of the Protocols to the press. No one in the British government considered making the full version of the report public.[22] The only instances of its publication outside of the US were a

---

19 "U.S. Board Bares Atrocity Details Told by Witnesses at Polish Camps," the *New York Times*, 26 November 1944, p.1., box 7, WRB, FDRPL.

20 "Two Million Executed in Nazi Camps' Gassing, Cremation Assembly-Line Methods Told by War Refugee Board," the *Washington Post*, 26 November 1944. box 5, WRB, FDRPL.

21 F. Hodel, memorandum, Re: Use of Reports on Oswiecim and Birkenau Forwarded by McClelland, box 7, WRB, FDRPL.

22 Gilbert, *Auschwitz and the Allies*, 290. The reason might be that there was no separate British governmental organization tasked with the organization of rescue initiatives on behalf of the "refugees." I argue in this article that the traditional offices in the American administration opposed the publication of the full version of the Protocols. It was only thanks to the efforts of Pehle (director of the War Refugee Board) that a full version of the Protocols was released. Michael Fleming has recently documented the efforts of the British government to supress and censor information about Auschwitz between 1941 and 1944; Michael Fleming, *Auschwitz, the Allies and Censorship of the Holocaust*

pamphlet in French entitled *Les Camps d'extermination* and later an abridged version of the Protocols under the title *Die Judenausrottung in Polen*, both released by private presses in Switzerland.[23] Excerpts from the reports were also broadcast in June and July 1944 by various national services of the BBC, including, for example, the Czechoslovak *Voice of the Free Republic*.[24]

Even in the United States, however, the path to publishing the report was not simple. Only when it was impossible to stop publication, did it become apparent that Pehle had not consulted with other American agencies or even with all the members of the WRB. The WRB, working under Pehle's directorship, was comprised of the Treasury Secretary, Henry Morgenthau Jr., the Secretary of War, Henry Stimson, and the Secretary of State, Cordell Hull. As it appears from the phone conversation between Morgenthau and Stimson that took place on November 27, 1944, a day after the Protocols were released, Pehle consulted only Morgenthau before the full version of the reports was relayed to the press. This phone conversation provides an interesting insight into the problematic responses to the Protocols on the part of the administration, and proves that an influential part of the government made an effort to stop the publication of the report. Hence it is quoted at length:

November 27, 1944, at 10.49 am:

"Stimson: I've just learned that there was some quite striking announcement put out as to the atrocities yesterday by the Committee ... on Refugees.

Morgenthau: Yes.

S: Well, it must have been done without anybody showing it to me so I was rather mortified by not knowing anything about it. ... I don't think Pehle ought to do that.

(Cambridge: Cambridge University Press, 2014). Fleming also argues that the Vrba-Wetzler report attracted far less attention of the British national press than it was the case with American newspapers (242). The fact that there was no governmental office in the British administration that would try to secure help for the persecuted Jews led to the situation that there was no significant pressure in the British government that could contribute to the publication of the report.

23 Kárný, "The Vrba and Wetzler Report," 562 and 567. See also Henryk Świebocki, ed., *London Has Been Informed... Reports by Auschwitz Escapees* (Oswiecim: The Auschwitz-Birkenau State Museum, 2002), 60.

24 Jan Láníček, "The Czechoslovak Section of the BBC and the Jews during the Second World War," *Yad Vashem Studies* 38:2 (2010): 123–153.

HMJr:	Well, I was under the impression, but I know he showed it to me.
S:	I know—I'm thoroughly—I'll probably be in thorough sympathy with any such announcement. I think it's important to get it out, but as long as I'm one of the Committee, I think I ought to know about it...

...

HMJr:	Have you asked McCloy [Assistant Secretary of War] whether he saw it?
S:	McCloy was the man who told me that it had come out. He didn't see it himself.
HMJr:	Well, I was under the impression...
S:	He heard of it through a row by Elmer Davis [director of the Office of War Information] who was annoyed that it hadn't been cleared through him. It hadn't been submitted to anyone here that I know of at all.
HMJr:	Well, that's wrong because I told Pehle to show it to McCloy. Now, I don't know...
S:	Well, I know, but he ought to show it to me. It's important enough— It's important enough. I had no...
HMJr:	I agree. I agree. I'll talk to Pehle. I don't know—I'd like to hear his side of the story.
S:	Yes, yes. I only just—McCloy is the one who brought it up as a thing which I ought to stop if possible. ... It hadn't been—he knew nothing about it.
HMJr:	Well, that's wrong.

...

| S: | Well, it's done now. It's done now. I'll look—I'll read the thing through. I didn't happen to see it myself, and I'll find that out."[25] |

As we now know, Pehle intentionally did not consult the Department of War, as the surest way to get the full version of the report published. That department evidently opposed the publication of the Protocols, because Stimson and McCloy also had their doubts about the veracity of "atrocity reports." Although Pehle himself admitted having doubts concerning "atrocity stories," as he referred to them, he concluded that, "after reading these accounts one cannot refute the conclusion

---

25 Morgenthau Diaries, Book 799, reel 230, image 19–21, FDRPL.

that such things do happen and are happening."[26] The day after the Protocols were
released to the press, Ira Hirschmann, a WRB envoy in Turkey, noted in a letter to
Pehle that, based on his own experience, he assumed that Pehle had published the
report "over the 'dead bodies' of some of his colleagues in the State Department."[27]
Pehle responded that the opposition was not so strong in the State Department,
but it was in other circles, which apparently was a reference to McCloy and Davis.
However, Pehle poignantly noted that this opposition was formed, "unfortunately"
at the moment when the release of the report could not be avoided.[28] Even Secretary Stimson personally resented this intrusion of Morgenthau and Pehle "into
matters of policy in respect to the treatment of Germany." Stimson penned in
his private diary that Morgenthau, "as a Jew is the last man who ought to do it."[29]

As mentioned in the phone conversation between Morgenthau and Stimson,
the main opposition came from the Director of the Office of War Information
(OWI), Elmar Davis. The OWI, created in 1942, was an American government
agency in charge of consolidating government information services during the
war. Laurel Leff emphasises that from the very beginning of his activities in 1942
Davis was reluctant to place too much emphasis on the persecution of the Jews in
American war propaganda. Notably, Davis was apparently concerned about anti-
Semitism in American society.[30] In November 1944, Davis' colleagues in the OWI
argued that the report might further encourage anti-Semitism in American society, since it would "prove" that in the concentration camps, the Jews persecuted
Jews (this was apparently a reference to the hierarchy among prisoners and the
role of *Kapos*). The OWI staff resented that the Protocols were published shortly
before the start of the sixth war loan, because they thought it might negatively
impact that loan.[31]

Furthermore when dealing with the Protocols, Davis primarily raised doubts
about the veracity of the report and enquired about its sources. Davis was rather

26 Pehle to Hirschmann, 28 November 1944, box 7, WRB, FDRPL.
27 Hirschmann to Pehle, 27 November 1944, box 7, WRB, FDRPL.
28 Ibid.
29 Richard Breitman and Allan J. Lichtman, *FDR and the Jews* (Cambridge, MA: The
    Belknap Press of Harvard University Press, 2013), 285.
30 Laurel Leff, *Buried by the Times. The Holocaust and America's Most Important News-
    paper* (Cambridge: CUP, 2005), 243–248. On anti-Semitism in American society, see,
    for example, Wyman, *Abandonment of the Jews*, 14–15.
31 Virginia M. Mannon, Memorandum to Files, 22 November 1944. Regarding: Mr. Elmer
    Davis' questioning of War Refugee Board's release of German atrocity stories, box 7,
    WRB, FDRPL.

sceptical about the incoming reports depicting the situation under the Nazis.[32] In a letter to Pehle, he raised absurd charges, arguing that because two of the authors of the report had worked as scribes in Birkenau, their escape might have been organized or allowed by the Germans. He alleged that the Germans might target the allied war effort by creating contempt for camp inmates, both Jews and Aryans. According to Davis, the Germans might want to influence American public opinion against the prisoners, even at the cost of publishing details from the camps that proved their crimes against the prisoners. Resenting the publication of the Protocols, Davis emphasised that the publication of the report was neither approved by his office nor by the Department of War nor by the State Department.[33] In this manner he distanced himself from Pehle's activities. It was evident that had Pehle asked for permission to publish the report, Davis would not have given it. Also Stimson, who otherwise appeared to agree with the need to publicize similar reports, warned Pehle at the end of December that he needed to be extremely cautious when giving such reports to the press. The Secretary argued that the horrific content of the reports was sure to invite further inquiry into the government's efforts to authenticate them.[34] As late as autumn of 1944, leading American officials were still suspicious of "atrocity stories" and did not want to be accused of spreading false propaganda that could potentially discredit the Allied information services.

The concerns of the OWI staff that overemphasizing the persecution of the Jews could be taken adversely by the public in the west and in Nazi-controlled territories, needs to be seriously considered in any analysis of the Allied reactions to the Nazi genocide of the Jews. The BBC home service in its radio broadcasts tried to avoid stressing the persecution of Jewish civilians, in part because of the prevailing anti-Semitic tendencies in British society.[35] Identical considerations can be documented in the United States, where in 1944 anti-Semitic sentiment among the public reached its peak.[36] In late October 1944, the US Army magazine, *Yank*, approached the WRB questioning whether the magazine could publish information on the atrocities committed by the Germans in Europe. The magazine

---

32 Laurel Leff, *Buried by the Times: The Holocaust and America's Most Important Newspaper* (Cambridge: CUP, 2005), 245–248.

33 Elmer Davis to Pehle, 23 November 1944, box 7, WRB, FDRPL.

34 McCloy to Pehle, 27 December 1944, box 7, WRB, FDRPL.

35 On this subject, see: Tony Kushner, *The Persistence of Prejudice: Anti-Semitism in British Society during the Second World War* (Manchester: MUP, 1989). See also the essay by Sukovata in this volume.

36 Leff, *Times*, 354.

intended to prepare an edition that would reveal to American soldiers the true nature of their enemy. This request came precisely when a complete transcript of the Protocols had arrived in Washington and Pehle offered a copy to *Yank*. However the editors decided not to proceed with the publication, because the report was, in their opinion, "too Semitic," meaning that it principally dealt with the fate of the Jews and could not convey any universal message; they would prefer information from other sources ("a less Jewish story"). The editors were concerned about latent anti-Semitism in the army and they thought that a story depicting the fate of the Jews would not appeal to the soldiers. A reporter for the *Yank* tried to get army clearance for an overseas edition, but found "a very negative attitude" in the Pentagon. According to representatives of the Pentagon, it was a "Hell of a hot story," and permission from the high military command was necessary for its disclosure.[37] As in the case with Davis, the US Army had reservations about the veracity of the story, and furthermore was also concerned about anti-Semitic sentiments among Americans. Low-ranking officials were not willing to approve its publication without consulting army commanders. Hence Pehle and the WRB were not successful in their efforts to get the help of the armed forces to ensure wider circulation and utilisation of the reports.

In contrast with Davis and the Pentagon, it is noteworthy that the otherwise sceptical American press, with minor exceptions, did not raise doubts about the veracity of the Protocols.[38] The majority of dailies and magazines brought the content of the reports to the attention of the public.[39] Subsequently, a Gallup Poll examined whether the American public regarded these reports as credible. The survey, published in early December 1944, found that Americans were "fully prepared" to believe that these events actually took place in Europe. Yet, as the report noted, the average American thought that the number of people killed

---

37 Virginia M. Mannon (Treasury Dept) to Pehle, 16 November 1944. Regarding: *Yank Magazine* and the German atrocity reports, box 7, WRB, FDRPL.

38 One exception was a veteran journalist Oswald F. Schuette, who contacted Stimson and expressed his doubts about the veracity of the reports. See: Oswald F. Schuette (National Press Building, Washington) to Henry L. Stimson (Secretary of War), 28 November 1944; Draft response for Stimson (prep. by Friedman) to Schuette, 2 December 1944, box 7, WRB, FDRPL.

39 Report on Press and Public Reaction to War Refugee Board. Release of Accounts of Auschwitz and Birkenau, box 7, WRB, FDRPL. See also two important studies on the subject of the responses of the American press to the news on the Holocaust: Leff, *Times*; Deborah E. Lipstadt, *Beyond Belief: The American Press And The Coming Of The Holocaust, 1933–1945* (New York: The Free Press, 1986).

in Nazi concentration camps was approximately 100,000.[40] Even at the end of 1944, the American public was not able to comprehend the scope of what was happening in Europe. The public's state of mind was certainly influenced by the US government, which, despite internal opposition, published the first detailed report about the extermination camps only at the end of November 1944. While the American press had been bringing news of the persecution of the Jews in Europe to the public since Hitler's rise to power, its reporting was not systematic and apparently lacked the backing of public authorities.

Unfortunately we have far less information about the Soviet response to be able to attempt any serious comparison. TASS–the official governmental press agency—reported on and quoted from the full version of the Protocols shortly after its release in late November 1944. Quite exceptional also was a direct reference to the Jews among the victims of the camps printed in *Pravda* and other major Soviet newspapers.[41] During the war, Soviet government policy predominantly avoided any differentiation of the victims based on their ethnic origin or religious affiliation; they were all "peaceful Soviet citizens." When analysing the Soviet response to the Holocaust we also need to take into account that overall, the Soviet Jews formed only a minor part of Soviet war victims and casualties.

The Auschwitz Protocols aroused profound outrage among politicians in the west but few were really willing to act. It is well documented that demands for action came mostly from non-governmental, Jewish sources. Even then, on both sides of the Atlantic, to quote Randolph Braham, "no measures [could have been undertaken] that might be construed as inconsistent 'with the successful prosecution of the war.'"[42] The Soviet administration also believed that only liberation of the camps by regular troops of the Red Army could rescue the prisoners.[43] We still do not know enough about the Soviet response to the Holocaust. Jeffrey Herf

---

40 "Gallup Poll Finds Mass Murders Underestimated," the *Washington Post*, 3 December 1944, box 5, WRB, FDRPL.

41 Karel C. Berkhoff, " 'Total Annihilation of the Jewish Population.' The Holocaust in the Soviet Media, 1941–45," *Kritika: Exploration in Russian and Eurasian History* 10:1 (2009): 94f.

42 Randolph L. Braham, *The Politics of Genocide: The Holocaust in Hungary, Volume 2* (New York: Columbia University Press, 1981), 1103.

43 Valkov (Soviet Embassy to the Czechoslovak Government-in-Exile) to Czechoslovak Minister of State, Ripka, 1 August 1944, LA-D, box 190, AMZV (Archive of the Czech Ministry of Foreign Affairs). Quoted in Jan Láníček, *Czechs, Slovaks and the Jews, 1938–48: Beyond Idealisation and Condemnation* (Basingstoke, UK: Palgrave, 2013), 212.

suggests that, "The Great Patriotic War was never a war to save the Jews."[44] But this is an inadequate statement, because we can also easily conclude that neither the Americans nor the British led the war against Germany to save the Jews (even though the German propaganda tried to portray the Allies as fighting for Jewish interests). We need to understand that all the reports about the persecution of the Jews were received at a time of global war. It was a war led by the Americans and their allies against a mighty block of enemy powers, a war whose outcome was in the balance for a long time, and a war that cost hundreds of thousands of lives–even millions of lives in the case of the Soviet Union. The whole war was predominantly and almost exclusively perceived through the lens of Allied national interests and the Allied efforts to end the war in the shortest possible time. Any policy that might have prolonged the war or diverted from the exclusive focus on the military dimension of the war was met with disapproval. We can document among the Allies an apparent abandonment of the principle of humanitarian interventionism, but that abandonment predated the war. The most notable case was the well-known American government's rejection to allow the more than 900 passengers of the *MS St. Louis* to disembark in the United States, once their Cuban immigration visas were cancelled in May and June 1939. The passengers had to return to Europe. Most of them survived the war in Britain and continental Western Europe, though 254 perished in the Holocaust.[45]

The most debated issue concerning the American response to the Holocaust was the proposed bombing of the Auschwitz camp complex and the railways leading to the camp.[46] From the moment they received the first proposals, the Department of War, especially Assistant Secretary McCloy, opposed the bombing of the concentration camps. McCloy argued that such an attack could be executed only with a diversion of considerable air power, which was needed elsewhere. The American forces were engaged in the landing on Normandy and later in supporting the Allied troops in France. At the same time they were attempting to break the German military machine and civil defiance in Germany by means of the constant bombing of German cities. Although Pehle repeatedly forwarded proposals to

---

44 Jeffrey Herf, "The Nazi Extermination Camps and the Ally to the East: Could the Red Army and Air Force Have Stopped or Slowed the Final Solution?" *Kritika: Exploration in Russian and Eurasian History* 4:4 (2003): 928.

45 Sarah A. Ogilvie and Scott Miller, *The St. Louis and the Holocaust: Refuge Denied* (Madison: University of Wisconsin Press, 2006), 194–195.

46 For selected essays on the subject, see: Michael J. Neufeld and Michael Berenbaum, eds., *The Bombing of Auschwitz: Should the Allies Have Attempted It?* (Lawrence, KS: University Press of Kansas, 2003).

bomb Auschwitz, only in November 1944 did he endorse them overtly, and only after receiving the full version of the Protocols.[47] This was the first time that a high-ranking American official directly supported the bombing of the Auschwitz complex, and it is clear that this was triggered by the Protocols. Pehle's demand, however, was rejected outright by McCloy.[48] There was in fact a shared notion on both sides of the Atlantic—in Britain and the United States–that military equipment should not be used for humanitarian purposes. In recent years the failure to bomb the camps has become one of the major points of contention among historians of the Allied responses to the Holocaust. Yet, as Breitman and Lichtman comment, "[T]hat was not the case at that time in the United States. Even American Jewish leaders knew little about Auschwitz, and most Americans would have agreed that the military's job was to win the war as quickly as possible."[49]

An important factor in McCloy's rejection of the bombing of the camps was that, as the Assistant Secretary of War, he had to take into consideration the fate of American POWs held in Nazi internment camps. As the liberation of Europe progressed and the collapse of Germany became increasingly imminent, the fate of those American internees in the last hours of the Nazi rule emerged as an issue.[50] Likewise, McCloy's concerns regarding the American POWs can help us find an explanation as to why the Assistant Secretary was reluctant to give any publicity to "atrocity stories."

In fact, similar concerns can be documented in a broader transatlantic perspective when we look at responses to Nazi racial policies from other Allied statesmen in Europe. In October 1944, the Czechoslovak government-in-exile approached the British Foreign Office and asked them to publicly support the Czech declaration against the German crimes committed against Jews and Czechs during the suppression of the Slovak National Uprising in the autumn of 1944. The British Foreign Office refused to support the declaration and only complied with the Czechs' request to forward the memorandum via private

---

47 Wyman, *America and the Holocaust, Vol. 12*, 175–176. Document no. 63. Pehle to McCloy, 8 November 1944.

48 Wyman, *America and the Holocaust. Vol. 12*, 184–185. Document no. 68. McCloy to Pehle, 18 November 1944.

49 Richard Breitman, "Roosevelt and the Holocaust," in Verne W. Newton, ed., *FDR and the Holocaust* (New York: St. Martin's Press, 1996), 109–127 and Allan J. Lichtman, *FDR and the Jews* (Cambridge, MA: The Belknap Press of Harvard University Press, 2013), 286.

50 Arieh Kochavi, *Confronting Captivity* (Chapel Hill, NC: University of North Carolina Press, 2005), 171–202.

channels to the Vatican. The British reluctance was based on their concern that another public declaration against Nazi crimes might cause German reprisals against British POWs.[51] Similarly, in October 1944, when the Allies prepared a declaration warning the Germans against the planned murder of the inmates in Auschwitz and Birkenau, the proposed declaration was opposed by the Dutch government-in-exile. The Dutch, "who had recently received reports of massacres of Dutchmen near Arnhem, were afraid that the issue of any declaration might merely lead to further murders and were consequently not in favour of the [...] proposal."[52] Hence in the last phase of the war, the western Allies were reluctant to issue public warnings or declarations concerning the Nazi persecution of the Jews, as well as other groups of prisoners because of possible repercussions for their nationals still in Nazi hands.

There is also evidence documenting the reluctance among the Allied nations to "inflate" the number of officially endorsed warnings. In July 1944 the Czechoslovak government-in-exile shared the first summary of the Auschwitz Protocols with other allies. At the same time they proposed a new declaration from the Allied countries that would reconfirm their determination to punish all those guilty of heinous crimes. The British side rejected this proposal and justified their decision by saying that sufficient warnings had already been issued and there was no need to prepare a new one. The British pointed to the official warnings given by Roosevelt and the British Foreign Secretary, Anthony Eden in March 1944, after the German occupation of Hungary.[53] The Americans shared the British view. The reason given was that the Protocols did not appear to contain any specific, concrete information about the future Nazi plans in Auschwitz; they just stipulated and described what had already happened. The only exception, providing specific details about planned German actions, was Vrba's and Wetzler's warning concerning the liquidation of the Theresienstadt family camp in Auschwitz-Birkenau planned for June 20, 1944. The planned liquidation of Jews deported to Birkenau from Theresienstadt was publicly condemned by the Czechoslovak government-in-exile, but not as a part of any broader allied declaration.[54] The Czechoslovaks did not initiate discussion on a general Allied declaration based on the Protocols until the beginning of July 1944, and

51 Minute on the file, 16 October 1944, FO371/38942, C13878/1343/12, The National Archives, London, (hereafter: TNA).
52 Notes by Allen, Foreign Office, 6 October 1944, C13825/131/25, FO371/39454, TNA.
53 Eden to Churchill, 3 July 1944, PREM 4/51/10, TNA.
54 Láníček, "The Czechoslovak Section of the BBC and the Jews during the Second World War," 137–138.

the Protocols did not contain any specific details about Nazi plans for the Jews after that date. Therefore the Americans and British did not deem it necessary to create another public declaration or warning.

This theory seems to be confirmed by the fact that the western Allies issued another warning, together with the Polish government-in-exile, only in October 1944. The publication of this declaration was triggered by an intelligence leak revealing the Nazi plan to destroy the camps in Auschwitz and murder all the prisoners before the arrival of the Red Army. But again the American and British governments were reluctant to take part in this declaration. Nevertheless a British official wrote that although the declaration would do neither any harm nor any good, because of the increasing Polish pressure and in the interest of Jewish and humanitarian organizations, he thought it was better to issue the warning. Apparently there was a fear in Britain that it "would be difficult to justify [their] own inaction to Allied governments and interested British circles and [they] should certainly be blamed later on if [a] massacre takes place and we have done nothing."[55] It is noteworthy, however, that the October 1944 declaration did not stress the uniqueness of the Nazi persecution of the Jews. The Allies protested against the mass execution of "the inmates" (the Jews were not explicitly mentioned) in the camps at Oswiecim and Brzezinka, where thousands of people from many European countries were imprisoned.[56] This story reveals another feature of the Allied responses to the Holocaust. In the very last phases of the war, the Allies published warnings against the planned Nazi massacres of the Jews, but only when detailed intelligence about specific actions was received. The Allies were sceptical about the impact of the warnings published in December 1942 and March 1944, but were at the same time concerned they might appear as not having done enough if in fact the received reports proved to be correct.

Understanding the Allied response to the Protocols helps us to identify the factors shaping bystanders' responses to warnings about the Nazi extermination campaign against the Jews. During the discussion in the House of Representatives and in the press, the only demands discussed were for a hard peace with Germany and postwar retribution against war criminals.[57] Furthermore, the departments involved in the rescue operations made no specific demands. It also seems that the long-established US governmental departments disregarded the newly created

---

55 Note by Ian Henderson, 9 October 1944, FO371/39454, TNA.
56 A copy of the declaration, 10 October 1944, FO371/39454, TNA.
57 Congressional Record – Appendix A4879, 28 November 1944, War Refugee Board on Atrocities. Extension of remarks of Hon. Emanuel Celler of New York in The House of Representatives, box 7, WRB, FDRPL.

WRB, although its chairman was accountable directly to Roosevelt. These ambiguities in the hierarchy of the US administration contributed to the fact that the only major response of the US government to the Nazi racial policy was the publication of the Auschwitz Protocols carried out by Pehle's office at the end of November 1944. It is noteworthy that there is no evidence that President Roosevelt himself ever read the reports of the Auschwitz escapees. By comparison British Prime Minister, Winston Churchill, and Foreign Minister, Anthony Eden read the report in July 1944, and responded by immediately demanding the bombing of Auschwitz. When representatives of the RAF rejected this demand, Eden deeply resented their decision.[58] Yet neither Churchill nor Eden subsequently insisted on the implementation of the military operation.

Indeed there are many similarities between the American and British responses to the incoming reports about the Nazi persecution of the Jews. If we follow the approach suggested by Marrus, we need to conclude that the suffering of the Jews did not figure prominently on the agenda of the Allied governments. There was a feeling that as long as Nazi Germany was capable of waging war against the Allies, all other issues were of secondary importance. Only the military defeat of the Nazis could, according to the Allies, save Jewish lives. Any military or diplomatic intervention was perceived as a dangerous diversion in the Allied military efforts. Furthermore, a part of the American leadership was very apprehensive about officially publishing reports that they did not entirely trust, an attitude that can be documented as well in the case of the British. Nonetheless we can only speculate about the reasons why the British did not consider publishing the Auschwitz Protocols. Both they and the Americans were sceptical about the content of "atrocity reports," but the British were also weary of the kind of response the report might evoke from the public, given the strong anti-Semitic sentiments that allegedly prevailed on both sides of the Atlantic. Similarly, both major Allies were anxious not to confirm the Nazi propaganda stories depicting the Allies as being in the Jewish clout. Moreover, being excessively apprehensive about their image as liberal democracies, both countries decided not to give prominence to the stories depicting the suffering of one particular group of victims and rather preferred the universalization of the Nazi persecution of the Jews.[59] What is even more important for a broader comparison, however, is that there is no available evidence that would suggest

---

58 Sinclair to Eden, 15 July 1944, Eden's handwritten remark: "He wasn't asked his opinion of this, he was asked to act." FO 371/42809, TNA.

59 Tony Kushner, *The Holocaust and the Liberal Imagination: A Social and Cultural History* (Oxford, UK: Blackwell, 1994).

any mutual influences that shaped the individual responses of the Allied governments. It is indeed striking that both of the major liberal democracies and also the minor Allies reached an almost identical conclusion about the way to respond to the information about the Nazi persecution of the Jews, and they reached their matching conclusion independently.

Hasia Diner

No Generation of Silence: American Jews Confront the Catastrophe in the Post-War Years

Abstract: *This essay challenges the widespread myth that survivors who came to America did not want to share their experiences. It richly documents the claim that survivors were not passive recipients of American benefactors, but actively shared their survival stories and participated in small-scale memorials.*

In late twentieth century America, the Holocaust came to assume tremendous prominence in American, Jewish, and indeed world consciousness. This emergence into bold and dynamic relief came about as the generation of Holocaust survivors had matured, had become fully integrated into America, and some had achieved a modicum of material comfort. With their children grown up and launched, the survivors seemingly turned back to the harrowing years of their suffering and made the story of what had happened to them and to their families a major point of public awareness. This way of seeing the history of Holocaust commemoration and the role of survivors in it, however, ignores a longer history of survivor work on behalf of remembering the catastrophe of the Jewish people. It also ignores the partnership in which they engaged with other American Jews in making an earlier memorial culture possible. From the late 1940s when the first of the *shearith hapletah*—the surviving remnant—began to come to America into the early 1960s, they functioned as memorial makers, as witnesses to the tragedy, and as collaborators with American Jewry in the project of keeping alive the memory of those who had perished and in helping to transform America and American Jewish life.[1]

The survivors who came to America functioned as more than recipients of American Jewish aid or as abstract symbols of Jewish survival. The Jewish women and men who made their way to the United States after the Nazi catastrophe told their stories, making an impact on the American Jewish scene. Their words and their actions entered into the communal culture. Survivors made links with

---

1   A form of this article was given as the Annual Monna and Otto Weinmann Lecture, sponsored by Janice Weinman Shorenstein, at the US Holocaust memorial Museum's Center for Advanced Holocaust Studies, 2011.

particular religious and communal organizations, Zionist groups, Hadassah chapters, synagogues, and the like, they addressed audiences and spoke about their Holocaust experiences. They made their voices heard in an American Jewish public world able to and willing to hear them.

This stands in direct contradiction to the often repeated, nearly universally accepted assertion that the survivors came to the United States and refused to talk about their brutal experiences. According to the dominant narrative, American Jews cajoled these "new Americans" into keeping quiet, demanding that they remain silent about the tragedies that had befallen them. Historians and others, including survivors when interviewed in oral history projects decades later, claimed universally that a kind of conspiracy reigned which forced them into silence for more than a quarter of a century.

The assertion that postwar American Jews ignored the Holocaust began in the late 1960s as young Jewish activists, aglow with the zeal of social and cultural protest so rampant in American society, blamed Jewish community leaders for their unwillingness to confront the horrors that had taken place under Nazi rule. Like young people from other ethnic communities who took their leaders to task, so too Jewish militants accused the rabbis, teachers, writers, and others who made up "the Jewish establishment" of not wanting to stand out as so very different from the rest of white middle-class America. This rendition of history continued into the 1980s as American Jewish historians began to study the postwar years and with little, and often no, documentation, asserted categorically that talk of the Holocaust had been a taboo subject until the late 1960s.[2]

Part of this widely accepted critique of postwar American Jewish communal responses to the Holocaust and its aftermath focused on the survivors. According to this rendition of history, the survivors who came to America found little or no space in the Jewish public arena for them to tell their story. No one seemed willing to hear what they had to say.[3]

---

2   See for example, Sherman Rosenfeld, "The Struggle for Shalom," in Jack Porter and Peter Drier, eds., *Jewish Radicalism: A Selected Anthology* (New York: Grove, 1973), 222–228; William Helmreich, *Against All Odds: Holocaust Survivors and the Successful Lives They Made in America* (New York: Simon and Schuster, 1992); Alan Mintz, *Popular Culture and the Shaping of Holocaust Memory in America* (Seattle, WA: University of Washington Press, 2001).

3   Edward Linenthal, *Preserving Memory: The Struggle to Create America's Holocaust Museum* (New York: Columbia University Press, 1995), 6 quotes, as do numerous other writers, Rabbi Irving Greenberg who described how in the world he grew up

While historians cannot actually know about "most" survivors and cannot re-construct what went on in their individual homes, work places, and other informal settings, the American Jewish public sphere has left a clearly marked paper trail which tells a different story. This story is one in which survivors functioned as active architects of a budding memorial culture as they, from the start, along with other Jews, attended memorial events, shared their experiences with audiences, and created institutions to hallow that memory. They wrote works to commemo-rate their tragedy even as they began building their new lives in America. They invited other Jews to listen to them and the Jews whom they met in America and who themselves had not endured the catastrophe, did not beg them to be still.

The American Jewish press paid attention to the survivors as builders of com-munities in America. Articles treated the survivors in heroic terms, heroic not as armed resisters, but as living embodiments of a Jewish will to survive as Jews.[4] In 1951, for example, the *Jewish Spectator* devoted a lengthy column to the dedica-tion ceremony of a synagogue, whose membership "consists mostly of German and Austrian Jewish refugees." The congregants of Ohav Sholom designated the building and the ceremony as a memorial to the synagogues Hitler had destroyed in Europe, and the magazine editor described in loving detail how, "as the bearers of the Holy Scrolls marched through the aisles toward the open ark, there was audible weeping among the throng of a thousand people," those whose previous synagogues had been destroyed by the Nazis.[5]

---

in, Holocaust survivors had little voice in the larger Jewish community and how they would not be heard until the latter part of the 1960s and beyond.

4   The only somewhat discordant note was sounded in one article by Weiss-Rosmarin in 1963, after the work of Bettelheim, Hilberg, and most importantly Arendt had entered into the general discourse. Weiss-Rosmarin, without referencing these three, com-mented that, "many diaries and memoirs of Nazi death-camp survivors stress that some Jewish "trusties" of the fiends outdid their masters in beastly cruelty. This fact has not received sufficient attention as yet. While it remains a moot question whether mass rebellion at the very inception of the Nazi terror could have prevented … the German death factories, it is clear that without the cooperation of officials of the "'Jewish self-governments'… the Germans could not have succeeded as well as they did." See, *Jewish Spectator* 27 (1963): 2.

5   *Jewish Spectator* 16 (1951): 10; the *Jewish Spectator* also provided a venue for the pub-lication of translations of Yiddish works by Holocaust survivors about that experience. Abraham Sutzkever, Rakhmil Bryks, K. Tzetnik, among others got their first non-Yiddish readership in this magazine. *Midstream* also published this kind of work. In 1962 it published a "condensation of a full-length play" based on Rakhmil Bryk's *A Cat in the Ghetto*, interpreted by Shimon Wincelberg. See, *Midstream* 8 (1962): 44–65.

Articles in English language Jewish publications featured interviews and profiles of survivors who had come to settle in various cities. Solomon Wider described in the pages of the *Pittsburgh Criterion*, how he, an inmate in Bergen-Belsen, had been "on more than one occasion … subjected to torture to lashes as punishment." He shared with Pittsburgh Jewish readers his anguish that on the last day before the liberation of the camp, "the Nazis burned alive my only sister and my two younger brothers." So too, the *Chicago Jewish Sentinel* published a two-page article, "Underground for Six Months! How would You Like to Live in a Hole In the Ground—Underneath a Stable?" In this piece reporter Lilian Elkin interviewed Mayer and Gita Friedman at length, as they related to her, and the Jewish readers of Chicago, their ordeal under the Nazis, their losses, and their survival.[6]

Survivors did not occupy a subterranean space in American Jewish life. Rather, their experiences and activities merged into the larger public culture of American Jewry. One survivor's experiences in the postwar American Jewish world demonstrate this. Johanna Spector "survived five years of concentration camp life during which she saw her husband killed." Before her ordeal, she had graduated from the Jewish Gymnasium of Libau, Latvia, and then enrolled at the State Academy of Music in Vienna where she "majored in piano and music history." She fell into the clutches of the Nazis while pursuing a doctorate in musicology at the University of Frankfurt-Am-Main, where she had hoped to write a dissertation on the history of Jewish music. Spector survived the camps and got a chance, through one of the National Federation of Temple Sisterhoods scholarships, to finish her studies in Cincinnati. Over the course of the 1950s, after completing her degree, she frequently spoke at Reform synagogues and at youth, women's, and young adult clubs sponsored by these congregations. Described in the newsletter of one such group, the Schallek Club of New York's Central Synagogue, as "a young lady who spent the war years in a German Concentration Camp," Spector shared with them "some of her horrible, almost inconceivable experiences." She did so at a cocktail party "sponsored by the Youth council," of the synagogue, "in behalf of the United Jewish Appeal."

Spector not only spoke about her ordeal on behalf of the Reform movement which had enabled her to restart her career, she also contributed to the creation of an American Jewish public culture on the Holocaust. In 1957, *Yedios* the magazine

---

6   "Laughter through Tears: a New American Who Arrives in Pittsburgh This Week Relates the Incredible Story of His Survival," *Pittsburgh Criterion*, 31 March 1950; "Underground for Six Months," *Chicago Jewish Sentinel*, 8 December 1949.

of YIVO (Institute for Jewish Research) reported that it had just received a gift: an illustrated volume of "ghetto and concentration camp songs." Johanna Spector, "through the good offices of the American Jewish Congress" contributed the volume that she had participated in creating. As it happened a "young German anti-Nazi artist ... heard the songs of the ghettos and concentration camps." Inspired, he "rushed home and painted for 36 hours without interruption." His work came to Spector's attention, and she "assembled and published—with music—the collection of 15 songs." The songs included not only the "well known Vilna Ghetto songs," but also various others, "sung in the Libau Ghetto and in the camps near." Johanna Spector, a survivor, had composed several of these.[7]

Spector's story reveals much about the activities of those who had lived through the Holocaust and made homes for themselves in postwar America. She, like so many, did more than just receive the assistance of Jewish communal charities, she helped to build the cultural life of her new home. She did not just attempt to blend in and shed her Holocaust experiences; several quite different American Jewish organizations, including the Reform movement, YIVO, the American Jewish Congress and the United Jewish Appeal, engaged her to share her memories with the larger Jewish public. Together they made it possible for her to communicate her horrendous experiences as a witness to the Holocaust to the American Jewish public.

In many communities, survivors, along with their American relatives and townspeople, organized Holocaust memorial events and invited others to join them. They participated in various city-wide memorial events, planned and attended by others from the local Jewish communities. At those events they told their stories, and shared their experiences of suffering and survival. Typically,

---

7   "Press Release, 6/3/48, National Federation of Temple Sisterhoods," collection 73, Box 37, Folder 1, American Jewish Archives, Cincinnati, Ohio, USA, (hereafter: AJA); *Schallek News* 2 (15 April 1949), 2, AJA 266, 1, 8; *Yedios* 65 (July 1957), 8; NFTS [National Federation of Temple Sisterhoods] also supported the studies of Hugo Gryn, "a surviver [sic] of Auschwitz, the Nazi concentration camp." At other times NFTS speeches and reports described as "a survivor of the horrors of Hitler's Europe." He, like Spector toured the country for the Reform movement and addressed various NFTS national gatherings. See, *Transactions XXI Biennial Assembly of NFTS....April 27-May 2, 1957*, in, AJA 73, 5/4.and "Report to the Committee on World Union for Progressive Judaism Activities," (31 October 1953), AJA 73, 39,1; at various points in the 1950s the NFTS took up the unnamed cases of "two former Displaced Persons and concentration camp survivors" for pre-rabbinic and rabbinic fellowships. See, "Dear Friend" from Gladys Harris, Chair, Committee on the Scholarship and Religious Education Fund (8 January 1954), AJA 73, 39, 3. [National Federation of Temple Sisterhoods]

Warsaw Ghetto memorial programs featured survivors participating in the ritualistic lighting of six memorial candles. In 1957, for example, the Chicago Yizkor Committee for 6 Million Martyrs included the "New Citizens Club" among the sponsoring organizations, and it announced that at that year's event, "the women who will light the six candles will remain on the platform throughout the evening's service ... [E]ach woman must be a Newcomer."[8]

This same ritual, with survivors prominently participating, took place across the country. In Pittsburgh such an event was organized under the auspices of the Jewish Community Council. In the 1958 ceremony, staged at the Young Men's and Women's Hebrew Association building, "Abe Salem of the Newcomers in Pittsburgh ... commented first, in Yiddish, on his memories of heroic comrades who died in the Warsaw Ghetto. He read the 'orders of the day' and ended his speech "with a poem glorifying these martyrs." The audience rose, "while one of the survivors of the ghetto lit memorial candles. *Mr. Jack Lipschitz,* of Warsaw, now of Pittsburgh, lit six candles in memory of the six million dead, following which Cantor Heiser chanted the memorial chant."[9]

Survivors addressed other communal gatherings, too, telling of their experiences. In 1951, according to the bulletin of a Reform congregation's youth group, "one of the last survivors of the Warsaw ghetto addressed Temple Israel," and talked to a Jewish youth group in Dayton, Ohio. In the early 1960s David Widowinsky, a veteran of that same ghetto spoke to both the annual Young Judaea Convention, held in Spring Valley, New York, and to the Society for the Advancement of Judaism, on the topic "My Credo as a Jew."[10]

Some survivors founded their own organizations, which they often named New Americans Clubs, and in New York they founded the Farband fun Yiddishe Katzetler un Partizaner, the association of former concentration camp survivors and partisans, called in English, United Jewish Survivors of Nazi Persecution. Others, or even the same women and men, joined other Jewish groups and participated in their ongoing activities. Of the six survivors who lit candles in the 1957 Yizkor Chicago ceremony, one represented the New Citizens Club and one a Newcomers branch of the Workmen's Circle. The other four stood on the stage not just as survivors, but also as members of Pioneer Women, Hadassah, the Women's

8 Chicago Yizkor Committee for Six Million Martyrs, Minutes, Meeting, 7 March 1957, 6, 5, 2, Spertus [Chicago] 14.
9 Minutes, Jewish Community Council of Pittsburgh (23 April 1958), 11,4 AJA 283.
10 NFTY, *Mimeo-Messenger* 2,4 (February 1951), 2,4 AJA 266; *The Senior* 20,1 (November, 1961), 2, 30, AJHS I-161; Society for the Advancement of Judaism, *Bulletin,* 23 March 1962, 12.

Division of the American Jewish Congress and the National Council of Jewish Women. A 1951 issue of *Mir Zeinen Doh*, (we are here), the publication of the former concentration camp survivors, included a column on "involvements with other organizations." It declared that, "the organization stands in a friendly camaraderie towards a large number of Jewish institutions. On the first level, the Jewish Labor Committee, the Workmen's Circle, and the Jewish Culture Congress," as well as a number of unions, and ORT (a Jewish Educational Organization), where two representatives of the survivor group sat on the executive board.[11]

Their connection to these well-established American Jewish organizations meant that survivor activities did not take place in secret nor did the survivors feel a need to obscure their personal histories. Survivors organized for themselves special branches of the Workmen's Circle and the Labor Zionist Organization. While they met separately, their activities got reported in the bulletins and reports of the larger organizations and they participated in programs that cut across branch lines.[12] Survivors living in the Bronx in the early 1950s founded a Workmen's Circle branch, named after "ghetto hero," Michael Klepfitch. Although it sponsored its own kindergarten, it did so at the Workmen's Circle, School 10, a school attended by other Bronx Jewish children.[13] Similarly, survivors who in 1959 founded Camp Hemshekh placed advertisements in the Yiddish press, seeking to enroll non-survivor Jewish children. They made clear what the camp stood for, and that "former partisans and *katseler* [concentration camp inmates]" had founded it.[14]

A whole array of other survivor activities became, if momentarily, part of the larger American Jewish communal culture. Dina Blumenfeld, the "famous Yiddish actress, star of the theater of the Warsaw ghetto," performed in New York in 1958. The Yiddish press advertised her performances, and actress Molly Picon devoted an installment of her weekly radio show to Ms. Blumenfeld, her artistry and the fact that she "underwent the entire terror of the Warsaw Ghetto. "Today," Picon told her listeners, she wanted to talk "not just about the actress, but also about her survival."[15]

---

11 *Mir Zeinen Doh* 1 (April 1951), 4.

12 See for the Labor Zionist "Newcomers Branch," n.d., 1,12, 0017 Spertus.

13 Farband Fun Gevezene Yiddishe Katzetler un Partizaner in New York, *Calendar for 1953*, 2, 918, YIVO 918.

14 Clipping, *Forward*, n.d.; clipping, *Morgen Zhurnal*, ME-18–29, folder 121, YIVO, RG 1400.

15 Flyer, 2 April 1958, 3, "Youth Section" folder, YIVO 1148; "Turkoff," 36, 681, AJHS P 38; Picon frequently devoted her radio show to memoirs by survivors as well as the

In the late 1940s individual survivors and groups of survivors began to publish memoirs and accounts of their Holocaust ordeals. Some turned to fiction to
express themselves. The *izkor ikher* provided one venue to share memories of the
horrific events as well as details of life before the catastrophe among themselves
and with the townspeople who had left for America decades earlier . Other works
in Yiddish like the memoirs of Aaron Tverski, *Ich Bin Der Korben Un Der Ades*
(I am the victim and the witness),[16] Shlomo Brynski, *Vehn Fundamentn Traisln
Zikh* (when foundations are shaken),[17] and *Lerer-Yizkor Bukh: Di Umgekumme
Lerer Fun Tsisho Shuln in Poilin* (the fallen teachers of the Tsisho schools in
Poland)[18] circulated only among Yiddish readers, although the English language
Jewish magazines and the *Jewish Book Annual* paid attention to them. Gerda
Weissman Klein's, *All But My Life*, on the other hand, came out in English under
the imprimatur of Hill & Wang, a major publishing house.[19] Kitty Hart shared
her Auschwitz ordeal in the 1960, *I am Alive*, a year after the Romanian survivor
Earl Weinstock, published, *Seven Years*.[20] So too S.B. Unsdorfer's 1961 *The Yellow
Star*, the "memoirs of a boy whose childhood was broken by Nazism and who
grew up in the concentration camps of Auschwitz and Buchenwald," and David
Widowinski's, *And We Are Not Saved*, a memoir dedicated "To the memory of
my mother … my teacher, and to the unknown Jewish child, who symbolize for
me the martyrdom of the Jewish people" represented just some of the books and
their dedications.[21]

---

     publication of *izkor ikher*. In 1947, for example, she spent the broadcast reading from
     Aaron Tversky's, *Ich Bin Der Korbin Un Der Ades*, (I am the victim and the witness),
     which had been published in New York in 1947. See, Picon Papers, 32, 551, American
     Jewish History Society [New York AJHS P-38 [Molly Picon Papers].
16   Aaron Tverski, *Ich Bin Der Korben Un Der Ades* (New York: Shulsinger Brothers, 1947).
17   Shlomo Brynski, *Vehn Fundamentn Traislin Zikh* (Chicago, IL: International Press,
     1951).
18   Committee to Perpetuate the Memory of the Fallen Teachers from the Tsisho Schools in
     Poland, *Lerer-Yizkor Bukh* (New York: Marstin, 1952–1954); in 1961 Dina Abramow-
     icz, essaying Yiddish writing in America for the *Jewish Book Annual: 1961* commented
     that "numerous…personal memoirs and diaries of the … *Hurban* … were added to the
     vast body of documentation of the catastrophe." (171).
19   Gerda Weissman Klein, *All But My Life* (New York: Hill & Wang, 1957).
20   Kitty Hart, *I am Alive* (New York: Coward-McCann, 1960); Weinstock, Earl, *Seven Years*
     (New York: Dutton, 1959).
21   S.B. Unsdorfer, *The Yellow Star* (New York: Thomas Yoseloff, 1961); Widowinski, David,
     And We Are Not Saved (New York: Philosophical Library, 1963); Berkowitz, Sarah Bick,
     Where Are My Brothers? (New York: Helios, 1965).

All sorts of publications, which were circulated in the ordinary course of post-war American Jewish public life, included the words of those who had survived the Holocaust. Youngsters who attended Brooklyn's Yeshivah of Flatbush revealed their Holocaust experiences to classmates in the school's 1953 yearbook. Abraham Fuksman's, "My Life Story," hid little. "I was born on May 1, 1940 in Baranowich, Poland. At that time, the Nazis started to attack Poland. I stayed with my parents a year and three months. On the sixteenth month, my parents gave me away to a Christian woman in order to save me. She baptized me, and I went to church every Sunday." He went on. "I did not know I was a Jew. I had no idea I had a real father or mother. As soon as the war ended with a casualty list of over 6,000,000 people, my mother and father came to take me back." His story continued. The woman who hid him, refused to give him up. His parents went to court to regain custody. They fled to Vilna, then to "Hungary, Czechoslovakia, and other countries," and spent time in a displaced persons camp in Austria, and finally, "on January 16, 1949, I arrived in Boston, Mass … Now I study in the Yeshivah of Flatbush." This seventh grader's life story, as he presented it to his peers, evinced no shame, reticence, or discomfort at having gone through this experience.[22]

Survivors turned to other media as well, and American Jewish institutions paid attention to their work. When the artist Luba Gurdus exhibited her work at the Stephen Wise Congress House in 1953, the pamphlet accompanying the exhibition noted that she had "spent the entire war in Poland, escaped from a Nazi collection center, was captured and imprisoned in Maydanek." The American Jewish Congress sponsored Gurdus's exhibit and drew attention to her experiences as a witness, in order to commemorate the tenth anniversary of the Warsaw Ghetto uprising. The New York press, including the *New Yorker*, the *New York Times*, and the *New York World-Telegram* commented in their reviews, reprinted by the American Jewish Congress in the exhibition catalog, that Gurdus "was there." Her work, "striking, gruesome and extremely moving drawings of life in a Nazi concentration camp," had been created "by a former inmate of Maydanek."[23] In 1951 a group of survivors used theater to narrate their own experience in a play they wrote and presented, *As Years Go By*. Sponsored by the United Service for New Americans, the four-act drama, "based on the actual experiences of their life from the time of Hitler's invasion to the present day," had been written and was performed by a group of survivors. A small work, staged in a synagogue in New

---

22 *Yeshivah Yearbook: 1953*, 36; Fuksman also contributed a version of this same life story in the Hebrew section of the yearbook.
23 "In Commemoration of the Tenth Anniversary," *Exhibition Catalog*, JLC, 2, YIVO 1148.

Jersey, the Yiddish press covered it. It reflected the willingness of some survivors to relate their experiences to the Jewish public and of American Jewish institutions to make such a telling possible.

The work of the survivors in the American Jewish scene and the awareness of American Jews that those who had experienced the Holocaust had a particular agenda also became apparent in the political realm. The clubs and associations they founded in their first years in America began with a political purpose. While the New York survivor organization reflected a deep cultural and social purpose, providing its members with a venue for getting together, singing Yiddish songs, listening to performances of familiar melodies from their former lives, participating in "programs spent at decorated tables in a friendly environment," and undertaking projects to address the job, housing, and other needs of the newly arrived survivors, they also engaged with American and worldwide Jewish politics. They tracked the fate of Jews remaining in Displaced Camps, paid attention to the work of the Claims Conference, and the like. But they also threw themselves into the political process. In 1950, before the details of the Claims Conference had been hammered out, they "sent a memorandum to Senator Herbert Lehman" telling him how they believed survivors should be compensated. That summer a delegation of 50 members went to Washington and met with Lehman and his staff. As described in *Mir Zeinen Doh*, "Senator Lehman greeted warmly those who had been rescued from Hitler's hell and he showed much understanding of their needs and suffering."[24] These details of the survivor group's visit to Lehman's office and its memorandum on the restitution process offer a small window into survivors' understanding of themselves as political actors who could, and did, speak for themselves. They learned the art of lobbying and did not shrink from stating quite clearly that they had a specific agenda, a result of their Holocaust experiences.

So too, starting in 1960, survivors in a number of American cities—New York, Boston, Cincinnati, Pittsburgh, and Washington D.C.—publicly challenged the Jewish "establishment" as Jews who had endured "Hitler's hell." Two events rocked American Jewry. First, starting on Christmas Eve, 1959 in Cologne, Germany, and then spreading rapidly around the world, what Jewish community-relations workers described as the "swastika epidemic," broke out in the United States. American Jews saw their synagogues and community centers defaced with the hated Nazi symbol. In a few instances bombs ripped through Jewish buildings.[25] At the same time the American Nazi Party lead by George Lincoln Rockwell, the "American Fuehrer,"

---

24 *Mir Zeinen Doh*, 4.
25 *AJY 1961*, 105–107.

blazed onto the headlines and into the American Jewish consciousness. Rockwell, clad in an S.S. uniform with a swastika armband, surrounded by similarly outfitted followers, organized rallies, addressing audiences with well-worn anti-Semitic canards, praising Hitler for his keen insights into the threat posed by "the Jews," and lauding him for his policies. In 1960 Rockwell threatened to set up pickets and disrupt showings of the movie "Exodus." The swastika outbreak and the Rockwell problem took place against the backdrop of the Eichmann Trial in Jerusalem, which focused attention on Israel, the Jews, and the story of the six million.

Rockwell in fact posed no threat to American Jews and the swastika-daubing episode came and went. But these events allowed survivors to shake up the American Jewish communal framework. Historically American Jewish organizations, the American Jewish Committee, Congress, the Anti-Defamation League, local community councils, and nationally, the National Community Relations Advisory Council (NCRAC), maintained a consistent posture on demagogues like Rockwell. Extending back to the 1920s, when Henry Ford issued the "Protocols of the Elders of Zion," the American Jewish consensus advocated quiet, behind the scenes action, but public silence. Anti-Semitic rabble-rousers ought, according to the regnant Jewish consensus, to be quarantined, ignored, and not allowed to command press attention. Counter-rallies, protests, organized jeering, or any public confrontation, only abetted their goal of generating coverage and drawing larger crowds. Most Jews had accepted this communal *modus operandi.*

But Rockwell generated a different reaction. In part this was because of his Nazi garb, in part because he claimed public attention simultaneously with the Eichmann Trial, and because he strutted onto the American Jewish scene when survivors had become reasonably well integrated into their communities. The established American Jewish organizations expected to proceed as in the past. In 1961 NCRAC decided that because Rockwell constituted "a nuisance, not a threat," established practices should prevail. This engendered fierce opposition from survivor groups around the country, particularly in the places where Rockwell appeared. He came to Boston with his storm troopers in January 1961 for the "Exodus" premier. Local survivors insisted that his appearance be addressed. The "New Americans' group" demanded a meeting with the Jewish Community Council, to air its opposition to relying on quarantine and quiet in the face of Rockwell's advocacy of a "program for crematoria and gas chambers" for America.[26] In

---

26 "Memo," 25 January 1961, box 1 folder 1 "American Nazi Party, 1961–1965," Julius Bernstein Papers in the Wagner Archives, Bobst Library New York University, New York (hereafter Bernstein Papers).

Chicago the same controversy flared, and contrary to the community consensus, survivors picketed Rockwell, as they did in Philadelphia, Boston, and Washington. They carried signs reading, "Remember Auschwitz."[27]

The "refugees'" actions troubled Council insiders. Those who, according to the executive director of the Boston Jewish Community Council, "bore mental and physical scars inflicted on them when they were inmates in Nazi concentration camps" engendered deep sympathy. Communal leaders recognized that the survivors had a unique perspective on this issue, different from most American Jews who had not experienced the Nazi ordeal directly. They saw the survivors as special, as both victims of catastrophe and witnesses to it. But on the other hand, what the survivors wanted deviated from the American Jewish consensus, hammered out over decades, as to what to do with loud, demagogic, anti-Semites. The Council, as a Jewish defense organization, had long maintained the policy of "quarantine," one which asserted that such individuals like Rockwell wanted publicity more than anything and that counter-demonstrations, noisy street confrontations only gave him exactly what he desired, press and media coverage. The Jewish Community Council, like its counterparts around the country, also considered it crucial to defend free speech regardless of the words' odiousness. As they saw it, untrammeled speech lay in the Jews' best interest and as such they had to defend it, even for those whom they despised. The Council also considered that it had an institutional stake in maintaining community discipline. The head of the Boston Jewish Community Council addressed this issue in January 1961 on his weekly radio show on WEEI (a talk radio station), expressing concern for the survivors but maintaining the rightness of the communal position.[28]

The local Jewish press covered this internal Jewish disagreement pitting survivors against the establishment. The newspapers editorialized, usually considering the Council's well-trod path appropriate, but at the same time remarking that, "One has to sympathize deeply with those in our midst who directly suffered at the hands of the Nazis. Their emotional reaction is understandable when they see the Nazi symbols in this free land." Even leaders of the council recognized this. Robert Segal speaking for the Boston Jewish Community Council, noted, "you can't explain all that to the survivor of Dachau who came early to the scene of Rockwell's Boston operation and stayed late to be sure that the American who imitates the German Nazis was given no chance to picket the movie or peddle

27 Clipping, 16 January 1961, ibid.
28 "Transcript of Radio show, WEEI 21 January 1961," 1, "American Nazi Party: 1961–1965" folder, Bernstein Papers.

his line. You can't explain it to the Hitler era survivor…. [T]hose with concentration camp experience cannot possibly be expected to adjust to the framework of a society dedicated to freedom to such a degree that even the most contemptible member of society is granted protection while uttering hatred. The man with the concentration camp serial number on his arm is wary of such nice distinctions."[29]

These articles in turn ignited a storm of letters-to-the editor from survivors who, as Segal had reflected, had little interest in "such nice distinctions." One letter, from a "Mrs. Fred M. Meyer, Brockton," published in Boston's *Jewish Advocate* deserves attention. Mrs. Meyer took the Council's Executive Director to task for his insistence on the conventional aloofness to anti-Semitic agitation. Mrs. Meyer not only argued against Segal's position, offering the opinion that "Rockwell has no right to appear in Boston and that he should have been stopped before he ever appeared," she also wrote her letter as someone "who had left Germany." She blasted Segal's articles as an "insult" to "us, who have lost our mothers and loved ones in the gas chambers." She and Segal differed because he "does not have the experience we had." Having had that experience, she considered herself entitled to express herself, staking out a distinctive survivor position and announcing it as such to the community.[30]

The survivors, ready to confront the Nazis in America, did not just chide the basically powerless Jewish agencies for their lack of willingness to aggressively confront Rockwell in public. In New York, "concentration camp survivors deluged city officials with their protests," demanding that Rockwell not be granted a permit to hold a rally at Union Square. In the other cities, individuals identified themselves as Jewish survivors of Nazi atrocities when interviewed by local, general newspapers.[31]

The groundswell of protest coming out of the survivor community represented the first time it had staked out a stridently particularistic position, divergent from that of American Jewry as a whole. This played a role in changing the communal response. Some Jewish agencies, historically committed to quarantine, began

---

29 Clipping, Bernstein Papers, ibid.
30 Clipping, 6 February 1961, in 1, "Co-ordination Committee, Jewish Culture Clubs," folder, Bernstein papers.
31 "Editorial," *Jewish Advocate*, 1, "American Nazi Party: 1961–1965," folder, Bernstein Papers. Similar confrontations between organized survivor groups and local Jewish community councils took place in Washington, D.C., Pittsburgh, and Cincinnati. The records of other Jewish communities would very likely reveal such clashes there as well. The *American Jewish Yearbook: 1961* reported on this exact struggle in New York. See, p. 108.

to shift under the specter of Rockwell and the example of the militancy of the survivors. The Jewish Labor Committee in 1960, in anticipation of Rockwell's appearance in New York, decided that "a request should be made by Jewish agencies of city authorities that they reject Rockwell's application for a permit," based both on the position that "the rights of freedom of speech did not include the right to advocate the extermination of an ethnic group," and "due to the nature of ... New York City ... with its heavy Jewish population and its large number of persons who had either experienced the Nazi terror, or who had members of their immediate families killed by the Nazis, the holding of such a meeting would inevitably result in bloodshed."[32]

This statement of the Jewish Labor Committee reflected the growing prominence of survivors in the American Jewish postwar world. The women and men who had suffered during the Holocaust era functioned as political players in the American Jewish communities where they settled. They participated in the ongoing activities of those communities, but also stood apart, holding differing views and carrying out independent actions. As Jews who had endured a singular experience they did not, as an organized group, shy away from discussing or sharing it with others.

All of this material, drawn from the archives and from the vast compendium of material produced by both the survivors and American Jewish institutions and organizations, stands in sharp contrast with the conventional narrative, which has emphatically claimed that when the survivors came to America they did not want to talk about what had happened. Conventional understanding of the postwar era purports that American Jews counseled, and indeed commanded them, not to talk, telling them that no one wanted to know or that they—the survivors—would be better off if they forgot and just went about the process of rebuilding their lives. In that narrative of the past, silence reigned and survivors either participated in the conspiracy of silence or were once again victimized by a callous, unthinking American Jewry.

To a certain degree the charges leveled against postwar American Jewry seem plausible. After all, starting in the 1980s and continuing well into the twenty-first century, communities and individuals launched oral history projects to record the memories of the survivors. Some of these projects became global in scope, financed, for example, by Steven Spielberg who used his considerable wealth to identify the remaining victims and preserve on videotape their recollections of

---

32 Emanuel Muravchik to JLC Field Staff, 3 August 1961, 1, "Co-ordination Committee, Jewish Culture Clubs," folder, Bernstein Papers.

what had happened. Laurel Vlock and Dr. Dori Laub, a psychiatrist and Holocaust survivor, launched a project in 1979 to use the new medium of videotaping to interview Holocaust survivors, based on a recognition that those who had endured the European catastrophe would begin to die in great numbers soon, as so many approached old age. Their early videotaping efforts then led to the creation of the Holocaust Survivors Film Project, Inc. that in 1981 eventually lead to the creation of the Fortunoff Video Archive at Yale University.

Likewise, by the 1980s, the survivors themselves, who had achieved a level of economic and political comfort in America, helped to reinforce the charge of post-war silence. They saw their children now educated, grown up and launched into the American world. These men and women entering into retirement and old-age began to organize themselves in more concerted ways in order to make sure that subsequent generations would know what had happened in the years of the catastrophe. In their own minds, and in those of their children, as well as in the impression of other observers, the projects of the 1980s and beyond had sprung up *de novo,* following no precedent, not growing out of previous undertakings of a similar nature, but on a more modest and spontaneous scale.

Yet the weight of the record of primary sources from the post-war era tells a different story, one in which women and men who had survived the catastrophe of the Nazis made it their business to testify and to remind the world of what they had endured. All of the examples cited here, which represent but a sampling of the material produced by and about the survivors, reflect an era when Holocaust remembrance had a kind of experimental and scattered quality to it. Each group, organization, or institution came up with projects of its own. No central institution existed to coordinate this: no specially funded, organized, and administered project had yet come into operation to systematically plan for memorializing the Holocaust and for making the survivors key players in such an enterprise. As such, in comparison to what came later, all that went on in the postwar period seems small, puny, and pale, lacking the institutional heft of the Holocaust memorialization culture as well as the high levels of activism undertaken by the remaining survivors in the late twentieth century.

But comparisons are ultimately unfair and analytically flawed. The women and men, the survivors and the American Jews of the postwar years occupied a very different world from that which came later, and which produced, for example, the United States Holocaust Memorial Museum and so many other undertakings. These more recent manifestations put the Holocaust at the center and make witnesses and heroes of the survivors. That invidious comparison has in essence blotted out the memory of the actions of the women and men who came to America in the late 1940s and 1950s and not only forged new lives for themselves but, as best they could, reminded the American and American Jewish world of what they had endured. Moreover, the history of these American Jewish women and men who participated in the public life of the Jewish community has faded from the collective memory, and their activities for and with survivors (and vis-à-vis the Holocaust more broadly) have disappeared from the memory of those who came after.

But the evidence should lead us to see the past as more complicated than that outlined in the dominant narrative. It should lead us to see the survivors in America and American Jews as women and men who did not shrink from talking about the Holocaust and acting as survivors of that defining event. They did what they believed they had to do, and what circumstances allowed them to. As they saw it, they could do no less, but they also could do no more. It would take a later era to allow for other projects reflecting the demands and opportunities of a different age.

Laura Hobson Faure

Towards Consensus? American Jewish Organizations in France after the Shoah

Abstract: *American Jewish organizations focused their attention on Europe in order to give humanitarian assistance to Jewish communities and they benefited from increased empathy after the Shoah. Philanthropy often bridged the gap between different Jewish factions in America.*

Exploring the mobilization of American Jewish organizations in France after World War II provides a concrete example of how American Jews responded to the needs of French Jews in the aftermath of the Shoah. Such an exploration offers insights into the actions, motivations and influence of various organizations. There is much to be learned about the postwar Jewish community inside the United States from analyzing the organizational dynamics and work of American Jewish organizations abroad. Indeed, historians have generally agreed that in the decade following World War II there was unprecedented integration of American Jews into US society. Yet the same historians disagree about the persistence of communal divisions among American Jews.[1] The study of American Jewish organizations

---

1 Writing in the 1950s, Nathan Glazer advanced the argument that pre-World War II distinctions between East European and German Jews were "wiped out," along with their class differences; Nathan Glazer, *American Judaism* (Chicago, IL: University of Chicago Press, [1957] 1972), 106. More recently, Arthur Goren highlighted the "functional consensus" (8) of postwar American Jewry, recognizing that while "pockets of animosity or indifference remained" (5), that "within the Jewish community, the divisive issues of the interwar years–class differences, the intergenerational tensions between immigrant and native-born, conflicting notions of Jewish identity, the assimilationist-radical deprecation of Jewish life and the strident polemics over Zionism–were vanishing or gone altogether." Arthur Goren, "A Golden Decade for American Jews 1945–1955," in Peter Medding, ed., *A New Jewry? America Since World War II* (New York: Oxford University Press, 1992), 10. Hasia Diner has a different approach, describing postwar Jews as " a small, internally divided people with no single voice to speak 'for' them," thus ascribing to a more diverse vision of postwar Jewry. Hasia Diner, *We Remember With Reverence and Love: American Jews and the Myth of Silence after the Holocaust, 1945–1962* (New York: New York University Press, 2009), 267. Riv-Ellen Prell characterizes postwar Jewish life as a "more complex story" (115) in which the "virtually every domain of Jewish life underwent changes with far-reaching consequences." (115) This

in France is a new angle from which to examine the question of postwar communal consensus and division, and thus sheds light on American Jewish identity
in a moment of transition. As Jews were gaining greater acceptance in US society
in the years following World War II, they were also facing new challenges such as
maintaining group cohesion during the Cold War, a time of great geographic and
social mobility.[2] Studying the relationships among American Jewish organizations
in postwar France provides a way to assess the ability and desire of American Jews
to work together toward the common goal of reconstructing European Jewish life.

Did American Jewish philanthropy in postwar Europe help American Jews
overcome their divisions or did it exacerbate them? In order to answer this question, I will analyze the origins of Jewish mobilization in the United States and
explore why France is an important place to study American Jewish aid. Secondly,
following Yehuda Bauer and more recently Maud Mandel,[3] I will focus on the
most active organization in the mobilization, the American Joint Distribution

moment of dynamic transition was, according to Prell, "as much about differences and
conflict among Jews as it was about a shared consensus." Riv-Ellen Prell, "Triumph, Ac-
commodation, and Resistance: American Jewish Life from the End of World War II to
the Six-Day War," in Marc Lee Raphael, ed., *The Columbia History of Jews and Judaism
in America* (New York: Columbia University Press, 2008), 116.

2   Prell, "Triumph, Accomodation and Resistance," 126–130.
3   Yehuda Bauer was the first to highlight the important role of the JDC in Europe in his
three-volume history of the JDC: *My Brother's Keeper: A History of the American Jewish
Joint Distribution Committee 1929–1939* (Philadelphia: The Jewish Publication Soci-
ety, 1974); *American Jewry and the Holocaust: The American Jewish Joint Distribution
Committee 1939–1945* (Detroit: Wayne State University Press, 1981); *Out of the Ashes:
The Impact of American Jews on Post-Holocaust European Jewry* (Oxford/New York:
Pergamon Press, 1989). More recently, Maud Mandel has addressed the role of the
JDC in the context of her work on the reconstruction of French Jewish life after the
Shoah. In particular, Mandel argues that the JDC used its financial aid as an incentive
to reform, and considers the JDC an example of American cultural imperialism; Maud
Mandel, "Philanthropy or Cultural Imperialism? The Impact of American Jewish Aid
in post-Holocaust France," *Jewish Social Studies* 9 (2002): 53–94. My research follows
in the footsteps of both Bauer and Mandel, yet differs from them in both scope and
methodology. First, I have chosen to focus exclusively on the American Jewish mobilization in postwar France, which allows us to discern the different approaches of the
various organizations, and places the JDC in comparative perspective. Secondly, I have
used both archival and oral history sources in order to understand what Americans
intended and accomplished, and how this aid was perceived and received by Jews in
France; Laura Hobson Faure, *Un "Plan Marshall juif," La présence juive américaine en
France après la Shoah, 1944–1954* (Paris: Armand Colin, 2013).

Committee (JDC), and describe its program and objectives in France in the decade following the Shoah. Finally, I will address the programs of the National Council of Jewish Women, the American Jewish Committee, the Hebrew Sheltering and Immigrant Aid Society (HIAS) and the World Jewish Congress (WJC), and analyze their relationships to the JDC.

The Origins of the Mobilization in the United States

Philanthropy often formed a bridge in American Jewish life, linking different factions of American Jewry, allowing for collective action.[4] The creation of the JDC in 1914 to help the victims of World War I, for example, united three fundraising initiatives that had been developed independently by Orthodox Jews, Socialist Jews and the philanthropic elite. Though the three groups maintained strained relations within the JDC, the committee remained intact, even expanding its work throughout Europe and the Soviet Union during the interwar years, and responding, to the extent possible, to the spread of Nazism and the outbreak of World War II.[5]

The spread and increasing virulence of Nazism gave rise to the United Jewish Appeal (UJA) in 1939, which built a unified national campaign engaged in fundraising for a variety of causes—Palestine, Europe and domestic welfare needs. The creation of the UJA was significant, as it reduced competition among the philanthropic causes of American Jewry. Once it was founded, the UJA coordinated fundraising and negotiated the distribution of funds according to the most urgent needs. As the leading distributer of American Jewish aid in Europe, the JDC became the prime beneficiary of the UJA, receiving 48.6 percent of collected funds in 1940.[6] These two institutions enabled American Jews to respond to the Shoah. Philanthropy in the name of survivors served the function of addressing their plight and also reinforced the Jewish identity of the American donors as they faced new challenges in the postwar period.[7]

---

4   Jonathan Woocher, *Sacred Survival: The Civil Religion of American Jews* (Bloomington, IN: Indiana University Press, 1986), 22–62.

5   On the creation of the JDC, see Bauer, *My Brother's Keeper,* 3–18.

6   Marc Lee Raphael, *A History of the United Jewish Appeal* (Chico, CA: Scholars Press, 1982), 10.

7   On the memorial functions of American Jewish philanthropy during this period, see Rachel Debligner, "'In a World Still Trembling': American Jewish Philanthropy and the Shaping of Holocaust Survivor Narratives in Postwar Ameirca (1945–1953)" (PhD Dissertation, University of California, Los Angeles, 2014).

Indeed, as World War II drew to an end, American Jews embarked on a new phase in their history, characterized by scholars as a "Golden Decade" or a "time for healing."[8] This period is considered an era of unprecedented tolerance towards Jews in America, a time during which social and economic barriers against them were lifted. As Nathan Glazer and others have analyzed, greater access to the American dream, coupled with general postwar economic prosperity, helped ease the class tensions that had divided American Jewry.[9] Like other Americans, Jews began to migrate from cities to the suburbs, where they often created new institutions from scratch. Synagogues with community centers were constructed, and Jews joined them in unprecedented numbers for social, if not religious reasons. Increasingly middle class, the Jewish population in the US, which numbered almost 5 million people in 1945,[10] was becoming more acculturated to American life. After the Immigration Acts of 1921 and 1924 restricted the numbers coming to America, there was a parallel tapering off of Jewish immigrant cultural associations. The significant number of Jews participating in the US Armed forces during World War II allowed the highly urbanized Jewish population to experience more rural parts of the country and meet Americans of other backgrounds, serving to strengthen their identity as Americans.[11] The American Jewish population was progressively becoming more homogenous just as its place in American society was rapidly changing. Philanthropy in the name of rebuilding European life aimed at helping others. Yet this action also provided postwar Jews an avenue to explore and assert their own Jewish identity in this moment of transition.[12]

---

8   Goren, "A Golden Decade for American Jews 1945–1955," 3–20; Edward Shapiro, *A Time for Healing: American Jewry since World War II* (Baltimore, MD: John Hopkins University Press, 1992).

9   Glazer, *American Judaism,* 106–128.

10 Michael N. Dobkowski, ed., *Jewish American Voluntary Organizations* (Westport: Greenwood Press, 1986) appendix 2.

11 Deborah Dash Moore, *GI Jews: How World War II Changed a Generation* (Cambridge, MA: The Belknap Press of Harvard University, 2004), 1–21.

12 It should be noted that American Protestants and Catholics also unified their philanthropic efforts in the name of European reconstruction. For example, the ecumenical World Council of Churches was established in 1942 in anticipation of postwar reconstruction needs and in 1946 merged with other Protestant and Orthodox organizations to establish the Church World Service. Kenneth Slack, *Hope in the Dessert, The Churches' United Response to Human Need, 1944–1984* (Geneva: World Council of Churches, 1986). For a discussion of Protestant, Catholic and Jewish aid efforts in comparative perspective after World War II, see Merle Curti, *American Philanthropy Abroad* (New Brunswick, NJ: Rutgers University Press, 1963), 513–526.

As a group, American Jews showed a strong determination to see Jewish life rebuilt in Europe. Roughly 550,000 American Jews had fought in the war. This number represented 11 percent of the entire Jewish population of the US, and 50 percent of all Jewish men between the ages of eighteen and forty-four.[13] With so many Jewish participants on the battlefields of Europe, there was no lack of reporting based on first-hand knowledge of the persecution of European Jews. Furthermore, the great majority of Jews in the US was of Ashkenazi origin and maintained strong cultural and familial ties to Europe.

Philanthropic efforts in the name of survivors of the Shoah were extensive and diverse, reflecting the "different strands of Jewish life."[14] Among other activities, Jewish women collected food, clothing and letters to send to Jewish orphans. Congregants listened to the letters and sermons of the rabbis who had served as chaplains in the US Armed Forces.[15] Well aware of the urgency of the situation, American Jews donated unprecedented amounts to the UJA. In 1939 this organization had been unable to raise 20 million dollars, yet it collected over 100 million dollars in 1946.[16] As a major recipient of the UJA, the JDC was able to finance its postwar programs, distributing over 194 million dollars of aid throughout Europe between 1945 and 1948.[17] JDC funds supplied European Jewish organizations with the cash needed to help surviving Jews, thus compensating for weak national aid in this moment of state building.[18]

Mobilizing in France

From 1944 through 1954, the JDC channeled 26.9 million dollars to the Jews of France.[19] France held great importance for the reconstruction of postwar European Jewish life. Three quarters of its Jewish population had survived the war,

---

13 Dash Moore, *To the Golden Cities: Pursuing the American Dream in Miami and L.A.* (New York: The Free Press, 1994), 10.

14 Diner, *We Remember,* 150–215.

15 Alex Grobman, *Rekindling the Flame, American Jewish Chaplains and the Survivors of European Jewry, 1944–1948* (Detroit: Wayne State University Press, 1993).

16 In 1939, the UJA raised $16,250,000. In 1946, a total of 132 million dollars were raised, of which 78 percent went to the UJA (Raphael, *A History,* 7 and 136).

17 Bauer, *Out of the Ashes,* xviii.

18 In France, with several minor exceptions, JDC funding was directed to Jewish organizations. However, these organizations may have at times had non-Jewish clients.

19 Report by Loeb and Troper, October 1914 through December 31, 1973, non-catalogued, The American Jewish Joint Distribution Committee Archive-New York (JDC-NY).

representing one of the highest survival rates in Western Europe.[20] At liberation, with its Jewish population of 180,000 to 200,000 individuals, France was home to the largest Jewish community in Western Europe.[21] France's ports provided access to the Americas and to Palestine, drawing in postwar Jewish migrants on their way to new lands. As a result, France was one of the rare places in Europe where the Jewish population was growing. By 1960, France had recovered its pre-war Jewish population figures.[22] Moreover, a diverse network of French Jewish welfare organizations had survived the war, providing a solid infrastructure into which American Jewish aid could be infused. And finally, France was the first country with a significant Jewish population that was liberated by the Allies, making Paris a hub for American Jewish reconstruction work.

The Joint Distribution Committee in France

The largest and most significant organizational response came from the JDC, which had played only a minor role in France until 1933. After that date, however, the JDC moved its European headquarters from Berlin to Paris, where it intensified its intervention in light of the Central European Jewish refugee crisis. It remained active in France throughout the war—even after the rupture of diplomatic ties between Vichy and Washington—and contributed an estimated 60 percent of the cost of the French Jewish resistance.[23] In December 1944, the JDC

---

20 Serge Klarsfeld estimates the total number of Jewish victims of the Final Solution in France at 80,000; Serge Klarsfeld, *Vichy Auschwitz. Le rôle de Vichy dans la solution finale de la question juive en France. 1943–1944* (Paris: Fayard, 1985), 180.

21 Doris Bensimon and Sergio Della Pergola estimate the population at 180,000 at the end of 1944; Doris Bensimon and Sergio Della Pergola, *La Population Juive de France: socio-démographie et identité* (Jerusalem: The Institute of Contemporary Jewry, Hebrew University of Jerusalem, Centre national de la recherche scientifique, 1984), 35. Annette Wieviorka estimates the Jewish population of France at just under 200,000 in the summer of 1944; Annette Wieviorka, "Les Juifs en France au lendemain de la guerre: état des lieux," *Archives Juives* 28 (1995): 5–6.

22 Anne Grynberg, "Après la tourmente," in Jean-Jacques Becker and Annette Wieviorka, eds., *Les Juifs de France. De la Révolution française à nos jours* (Paris: Liana Levi, 1998), 267.

23 Lucien Lazare, *La Résistance juive en France* (Paris: Stock, 1987), 282. See also Laura Hobson Faure, "'Guide and Motivator' or 'Central Treasury'? The Role of the American Jewish Joint Distribution Committee in France, 1942–1944," in Jacques Sémelin, Claire Andrieu, and Sarah Gensburger, eds., *Rescue Practices Facing Genocides: Comparative Perspectives* (London and New York: Hurst and Columbia University Press, 2011), 293–312.

sent its first postwar American representative to France and began responding to the needs of Jewish orphans and refugees. Insisting on the temporary nature of its aid, the JDC rarely offered direct services to Jews in France, but instead funded a network of Jewish welfare organizations of diverse ideological affiliation—from Communist to Ultra-Orthodox. The JDC covered 72 percent of the expenses of Jewish welfare organizations in 1946, 54.5 percent of these costs in 1949, and 40 percent in 1952.[24] It is estimated that the JDC aided 50,000 individuals in France in 1945 alone, which represents between 25 and 28 percent of the estimated Jewish population at that time.[25] The JDC's marked distance from the assisted population ran parallel, somewhat paradoxically, with their deep-seated intervention within the aid agencies themselves.

Like other American Jewish organizations that would come to France, JDC's reconstruction work in France was based on a distinct vision of the American Jewish community, and not on pre-war French Jewish life. As a welfare organization, the JDC focused on refashioning French Jewish social services. The JDC encouraged a centralization and professionalization of French Jewish institutions that mirrored American Jewish welfare. Indeed, in the US, a movement to increase the centralization of Jewish welfare had begun in the late nineteenth century, setting up federations to collectively raise and distribute funds on the municipal level in order to increase efficiency and eliminate the duplication of services. In keeping with national trends in social work, Jewish organizations underwent an intense professionalization process after World War I, modifying the names of organizations, and incorporating trained social workers into their ranks.[26] An early example of this American influence in France can be observed in March 1945, when the JDC facilitated the merger of three aid committees to form the *Comité juif d'action sociale et de reconstruction* (COJASOR), in order to establish a central family services agency in France.[27]

The efforts of the JDC to reform French Jewish welfare practices intensified as the postwar emergency situation stabilized. In 1946, the new country director

---

24 Statistical Report France, Country Directors Conference, October 1952, Laura Margolis Jarblum collection (non-catalogued), The American Jewish Joint Distribution Committee Archives-Israel (JDC-I).

25 JDC Primer, 1945, page France-8, non-catalogued, JDC-NY; percentages based on a Jewish population of 180–200,000 individuals.

26 Herman D. Stein, "Jewish Social Work in the United States, 1654–1954," *American Jewish Yearbook* 57 (1956): 44–59.

27 Relief situation in France, January through June 1945, 17 August 1945, Folder 247, France 1945/54, JDC-NY.

for France, Laura Margolis, shifted JDC policy to create institutions designed to ensure the long-term survival of the French Jewish community. The JDC continued to support local Jewish organizations, but American welfare concepts and structures were pointedly introduced into the practice of French agencies during Margolis' tenure, from 1946–53.

For example, the JDC established a short-lived nursing school in Paris in 1948, making use of American faculty and methods. More significantly, after failed attempts to reform social work practices within European Jewish social agencies, the employees of the JDC opened an American school of social work in Versailles which functioned from 1949–1953. Herman Stein, a former graduate and faculty member of Columbia University School of Social Work, recruited for the JDC from his alma mater. Named after the former JDC chairman Paul Baerwald, the school trained roughly 120 students from Europe, North Africa and Israel. The school closed its doors in the fall of 1953, but its faculty remained active until the late 1950s, providing staff training in social work to Jewish organizations in Europe and North Africa.[28]

Perhaps most significantly, however, in the fall of 1947, the JDC began working with leaders from French Jewish institutions to create a centralized fundraising body modeled after the American United Jewish Appeal. To do so, the head of the JDC hired Harry Rosen, a specialist in community organizing from the United States. Rosen struggled to understand French Jews, and they struggled to understand him.[29] After multiple conflicts, Rosen was sent home, and Laura Margolis took over his work.[30] In 1949, the *Fonds Social Juif Unifié* (FSJU) was established, uniting the fundraising campaigns of most Jewish welfare organizations under a common umbrella. The JDC saw the *Fonds Social Juif Unifié* as the organization that would carry on its welfare work once French Jews were able to operate on their own without JDC help. In 1953, the JDC began transferring its programs and French employees to the FSJU.[31] Even though the JDC was still active in French

---

28 Laura Hobson Faure, "Le Travail social dans les organisations juives françaises après la *Shoah*: création *made in France* ou importation américaine?" *Archives juives, Revue d'histoire des Juifs de France* 45 (2012): 43–60.

29 Letter from H. Rosen to P. Skorneck, 22 June 1948, File 287, France 1945/54, JDC-NY.

30 Laura Margolis Jarblum Interview, page 34, (128) 56, Oral History Division, Hebrew University of Jerusalem.

31 Memo from Ester Hentges, 13 April 1953, File 287, France 1945/54, JDC-NY.

Jewish life in the 1960s, it was the FSJU, for example, that organized the emergency measures to assist Algerian Jews in the summer of 1962.[32]

In the early 1950s, Jewish community centers like those popular with American Jews after World War II, were introduced in France by the JDC.[33] The newly formed education department of the JDC designed the French centers, which sought to cultivate pluralism in French Jewish life. The first postwar community center in Paris opened its doors in 1955, and by June 1956 it had 800 members.[34] By the end of 1957, Paris, Lens, Belfort, Rouen and Lyon all had this same type of structure.[35]

The Fonds Social Juif Unifié and the Jewish community centers still operate in France today. Likewise, social work has gained greater professional recognition within Jewish organizations due to efforts of the JDC. Maud Mandel has affirmed that the JDC acted as a centralizing force in Jewish welfare organizations in France, where it asserted an American influence on their structures. The JDC, however, was not the only American Jewish organization to establish a program in postwar France. Others also came, bringing their own visions for reconstruction. At times these visions were in accord with the JDC, at times they stood in opposition to it.[36]

Complementing or Challenging the JDC?

The presence of multiple American Jewish organizations in France poses the question whether the ideological and class divisions that characterized interwar American Jewry were substantively changed in the postwar era. Strictly speaking, the United Jewish Appeal was the representative philanthropic body for the American Jewish community. By giving money to the UJA, which in turn provided funds to the JDC for postwar reconstruction in Europe, American Jews were acting in accordance with the principles of centralization and efficiency

---

32 Colette Zytnicki, "L'accueil des Juifs d'Afrique du Nord par les institutions communautaires (1961–1965)," Archives Juives 31 (1998): 95–109; Laura Hobson Faure, "L'immigration des Juifs d'Algérie en France métropolitaine. L'occasion pour les Juifs français de recouvrer leur indépendance face au judaïsme américain dans la France d'après-guerre?" Archives juives 42 (2009): 67–81.

33 As Maud Mandel points out, Turkish Jewish immigrants did open a community center in Paris in the 1920s. Yet this structure was not widespread until the 1950s. Mandel, "Philanthropy or Cultural Imperialism," 80.

34 Executive Committee minutes, 29 January 1957, File 151, France 1945/54, JDC-NY.

35 Ibid.

36 Mandel, "Philanthropy or Cultural Imperialism," 53–94.

dominant in American Jewish welfare organizations. Yet in the field things were not so simple. The very presence of organizations other than the JDC in postwar France suggests that American Jews were not convinced that the JDC alone could serve all their philanthropic needs. This stands in contradiction to Arthur Goren's analysis of postwar American Jewish life, where he affirms communal consensus in philanthropic matters:

> The blurring of differences during the early postwar years enabled the national coordinating agencies of American Jewry to flourish, particularly those agencies that guided fund-raising campaigns and the policy-making implicit in allocating the funds. The local communities channeled vast sums of money and political influence to these bodies through their federations. They, in turn, dispersed overseas relief, aid to Israel, support for the community relations organizations and help for the national denominational and cultural institutions.[37]

While Goren's analysis suggests that American Jews were running a well-oiled philanthropic machine, Hasia Diner presents a different view, pointing out that:

> American Jews, both youth and adults, faced an unprecedented reality in the postwar era. Divisions derived from decades earlier persisted, but the fundamental changes, some wrought by the Holocaust, others by the affluence, suburbanization, and liberalism of the era, meant that different strands of Jewish life each had to decide how to cope with the new environment.[38]

Diner suggests that each faction of American Jewry sought solutions to the challenges of the postwar world on its own, implying a more diverse and potentially divisive approach to philanthropy. Like Diner, Riv-Ellen Prell, referring to American Jewish organizations during the Cold War, also emphasizes conflict.[39] The case of American Jewish mobilization in postwar France allows us to test these scholarly assessments. By looking at the relationship between the JDC and other American Jewish organizations in France, we will be able to understand the inter-organizational practices of American Jews during this period better.

Both the National Council of Jewish Women (NCJW) and the American Jewish Committee (AJC), for example, sought to collaborate with the JDC by establishing complementary programs that focused respectively on Jewish women and Jewish political life in France. The NCJW, founded in the US in 1893, functioned through local chapters, and built a network for Jewish women across the US. Over 15,000 women joined the NCJW between 1920 and 1927, increasing membership from

37 Goren, "A Golden Decade," 4.
38 Diner, *We Remember*, 324.
39 Prell, "Triumph, Accommodation, and Resistance," 128–130.

36,500 to 51,000.[40] By the 1960s, the organization had over 100,000 members.[41] The women of the NCJW were often affiliated with the Reform movement, and often, their husbands were involved in the AJC. Socio-economically, the members of the NCJW were primarily from the middle and upper classes, and were able to coordinate a personalized approach to aiding European Jews. In 1945, for example, the National Council for Jewish Women coordinated a "Ship-A-Box" program. They collected donations of food, clothing and toys, which they sent to Jewish children's homes in France from 1945 until at least 1949. There is some evidence that the program may have been extended to North African children in transit camps in Marseilles who were awaiting transit to Israel.[42]

The NCJW intensified its European activities in 1946, sending Ms. Gloria Wagner to represent it in France. The JDC explicitly collaborated with the NCJW and provided office space for Ms. Wagner in their Paris office. Informed by the JDC of the needs of Jewish women in France, the NCJW developed two new programs: a home for young Jewish women in Paris, and a scholarship program to send Jewish women to the United States to study welfare related topics at American universities. The NCJW women's home opened in Paris in the summer of 1947, and offered room and board to forty young Jewish women. The director of the JDC pointed out that the needs of this population were particularly acute due to the fact that women of this age were too old to live in children's homes, but were as yet unable to earn enough to support themselves. This need was intensified in 1947 when the JDC, in a cost-cutting measure, changed its policy and required that the organizations that ran children's homes "clean house" of children who were over the age of eighteen.[43] Thus, while this work was technically welfare work and under the domain of the JDC, the JDC organized through the NCJW in order to help a small yet specific population that was "falling through the cracks" of its own program.

40 Faith Rogow, *Gone to Another Meeting: The National Council of Jewish Women, 1893–1993* (Tuscaloosa, AL: University of Alabama Press, 1993), 167–174.

41 Encyclopedia Judaica, "National Council for Jewish Women," *Encyclopedia Judaica* (New York: Keter, Macmillan Reference USA, 1972), 871.

42 Letter from C. Passman to JDC Headquarters in NY, 2 September 1949, File 260, France 1945/54, JDC-NY.

43 Letter from Laura Margolis to Hortense Goldstone, 15 October 1947. File 291, France 1945/54, JDC-NY.

The JDC also welcomed the decision of the American Jewish Committee to open an office in Paris.[44] The AJC was established in 1906 as an elite committee to advocate for Jewish civil rights. It thrived as one of the most powerful Jewish organizations in the United States due to its distinct social and political characteristics linking it to upper-class American Jewish men of German descent, most of whom were affiliated with the Reform movement. A 1944 decision to break with the committee format and establish local chapters in the United States allowed the AJC unprecedented growth. By 1949, its membership had increased from 400 individuals to 18,000.[45] In spite of its rapid growth, the AJC's postwar organizational style as well as its membership profile, described as "moderate, judicious, deliberate, with a preference for anonymity and an aversion for the dramatic,"[46] remained remarkably similar to the interwar period.

In April of 1947, when the AJC opened its office in Paris, it was under the supervision of Joel Wolfsohn, AJC European Director of Foreign Affairs. Zachariah Shuster, a polyglot writer and publicist, was chosen to manage the new Paris office.[47] In 1951, Abraham Karlikow, an American journalist and former employee of the public relations department of the JDC, began working for the AJC.[48] He eventually became the director of the office, which at its peak employed about a dozen individuals. Under the direction of Shuster and then Karlikow, the AJC's

---

44 Re: Herbert Katzki, 7 April 1947, File: Key People FO-EUR 47, Box 14, FAD 41, RG 347.7.41, AJC, YIVO. Furthermore, writing to his superiors in New York, the JDC director for France suggested the AJC was needed to deal with restitution issues: "Here… there is the need of a qualified American expert, one of the American Jewish Committee. I cannot understand why they haven't yet sent someone over here to deal with this kind of problem…Can you bring added pressure on AJC to send over a really competent person to guide the local people?" Letter from Arthur Greenleigh to Moses Leavitt, 7 April 1945, File 247, France 1945/54, JDC-NY.

45 Naomi Weiner Cohen, *Not Free to Desist: The American Jewish Committee, 1906–1966* (Philadelphia, PA: Jewish Publication Society of America, 1972), 338.

46 Ibid.

47 According to one former AJC employee, Shuster "spoke everything," including Russian, German, French and English; Telephone interview conducted by author with former AJC employee, 3 August 2005. See also New York Public Library, American Jewish Committee Oral History Collection, Zachariah Shuster interview conducted by Mitchell Krauss, 6 June 1972.

48 Telephone interview conducted by author with Abraham Karlikow, 27 October 2005. See also New York Public Library, American Jewish Committee Oral History Collection, Abraham Karlikow interview conducted by Mimi Harmon, 15 October 1980; Abraham Karlikow interview conducted by Irma Krents, 18 April 1988.

Paris office served as a base from which to closely survey the political situation of Jews behind the Iron Curtain and in North Africa. Nonetheless, the situation of the Jews in metropolitan France quickly became a central preoccupation of the AJC. While their situation was perhaps less urgent, their status as the largest Jewish population in Western Europe demanded attention.

Fully engaged in dispelling the "Jew-equals-Communist" myth in the United States, the AJC was dismayed by the strong support for Communism among the Jews of France.[49] Shuster saw this as an opportunity to educate the Jews of France on Jewish life outside of their country. In a memorandum to the Department of Foreign Affairs of the AJC, he shared his observations:

> One reason for the extremism of Jewish life in Europe is the fact that the sources of information are slanted in a narrow and partisan way. The lack of information is particularly obvious with regard to the Jewish community in America and the political and social trends in it. There is a great thirst for knowledge and even more for proper analysis of the Jewish situation in the world.[50]

The AJC thus committed itself to providing the Jews of France with a "proper analysis" of Jewish life in broader perspective. The Paris office of the AJC saw potential in creating a magazine modeled on *Commentary*, which the AJC published in the US beginning in 1945.[51] After an initial brochure was sent to a select number of individuals, a trial issue of the new magazine, *Evidences*, appeared in France in May 1949. Edited by journalist Nicolas Baudy, *Evidences* published articles on a variety of topics linked to Jewish life and European society. Its contributors included Raymond Aron, David Ben Gurion, Léon Blum, Bernard Blumenkranz, Albert Camus, Martin Buber, and René Cassin, among others.[52] A handpicked group of three thousand individuals, "chosen for the influence they [had] on general public opinion, Jewish affairs, or events affecting Jews,"[53] received a free subscription to

---

49 Peter Novick, *The Holocaust in American Life* (Boston, MA: Houghton Mifflin Company, 2000), 85–102. For a larger analysis of the AJC and the JDC during the Cold War in France, see Laura Hobson Faure, *Un "Plan Marshall juif,"* 177–223.

50 Memo from Z. Shuster to Foreign Affairs Department, 11 April 1947, File: France 1945–49, Box 18, FAD 1, RG 347.7.41, AJC, YIVO.

51 By 1960, *Commentary* had a circulation of 20,000; Edward Shapiro, *A Time for Healing*, 27. Memo from Z. Shuster to Foreign Affairs Department, 11 April 1947, File: France 1945–49, Box 18, FAD 1, RG 347.7.41, AJC, YIVO.

52 Robert Attal, "Index de la revue 'Evidences' (1949–1963)" (Jerusalem: unpublished manuscript, 1972).

53 Facts About Evidences, 2 March 1950, File: Evidences, 1947–1962, Box 18, FAD 1, RG 347.7.41, AJC, YIVO.

Evidences. According to the AJC's own records, in its first year, seventy-percent of the articles in *Evidences* covered Jewish subjects or were designed to appeal to a Jewish audience.[54] The very fact that the AJC compiled this statistic shows to what extent its publication was part of a conscious effort to form public opinion. The clear orientation of the AJC program—focused on political matters and not on welfare—facilitated smooth relations between the AJC and the JDC.

While the JDC may have worked in harmony with the AJC, it clashed with US immigrant and Zionist organizations which were not affiliated with the United Jewish Appeal, but had independent programs operating in France. The Hebrew Sheltering and Immigrant Aid Society (HIAS), for example, which was established at the end of the nineteenth century to assist Eastern European immigrants in New York, established a European presence to assist Jews in emigration under the name of HICEM in 1927.[55] After World War II, HIAS dissolved HICEM, but continued to function on its own in Europe.[56] By April 1945, HIAS had reestablished offices in Paris, Lyon, Marseilles and Nice, and later it expanded to five other French cities.[57] Conflict between HIAS and the JDC erupted in the summer of 1946 when the JDC opened an emigration office in Bordeaux in the same building utilized by HIAS. Concerned with maintaining good relations with the American Consul, the HIAS representative in Bordeaux wrote to his superiors for clarification on how to deal with cases that concerned the two organizations.[58] The director of HIAS-France forwarded this letter to New York, to show them the "effect made by [the] appearance of another 'competing' organization."[59] He continued:

54 Ibid.

55 HICEM was a partnership between HIAS, the Jewish Colonisation Association and Emigdirect; see Eli Lederhendler, "Hard Times: HIAS Under Pressure, 1925–26," *Yivo Annual of Jewish Science* 22 (1995): 105–129; Valery Bazarov, "HIAS and HICEM in the system of Jewish relief organisations in Europe, 1933- 41," *East European Jewish Affairs* 39 (2009): 69–78.

56 Mark Wischnitzer, *Visas to Freedom, the History of HIAS* (Cleveland: World Publishing, 1956), 205.

57 Hobson Faure, *Un "Plan Marshall Juif,"* 301.

58 Letter from HIAS Representative in Bordeaux to Director in Paris, 2 August 1946, File 79, Reel 19.6, Records of Postwar HICEM/HIAS 1945–1953, France IV, Series 4, RG 245.5, YIVO.

59 Letter from Director of HIAS-France to Asofsky (HIAS-New York), 6 August 1946, File 395, Reel 19.6, Records of Postwar HICEM/HIAS 1945–1953, France IV, Series 4, RG 245.5, YIVO.

You certainly will be aware of the shade of contempt in the words of the Bordeaux Consul when saying 'that they don't want, under any pretext, 'rivality' [sic] between different organizations in order to get a success more or less important.'

I understand indeed that in order to make peace you need at least two parties, but to make war, the wish of a single one is quite enough, I dare say that peace does not depend only on you. I believe useful to show in discussions that there was no sense in creating a new organization [the JDC] in Bordeaux: As said beforehand, the total amount of emigration cases in the Bordeaux district has been centralized by our office and the lack of complaints and, on the contrary, lots of compliments we get, show that our Office works at everybody's satisfaction.[60]

The "war" between HIAS and the JDC continued in Europe until the passage of the Displaced Persons Act of 1948. When faced with what they thought was the real possibility of evacuating the DP camps, the JDC and HIAS finally joined forces to establish a shared office in Frankfort in July of 1949.[61] More significantly, the position of HIAS within the complex of American Jewish welfare organizations was further clarified in 1954, when it merged with the immigration departments of the JDC, the National Council of Jewish Women, and the United Service for New Americans. The new organization, United HIAS Service, marked the completion of the "integration" of HIAS into the American Jewish Welfare establishment, and as a result, it finally began to receive funds from the UJA. It was also allowed to maintain independent fundraising.[62]

The World Jewish Congress (WJC), created in 1936, represented the immigrant and Zionist elements in American Jewry through its collaboration with the American Jewish Congress, which funded the majority of its work in Europe. Though not officially an American organization, WJC deserves consideration here because the majority of its funding, as well as the drive behind its French program, came from the United States. The WJC had been headquartered in Paris before the war, and reestablished an office there in the fall of 1945.[63] Determined to play a role in French Jewish life, it designed an extensive program that included political advocacy on matters involving Jews, relief work, and cultural activities.[64] Even though the WJC's primary focus was political, in the years following the war it contributed general relief to French Jews through shipments of food, clothing

---

60 Ibid.
61 Bauer, *Out of the Ashes*, 186.
62 Wischnitzer, *Visas to Freedom*, 257–270.
63 Paris Office of the WJC, Program for the next 6 months, 29 October 1945, H112/1 France, Cahn-Debre, Sylvain, 1945, WJC (361), American Jewish Archive (AJA).
64 Ibid.

and medicine.[65] Mrs. Louise Waterman Wise, the wife of Rabbi Stephen Wise, mobilized the women's division of the American Jewish Congress in the name of European Jewish children, forming the American Committee for the Rehabilitation of European Jewish Children. The goal of this committee was to establish and fund children's homes, and when possible, to carry out the reunification of children with their surviving relatives. This committee utilized the infrastructure of the WJC, and through it, opened eleven homes in four countries.[66] In France, the WJC worked in collaboration with French Jewish organizations to run six children's homes.[67] By the spring of 1947, 255 children were being cared for in these institutions, and, the WJC also supported another 410 children living with foster families in France.[68]

It is likely that the welfare efforts of the WJC were a source of frustration to the JDC, which considered itself the direct, and only legitimate emanation of American Jewish aid to the Jews of Europe.[69] Indeed, these two organizations had fought over the assistance to the children who had escaped from France to Spain during World War II.[70] Nevertheless, the leaders of these organizations appeared to turn the page in the postwar years. In 1946, Nahum Goldmann of the WJC wrote to inform a colleague that he was negotiating with Joseph Schwartz of the JDC to establish "good neighbor relations and friendship."[71] In 1947, these efforts led to an accord by which the American Jewish Congress (the source of the WJC money) agreed to stop raising funds independently and join the United Jewish Appeal. In exchange, the JDC was to finance the homes previously funded by

---

65 Leon Kubowitzki, *Unity in Dispersion: A History of the World Jewish Congress* (New York: World Jewish Congress, 1948), 301.
66 Ibid., 302–305.
67 Foster Children in Europe, 30 April 1947, D 73/9, WJC (361), AJA.
68 Ibid.
69 Re: Herbert Katzki, 7 April 1947, File: Key People FO-EUR 47, Box 14, FAD 41, RG 347.7.41, AJC, YIVO. Katzki, secretary of the JDC, enthusiastically welcomed the American Jewish Committee to France, stating that its late arrival "permitted the World Jewish Congress to gain influence."
70 During World War II, Jewish children were evacuated from France to Spain by members of the Jewish resistance, both the WJC and the JDC opened children's homes to receive them. The JDC opened its home in Spain, leaving the WJC home in Portugal empty; Haïm Avni, "The Zionist Underground in Holland and France and the Escape to Spain," in Yisrael Gutman and Efraim Zuroff, eds., *Rescue Attempts During the Holocaust. Proceedings of the Second Yad Vashem International Historical Conference. Jerusalem, April 8–11, 1974* (Jerusalem: Yad Vashem, 1977), 555–590.
71 Letter from N. Goldmann to A. Tartakower, 31 July 1946, H115/9, WJC (361), AJA.

the American Jewish Congress, and to allow their organization in the field—the WJC—to continue to manage the homes.[72]

Conclusion

The intangible bonds of Jewish solidarity that inspired American Jews to enlist in the armed forces, send packages to Europe, and give money to the United Jewish Appeal expanded into an aid program that assisted almost one quarter of the Jews in France in 1945 alone. Yet the JDC did not only distribute money. It brought American concepts and social welfare practices to France, and it sought to reform French Jewish life according to an American model. In a sense American Jews created their own "Marshall Plan." Its heritage is still present in France today.

While Jewish solidarity formed the major impetus for this mobilization, it was also characterized by each organization's desire to disseminate its ideology. "Setting up shop" in France was thus not only a means of expressing solidarity—it was a way of asserting one's own particular vision of Jewish life.

The study of the relationships among Jewish organizations in postwar France suggests that the ideological and class divisions that characterized American Jewry in the interwar years were not immediately extinguished after World War II, and indeed, were even carried across the Atlantic in the baggage of the various organizational representatives. While this fact lends support to conflict-driven assessments of postwar American Jewry, we can also detect distinct moves towards consensus and centralization, as observed by Arthur Goren. Indeed, this can be seen in the examples of the HIAS and the WJC in France: by 1954, both organizations had been "integrated" in their own particular manner into the United Jewish Appeal, thus allowing for greater coordination of overseas welfare.[73]

After World War II, American Jews were faced with a moment of change and uncertainty. As a result of the Shoah, they had become the largest Jewish community in the World. This shift in the dynamics of world Jewry took place during a period of rapidly increasing acceptance of Jews into US society. This article has shown that while American Jews responded *en masse* to help European Jewry after the Shoah, they did not all do so along the same path. Jews did not choose

---

72 Letter from L. Kubowitzki to S. Cahn-Debré, S. Perl, 20 March 1947, D 73/9, WJC (361), AJA; Agreement between the World Jewish Congress and the American Joint Distribution Committee, 26 December 1947. File 249, France 1945/54, JDC-NY.

73 A similar arrangement was reached between the JDC and the orthodox group Vaad Hatzalah in 1948; Alex Grobman, *Battling for Souls: The Vaad Hatzala Rescue Committee in Post-Holocaust Europe* (Jersey City: KTAV, 2004), 235–240.

to support the same philanthropic organizations, and in fact asserted the diversity of American Jewish life by giving to multiple causes, and by supporting organizations that originally worked outside the auspices of the UJA. A study of American Jewish mobilization in postwar France provides us with a textured portrait of American Jewish identities in the decade after World War II. In that decade, differences were initially asserted, then recognized, and eventually negotiated in exchange for group cohesion. Immigrant and Zionist organizations entered into agreements with the JDC and the UJA where their identities were taken into account. In the same way the UJA was slowly accorded the role of sole voice of American Jewish philanthropy abroad. Dissent gave way to consensus, yet minority identities endured. From cacophony to concert, American Jews increasingly spoke with one voice, and, as a group, moved from the periphery to the mainstream in postwar American life.

Zohar Segev

National Identity, Cultural Revival, and National Struggle: The World Jewish Congress, American Jewry, and the Challenge of Jewish Diaspora in the Shadow of the Holocaust

Abstract: *By actively supporting the restoration of Jewish communities in the European diaspora, American Jews justified their own choice of remaining in the US, next to the Zionist ideal of resettling in Palestine. American Jewish support for European Jews created a clear role for American Jews that broke the potential monopoly of the state of Israel as the sole guardian of Jewish rights.*

The dramatic triangle of the Holocaust, the survivors, and the state of Israel provided the framework and background for the absorption of the survivors into it, at the same time as it strengthened the ethnic and national identity of Diaspora Jews, in particular those in the United States. When founding a Jewish state became a realistic possibility, and it was subsequently established, it by no means ended the activity in favor of a nationally oriented Jewish Diaspora. Rather it accelerated it. Israel's establishment challenged the Diaspora leaders who held Zionist views. They had to find new ideological and organizational content once the state was formed. Along with the vast effort involved in founding Israel and preserving it during the first hard years, there was an equally difficult, complex undertaking: to rehabilitate European Jewish life after the Holocaust and to enable Jews who so desired to reintegrate into their places of origin.[1]

The historical conversation regarding the Jews of the United States and the Holocaust revolves around two central themes. The first and most conspicuous one sharply criticizes American Jewry for its inactivity in rescuing Jews during the Holocaust. The second and closely linked issue is American Jewry's crucial contribution to the establishment of the Jewish state through its political struggle within the American arena. Personal and communal shocks following the Holocaust, and a deep dissatisfaction with hopeless rescue operations led American Jews to throw their full weight and influence behind the establishment of a Jewish state

---

1 See also, Zohar Segev, "Remembering and Rebuilding: The World Jewish Congress, in the shadow of the Holocaust," *Journal of Modern Jewish Studies* 14 (2015): 315–332.

when international arrangements were coordinated after World War II. The full significance of such a readiness to act in America as an ethnic group with specific political goals becomes more outstanding in light of the opposition of Presidents Franklin D. Roosevelt and Harry S. Truman to the establishment of a Jewish state. Indeed, the Jewish vote wielded as a political instrument changed the United States Government policy with regard to establishing a Jewish state in the Middle East.[2]

These are absorbing issues, each of which deserves attention. In the present essay, however, they introduce us to the fascinating triangle of the Holocaust, the survivors, and the state of Israel within the American Jewish context. Hitherto, research and related scholarly discourse have focused mainly on these three points of the triangle within the Israeli context. In my view, however, such a discussion is incomplete unless it addresses the dramatic developments in the Jewish world at large, and in the United States in particular. The complex relationship between the Holocaust, the survivors and the state of Israel constitutes a hothouse, as it were, for the intensive growth of an ethnic Jewish identity in the Diaspora, and for the creation of a significant Jewish community flourishing alongside Israel and able to support it. This is by no means an anti-Zionist view. Political, organizational, and ideological processes existed among American Jews in all sectors. Thus, for instance, American Zionists sought to mold Israel in general, and at the same time to impact Israel's relationship to American Jews in such a way that American Zionism would continue to prosper after the state was established.

In this essay I would like to explore the role of the World Jewish Congress (WJC) in the 1940s and 1950s. What was unique about WJC activity was that its leaders sought to cultivate relations between Israel and the Jews of the United States just as the American Zionists did. But they were also intensely and resolutely absorbed in rehabilitating the Jewish Diaspora and in helping the survivors who so desired to reintegrate into Europe. WJC leaders were neither fazed by the plight of the survivors nor by the terrible destruction of European Jewish communities. Quite the opposite was true. They saw these things as a way to justify an international Jewish organization with two objectives: to preserve the rights of world Jewry by representing them in the new post war international organizations, and secondly to foster an ethnic identity with national characteristics. WJC believed

---

2   For unmistakably example of criticism see David S. Wyman, *The Abandonment of the Jews: America and the Holocaust, 1941–1945* (New York: Pantheon Books, 1984). About American Jewry's outstanding contribution to the establishment of the Jewish state, see H. D. Shapiro, *From Philanthropy to Activism: The Political Transformation of American Zionism in the Holocaust Years 1933–1944* (Oxford, UK: Pergamon Press, 1994); Marc Lee Raphael, *Abba Hillel Silver* (New York: Holmes & Meier, 1989), 135–164.

that these steps would assure the continued existence of the Jews in the Diaspora and allow individuals and communities to contribute to a better post-war world by fostering both the interests of Jews as well as other minorities. WJC activists in Europe did not ignore the centrality of Jews living in Palestine after World War II. At the same time, however, they worked to establish a new ethnic reality in Europe, one in which Palestine would be important—but not all-important.

Though defined as an international body, WJC was in fact an American Jewish organization that had been established by Stephen Wise, a Reform rabbi and one of the most important American Zionist leaders until his death in the 1940s.[3] The WJC center was in the United States. Its offices in Europe and South America were financed by American sources and reported to the WJC organization in the United States. In the US, enthusiasm for Zionism predated World War II and was obviously reinforced after the war broke out. The founding session of the WJC took place in Geneva in August 1936 with 280 delegates from 32 countries in attendance. While it was a new organization, the WJC continued the tradition of the American Jewish Congress founded in 1918, and the Committee of Jewish Delegations of 1919. It functioned as a voluntary body representing Jewish communities and organizations throughout the world in dealing with government and international authorities, and it worked to encourage social and cultural life in its member communities. To date researchers have focused on the Jewish leadership of the 1940s and 1950s that criticized the WJC for minimal rescue efforts during the Holocaust and a failure to draw broad segments of the Jewish community into their organization and activities during, and immediately after World War II.[4] Nevertheless, the WJC archive reveals a far more complex reality.[5]

---

3 For information on Wise, see Melvin I. Urofsky, *A Voice that Spoke for Justice: The Life and Times of Stephen S. Wise* (Albany, NY: State University of New York Press, 1982); Robert D. Shapiro, *A Reform Rabbi in the Progressive Era: The Early Career of Stephen S. Wise* (New York: Garland Publications, 1988).

4 See, for example, Rafael Medoff, *The Deafening Silence* (New York: Shapolsky, 1987). A detailed survey of research along these lines can be found in: Gulie Ne'eman Arad, "Cooptation of Elites: American Jewish Reactions to the Nazi Menace, 1933," *Yad Vashem Studies* 25 (1996): 32–33.

5 For general information about the WJC see, Leon A. Kubowizki, *Unity In Dispersion: A History of the World Jewish Congress*, (New York: WJC, 1948). (From here on, Kubowizki, *World Jewish History*); Isaac I. Schwarzbart, *25 Years In the Service of the Jewish People* (New York: WJC, 1957). On the WJC as an American organization see, for example, the unpublished autobiography of Dr. Arieh Tartakower, head of the Cultural Department. Central Zionist Archives, Jerusalem (hereafter CZA), 352/C6, 2.

The horrors of the Holocaust prompted the leaders of the WJC to increase their activity on behalf of European Jewry in the aftermath of the war. They opened cultural and educational institutions in Europe, reclaimed Jewish property, and secured compensation for survivors and for the Jewish people as a whole. At the same time the WJC worked to insure the prosecution of war criminals and they sought a European political order that would prevent future anti-Semitic activity.

Social Work

An outstanding example of the WJC's European activity was its plan to train American Jewish social workers to work in Europe on their behalf. Planning began at the end of November 1944, and graduates were to leave for Europe as soon as the political and security situation allowed. The training program would be a joint undertaking of the WJC and the New School for Social Research in New York. The curriculum was designed and the staff selected in collaboration with the noted philosopher and sociologist, Prof. Horace M. Kallen. A position paper appended to the curriculum reveals the concern of WJC leaders for the challenges the Jews would face once the war was over. They thought the social workers would require Jewish education in order to address these challenges. Among other things WJC officials noted the need to save hundreds of thousands of Jews from starvation and disease, they recorded the need for mass organization and transportation of Jewish refugees, and the necessity of enlisting huge contributions for the resettlement of displaced Jews in Europe. The authors of the papers, who were members of the aid and welfare committee of the WJC, laid special emphasis on the social and economic challenges involved in resettling displaced Jews within the fabric of European life. They identified as the most important instrument to attain this goal, the training of a significant group of social workers that could deal with welfare and rehabilitation. As the traditional, long-established Jewish social support system had not survived the Holocaust, WJC felt that the only way to train new cadres for these tasks was by establishing a special study program in New York for Jewish social workers.[6]

The syllabus for the training course provides a perspective on the goals of the undertaking and reveals something about the worldview of those who planned it. The curriculum included courses dealing with citizenship problems in the welfare context. It organized discussions of Jewish community life, and lectures about

---

6 "Plan to train American Jewish social workers," 16 November 1944, The Jacob Rader Marcus Center of the American Jewish Archives, Cincinnati, Ohio (hereafter AJA) 361 C-69/1.

welfare activity in conjunction with governments, international organizations and the private sector. The task they set themselves was huge because WJC hoped to do this not only in Western Europe but also in central and Eastern Europe, where the Jewish communities had been almost completely wiped out and, moreover, the local population opposed their return.[7]

Additionally the course schedule shows that the WJC leaders wanted to advance the rehabilitation of Jewish life in Europe, even as they recognized the importance of a Jewish state in Palestine. A ten-hour course on the importance of refugees returning to their former homes also held a discussion of the national home, and gave particulars on the illicit ways to enter Palestine. Even with that, however, only a minor place in the curriculum was accorded to promoting Palestine as a refuge for the displaced, thus indicating the tremendous importance WJC leaders attached to rehabilitating refugees into post-war Europe.[8]

The social workers' training program is only the tip of the iceberg of a wide-range of activities supporting rehabilitation in Europe. Other actions included the registration of private and communal Jewish property in Poland based on pre-war numbers, not only as a basis for compensation claims, but also to create a foundation upon which to rebuild communities. Educational centers were established with curricula in Hebrew and in Yiddish, prayer books were printed and distributed, European Jewish schools were "adopted" by American Jewish institutions with a promise of support, and basic books on Jewish history were produced. Visiting lecturers were engaged, scientific periodicals established, and adult education programs using the then-modern radio and gramophone were launched.[9]

Caring for Orphans

Within WJC activity on behalf of displaced Holocaust survivors, the children received special attention. The archives tell of an impressive system set up by leaders of the WJC in Europe that went far beyond what they had initially set out to do to rescue and rehabilitate children. In the nature of things, caring for the children meant setting up an educational system. From early in 1943 WJC leaders stressed the need for a special organization to care for the children once the war was over.

---

7   Ibid.
8   Ibid.
9   See memorandums at the WJC papers: 20 March 1946, AJA, 361 E-10/14; etc. 24 September 1948, AJA/

Indeed, in 1944, under the leadership of Stephen Wise, the Children's Department coordinated the collection of funds to rehabilitate orphans.[10]

The Children's Department had two main goals. The first was the creation of a network to enable adoption in the United States and in Palestine and the second was the restoration of Jewish life in Europe. The decision to promote the adopting process in the US and Palestine was reached to compensate for the shortage of Jewish families available in Europe after the War.[11]

Working toward the second goal—restoring Jewish life in Europe—WJC leaders built orphanages and supported existing and newly created children's homes economically and educationally. Although designated as orphanages, WJC institutions also served children of single parents who could not give their children adequate care in post-war Europe. The leaders were well aware of the formidable task of caring for children after their traumatic wartime experiences. The best way to do this, it was felt, was to have the children adopted by European Jewish families, though they knew that few such families were equal to the task. Hence the institutions offered the children both educational and psychological support.[12]

The Mizrahi movement, the Jewish Agency and various Orthodox associations chose to transfer authority over their orphans' homes in Europe to the WJC. The fact that the WJC took them on shows how committed it was to this supremely important undertaking. It also shows the strength of its economic and organizational power. That strength allowed the WJC to take over responsibility for institutions previously run by other groups. Written agreements document that the WJC assumed the major financial burden and an ongoing administrative responsibility for these institutions. While educational material was adapted to the outlook of the founding associations, a broad WJC-established curriculum was preserved.[13]

In 1946 the WJC took care of more than 1600 children in 13 homes.[14] Establishing and maintaining them was a complex challenge. Aryeh Leon Kubowitzki, director of the WJC rescue services explained this challenge in a letter dated April 1945, to Dr. Yaakov Helmann, an activist living in Buenos Aires. The letter writes of the need for a strong professional organization to help the children and tells of the efforts of the WJC to ensure the ability of the children to reintegrate into

---

10 An official statement of the WJC about Jewish Children in Europe, November 1944, AJA, 361 C-98/7.
11 Protocol, WJC Children's Department, 25 January 1946, AJA, 361 D-71/11.
12 Leon Kubowitzaki, 26 April 1945, AJA, 361 D-71/6.
13 25 January 1945, AJA, 361 D-71/25; 6 March 1946, AJA, 361, D-71/11; 18 February 1947, AJA, 361 D-71/12.
14 15 January 1945, AJA, 361 D-71/12.

the European society in the future. The writer reports that the WJC established a home in Switzerland for Italian Jewish children—a home made possible by Dr. Helmann's contribution—but that it would run out of money by July of that year. He goes on to write that the orphanage went into operation in December 1944, before which the children were in the care of the International Red Cross or Swiss philanthropic associations. Given the emotional and bureaucratic difficulties these children presented (and faced), philanthropic agencies were by no means eager to engage with them, so they had been distributed among institutions and private homes. Only with great effort did the WJC manage to bring together 55 children aged 8 to 16. Kubowitzki writes that the children were now housed in what was formerly a secondary school, rented by the WJC, and that they followed the Italian school curriculum. The orphans' home, he continued, was run by a committee that included Dr. Gerhardt Ringer, the WJC representative in Switzerland who also represented the International Red Cross, and by a rabbi described as a spiritual advisor and counselor. Among the children's varied activities, Kubowitzki stressed the house news bulletin that they regularly issued.

The fact that it was the curriculum of the Italian Ministry of Education that was adopted by the orphanage is significant. It shows that it was the purpose of the WJC in their orphan's homes to prepare the children to continue their lives in Europe.

The orphanage budget was based solely on WJC members' donations, some 6000 or 7000 Swiss francs a month, with only a nominal sum from the International Red Cross. The purpose of the Kubowitzki letter was clearly to ask for donations to save the home from closing.[15] This request for donations from Argentina was part of a general effort to fund the network of WJC orphanages in Europe. American Jewish families and institutions made financial pledges to maintain a child in a WJC home. The target sum for each pledge was three hundred dollars a year, in addition to food parcels for the adopted child. To increase commitment and strengthen the bond, the WJC leadership made a point of sending "their" child's picture and history to each supporting family who, if they wanted to, could establish direct contact with the child. Another means of supporting the children was for American families to send regular food parcels to Europe. In 1946 some 7000 parcels were sent every month.[16] For many there was long-term commitment to the child that the families had contacted through the WJC.

---

15 Leon Kubowitzaki, 16 January 1945, AJA, 361 D-71/2.
16 30 January 1946, AJA, 361 D-71/11. 10 January 1946, AJA, 361 C-3/204.

Legal Interventions

Establishing and maintaining orphans' homes was not the only way the WJC worked to rehabilitate Europe's Jewish children. WJC leaders knew well that during the war, in a desperate attempts to save lives, children had been taken from their parents and given to non-Jewish families or Christian religious institutions. After the war legal battles were fought throughout Europe for the return of these children to their parents or other relatives, or failing that, for an order to put the children into WJC children's homes. In addition, the WJC provided financial support to those parents and relatives who took in children, believing firmly that supporting these Jewish families was one of the organization's main tasks in post-war Europe.[17]

WJC efforts to care for the orphans in Europe reveals the desire of its leadership to restore them in the Diaspora, work that ran parallel to the WJC's support for the nascent Jewish state and their effort to strengthen the Jewish community in Israel. From the WJC leadership's perspective reintegration into their former communities in Europe was the best solution for the children and for the Jewish People. School curricula for the wards of the European children's homes also reflect this view. Both regular and enrichment programs stressed the special status of Palestine as the home of the Jewish people but it was put alongside instruction that in fact prepared pupils for living in Europe as a way to fortify renewed Jewish community life there. Among the things the children were taught were the Jewish dietary laws, prayers, and Sabbath customs; this training was given with the idea being that familiarity with Jewish traditions and the observance of customs were essential if Jewish communities were to have a future in Europe. Significantly, rabbis filled the main spiritual leadership roles in the orphanages and all other educational institutions, the food was kosher, and the Sabbath scrupulously kept. In addition, the curriculum included Jewish history and instruction in the Yiddish language.[18] This last was especially significant, given the opposition of, first, the Zionist and, then, the Israeli establishment to Yiddish as a linguistic symbol of Diaspora existence—as against Hebrew, the symbol of renewed Jewish life in Palestine, where Yiddish was clearly irrelevant. The creators of the curriculum created a cultural and educational mélange that combined religious and traditional components with modern aspects of Jewish life in Europe and elsewhere. Such a mixture constituted a powerful tool for reinforcing nationalist sentiments, as

---

17 26 November 1945, AJA, 361 D-71/6.
18 25 January 1946, AJA, 361 D-71/11.

many scholars of both Jewish and worldwide issues of nationality have observed.[19] While WJC activists appreciated the significant position that the Jewish center in Palestine occupied in post-war Jewish life, they actively engaged in shaping a new ethnic reality in Europe in which Palestine was an important element, but was not the singular goal.[20]

Global Interest Organization

The WJC acted not only within Jewish communities after the war but also in the wider civic world. Its leaders felt it was their right and duty "as representatives of the biggest Jewish organization in the Diaspora," to support the trials against war criminals, and in its committees there was sharp criticism of the activity of other Jewish agencies vis-à-vis the Nuremberg trials. WJC documents reveal a struggle to restore Jewish property and to safeguard the rights of Jews and of other minorities within post-war political arrangements. Special attention was given to obtaining compensation both for individual survivors, and for the Jews as a people. This presents a topic for further investigation, especially in view of the current discussion on the role and the function of the Compensation Committee. WJC leaders held that not only individual survivors but also the Jewish people taken together were entitled to compensation. It was no accident that compensation funds were allotted to cultural institutions, community organizations and educational projects. This emerged from a worldview that recognized the damage wrought by the Holocaust was against the Jews as a people, that the immense damage demanded immense funds for repair, and that such funds could only be available from compensation moneys.[21]

The WJC regarded itself as the general representative of the Jewish people outside Israel, and in fact as the primary representative of all the major Jewish organizations.[22] Hence it demanded control—and that the money *not* be sent to the

---

19 See, for example, Benedict Anderson, *Imagined Communities: Reflections on the Origin and Spread of Nationalism* (London: Verso, 1983), 17–40.

20 Post-War Work Plan of the WJC's Child Care Division (no date specified), AJA, 361 D71/11.
    The full significance of the educational and pedagogical program instituted in the WJC children's homes becomes evident in relation to the very different programs adopted in the children's homes run by the youth movements, the chief objective of which was to prepare the children for migration to Palestine.

21 26 November 1944, AJA, 361 A-68/11.

22 Other Jewish organization, especially the American Jewish Joint Distribution Committee did not accept this perspective. About the tension between the two originations

Israeli government—of very considerable sums to reestablish functioning Jewish communities in the Diaspora. An outstanding expression of this self-perception was the WJC's attempts to obtain official status within the United Nations. Its committees submitted papers, sent memoranda, and supplied data to United Nations committees dealing with minority issues, aid and welfare. Stephen Wise came out sharply in public against regarding Zionism as the only organizational factor in post-Holocaust Jewish life. Nahum Goldmann, a founder of the WJC and its president after Wise's death in 1949, stressed in 1948 that the WJC, not the Israeli government, spoke officially for Diaspora Jewry. In this spirit a report on WJC activity in the United Nations insisted that the WJC, not the Israeli government had defended Jewish rights throughout the world. In fact, in 1947 WJC leaders requested and received recognition from the UN as a non-governmental organization with consolatory consulting status, which legally and internationally recognized their unique position.[23]

Such organizational and political activity of the WJC revealed their internal ideological position and this is turn was reflected in a wide range of speeches, articles in periodicals, and the proceedings of meetings. One example is Stephen Wise's address to the European branch of the WJC in August 1945. There he mentioned the importance of the *Yishuv* (the Jewish community in pre-state Israel), and defined the Jews of the world as one people with a common faith, a common future, and a common fate. The two main problems facing the Jewish people at the war's end according to Wise, were opening the gates of Palestine and renewing Jewish life in the liberated lands. Wise added that the WJC had exerted all its influence to open those gates, and placed itself at the disposal of the Zionist movement in its just struggle. But the WJC was the only body able and willing to deal with renewing Jewish life in Europe. Again Wise stressed that the WJC was at the same time working to establish a Jewish state and to revive Jewish life in Europe. Wise emphasized that the latter was a most significant project that challenged those who saw Zionism as the sole solution for the Jewish people and opposed reorganizing life in the Diaspora. As a Jew, Wise concluded, he did not see his own Zionism as preventing him from dealing with Jewish existence throughout the world and he did not see Palestine as the sole solution.[24]

---

see, letter from the JDC's Vice President Joseph C. Hyman to Wise, 7 July 1944, AJA, 361 H296/4.

23 Nehemia Robinson, *The United Nations and the World Jewish Congress* (New York: WJC, 1955).

24 19 August 1945, AJA, 361 A-9/10.

Conclusion

Wise's explanations and the WJC agenda in the mid-1940s correct the narrow understanding of the WJC founders' motives, which contemporaries and researchers alike have taken as a purely Zionist project. Concern for world Jewry and especially the Jews of Eastern Europe was the basis for establishing the WJC in 1936. Indeed the ideology and activity of the Zionist movement in the 1930s shows that the JWC shared this purpose. But WJC leaders maintained that although the Helsinki Convention in 1906 resolved that the Zionist movement, "work in the present among the Jews of the Diaspora," the movement could not actually do so since most of its energy was invested in Palestine. Hence WJC leaders believed that the need arose for a complementary and supportive international Jewish organization working towards the same goals.[25]

Doubts about the need for the separate existence of the WJC, friction between its institutions and those of organized Zionism, and the structural problems involved in the parallel functions of the two organizations were all apparent throughout the 1940s and 1950s. These difficulties rose out of the very existence of the WJC alongside the Zionist movement. This is the main topic of a secret letter sent to Goldmann and Wise in June 1943 by Dr. Jacob Robinson, founder of the WJC's research institute (the Institute of Jewish Affairs), the Jewish Agency's legal advisor, and subsequently the WJC's representative at UN discussions.[26] Robinson's letter notes that he was writing to them precisely because they were prominent officeholders both in the Zionist movement and in the WJC. He describes the relationship between the two movements as a grave conflict. In his view, the WJC's attempt to separate its work with European Jewry from the issue of Palestine in order to set an agenda separate from that of the Zionist movement, had generated serious ideological and practical difficulties for the organization.[27] Defining themselves as Zionists, WJC leaders worked for the establishment of a Jewish state and at the same time sought to strengthen Diaspora Jewry's ethnic identity, of which Zionism was a central component.

The Zionist view of Wise, Goldmann, and their colleagues in the WJC leadership was defined as international, but their organization operated as an American Jewish body. American Zionists did not center their ideology concerning Aliyah (emigration) to Palestine as most European Zionists did, and as Richard

---

25 Goldmann, Memorial addresses at the preparatory convention and foundation conference of the WJC, Z-6/2273, CZA, 10 August 1936.
26 Letter from Robinson to Goldmann, 25 March 1943, CZA, A-243/73.
27 Ibid.

James Horatio Gottheil, one of the founders of the American Zionist movement has explained: Zionism was the first and foremost means of maintaining Jewish solidarity in the country of residence. Since religion could no longer do so in an increasingly secular population, and living in the United States where rising nationalism obliged the Jews to integrate to such an extent that continued Jewish existence was threatened, Gottheil maintained that Zionism was the only solution.[28] Hence WJC leaders saw no contradiction between strengthening the national and ethnic identity of Diaspora Jews after the Holocaust and supporting the establishment of a Jewish state. On the contrary: Zionism was a political and social process granting legitimacy and modern content to Diaspora existence everywhere, and in the United States in particular. From The American Zionist perspective, Zionism enabled Jews to live in the modern world and at the same time to preserve a unique ethnic and cultural heritage of major importance, not only for them but also for humanity at large; Zionism is historically significant not only because it established a sovereign Jewish state, but also because it created new patterns for Jewish existence throughout the world. A by-product of the tremendous effort of world Jewry to build a national home was the welding of the world Jewish community into a political force with common objectives and active institutions.

This outlook is reflected in the establishment of the WJC in 1936. The Nazi rise to power in 1933 revealed the need for a Jewish organization that would struggle for Jewish rights in their home countries and engage in institutionalized philanthropy on their behalf. The situation in central and Eastern Europe was bad and worsening, and the anti-Jewish propaganda from Germany reinforced the readiness of American Jews to act as an organized ethnic group towards Jewish goals. This was a convenient basis for WJC activity on the American scene, at the time perhaps the only place, where effective Jewish political activity could be carried out. For its founders it served another purpose too. Through the WJC the founders could act independently of, and not subject to, the Zionist establishment, following their own political agenda in the crucial years after the Holocaust and the end of World War II.

The WJC agenda after World War II reveals the importance of Diaspora nationalism. The purpose of my paper is to show that leaders of the WJC sought to structure the Jewish people using the pattern of Diaspora nationalism not instead of, but parallel to the Jewish state. While they did not explicitly use the

---

28 Richard J. Gottheil, *Zionism* (Philadelphia, PA: The Jewish Publication Society of America, 1914), 103–104.

phrase Diaspora nationalism to explain the nature of their work after World War II, their ideological explanations and their activities in fact expressed that very idea.[29] Researchers and observers at that time took a critical view of the concept[30] because they feared that Diaspora nationalism would undermine support for the state of Israel. By contrast WJC leaders regarded Jewish national existence in the Diaspora in a most favorable light, maintaining that it could and that it must continue alongside Israel, principally because it justified the existence of the Jewish community in the United States.

The harsh, complex reality in postwar Europe particularly for Jews seriously impeded the WJC work among the Jewish communities of Eastern Europe. Continued anti-Semitism, pogroms, xenophobia, appropriation of Jewish property by former neighbors, total takeover of the communal physical infrastructure by the state, and demographic annihilation created ominous conditions.[31] This situation was made worse by the emerging Cold War and the widening gap between east and west. These factors combined to prevent the realization of the national Diaspora concept in Europe.

By contrast, in the American arena the situation worked the opposite way and strengthened the national cohesion. The means for achieving the WJC goals in Europe strengthened Jewish organizational and financial infrastructure in the United States. The increased Jewish participation in American life gradually improved their socioeconomic status and their acceptance by American society as

---

29 Jasmin Habib, *Israel, Diaspora, and the Routes of National Belonging* (Toronto: University of Toronto Press, 2004), 27–36; David Mittelberg, *The Israel Connection and American Jews* (London: Praeger, 1999), 21–35; Michael Doorley, *Irish-American Diaspora Nationalism: The Friends of Irish Freedom, 1916–1935* (Dublin: Four Courts, 2005); Smadar Lvie and Ted Swedenburg, eds., *Displacement, Diaspora, and Geographies of Identity* (London: Duke University Press, 1996), 1–25; Robert M. Seltzer, *Simon Dubnow's "New Judaism", Diaspora Nationalism and the World History of the Jews* (Boston, MA: Brill, 2014); Kirsten Heinsohn, "Diaspora as Possibility and Task the Plea of a German Jewish Woman," in Susann Lachenicht, Kirstern Heinsohn, eds., *Diaspora Identities, Exile, Nationalism and Cosmopolitanism in Past and Present* (Frankfurt & New York: Campus Verlag 2009), 130–147.

30 We can understand the critical view: 1. Because the fear that the Diaspora Nationalism concept would undermine the support for a Jewish state 2. The conclusion, after the holocaust, that there is no future for Jewish existence in Europe.

31 Pieter Lagrou, "Return to a Vanished World: European Societies and the Remnants of their Jewish Communities, 1945–1947," in David Bankir, ed., *The Jews Are Coming Back: The Return of the Jews to their Countries of Origin After WWII* (New York: Berghahn Books, 2005), 1–24.

an ethnic community with unique features. As a result of its European activity, American Jewry developed a strong sense of responsibility for world Jewry while simultaneously strengthening its own feelings of ethnic identity.

David S. Frey

Echoes of the Shoah: The 1951 Resettlement of Budapest's Jews

Abstract: *A series of large-scale expropriations and evictions of the heavily Jewish Budapest middle-class in 1951 revealed that the fragility of the implementation of the human rights provisions in the Hungarian constitution. The American Legation and the State Department collected evidence of human rights violations, which stirred a debate that was the opposite of a "Holocaust silence."*

When Hungary promulgated the basic law that transformed it into a republic in 1946, the transitional constitution's preamble guaranteed "natural and inalienable human rights for all citizens."[1] It specifically enumerated natural rights as personal freedom; the right to life without oppression, fear or want; the right to private property; the right to personal security and work; freedoms of thought, expression, religion and assembly; and more.[2] Hungary's commitment to individual human rights was theoretically bolstered in September 1947, when the series of peace treaties between the Allied and Associated Powers and the former Axis satellites of Hungary, Romania, and Bulgaria all came into force. As part of these treaties, the defeated countries became legally obliged to provide fundamental human rights and freedoms to the populations over which they presided. Article one of the political clauses segment of the Hungarian treaty obliged the state to guarantee to all persons under Hungarian jurisdiction, without distinction as to race, sex, language or religion, the enjoyment of human rights and fundamental freedoms, including freedom of expression, of press and publication, of religious worship, of political opinion and of public assembly. Further, the treaty asserted that "laws in force in Hungary shall not, either in their content or in their application, discriminate or entail discrimination, between persons of Hungarian nationality on the ground of their race, sex, language, or religion, whether in reference to their persons, property, business, professional, or financial interest, status, political or

---

1 András Körösényi, *Government and Politics in Hungary* (Budapest: Central European University Press, 2000), 145.

2 "Legal Article 1 of 1946, concerning the form of the Hungarian State," *Országos Törvénytár* [National Legal Register], 1946, 1 (20 February 1946). http://www.rev.hu/sulin et45/szerviz/dokument/torvenycikk1.htm (Accessed 1 December 2016).

civil rights, or any other matter."[3] Article XVIII even stipulated compensation and indemnification for those who had suffered from legal discrimination, persecution, and deprivation of property between 1938 and 1945, meaning Jews.[4]

Even before the proverbial ink was dry, these stipulations became problematic. Hungary was already under the *de facto* control of the Soviet Union, and the increasingly Soviet-determined government began, in the opinion of the US State Department, "to flout [its] Treaty obligations in respect to human rights."[5] Using so-called "salami tactics," which included detentions without charge, beatings, extortion and other violations of the civil rights which they had agreed to protect, Hungarian communists gradually asserted control. Non-communist politicians fled the country rather than be jailed or killed, or they joined the Hungarian Socialist Workers Party. By 1948, American and Allied diplomats became convinced that Hungary had no intention of honoring its constitutional and treaty obligations. The State Department responded by creating a small and secret program called the Treaty Violations Program, better known by its acronym TREVI. The TREVI program's charge was to document and publicly protest violations of the human rights stipulations of the peace treaties between the Allied Powers and the former Axis satellites of Hungary, Bulgaria, and Romania.[6]

The TREVI bureaucrats were overwhelmed from the endeavor's inception, tasked with deposing the hundreds, if not thousands of refugees from communism, not to mention the thousands of victims of abuse who remained inside Hungary. In 1949, the arrest, detention and show trials of Americans working in Hungary and Hungary's Prince Primate József Cardinal Mindszenty became top priorities for the officials assigned to Hungary. And when Hungary began forcibly transferring upwards of 50,000 political prisoners and criminals, in some cases

---

3   1947 18th Law, codified in the 10 Feburary 1947 Paris peace negotiations. http://www. hunsor.se/dosszie/1947parizsibeke.pdf (Accessed 1 December 2016).

4   Kinga Frojimovics notes that in 1993, the Hungarian Constitutional Court ruled that Hungary had not carried out the provisions of Article XVIII, and that Parliament should pass law to do so. Frojimovics, "The Role of the World Jewish Congress in the Reestablishment of Jewish Communal Life in Hungary after the Holocaust," in Judit Molnár, ed., *The Holocaust in Hungary: A European Perspective* (Budapest: Balassi Kiadó, 2005), 308, ft.17.

5   EUR/EE Stevens to EUR/EE Leverich, "Memorandum on Human Rights (TREVI) Project," 27 May 1954, 2. RG 59, 1950–54 Central Decimal Records File, #760.00/ 5-2754. National Archives Records Administration, Washington DC, (hereafter NARA).

6   The TREVI program was overseen by the Legal Advisor, and had representation within the State Department from the Southeastern Europe political desk, Research & Intelligence, Public Affairs (VoA), and United Nations Affairs.

to Soviet gulags, in other cases to work camps in eastern Hungary in 1950, the stakes rose further. TREVI activity reached a fevered pitch in the spring of 1951, not only as the trial of the acting head of the Roman Catholic Church in Hungary, Archbishop József Grosz, attracted global attention, but as Hungarian authorities initiated a new terror campaign.

This essay examines that four-month campaign, a series of large-scale expropriations and evictions that inordinately affected the still heavily Jewish Budapest middle class. The American Legation in Budapest and the TREVI program collected reams of evidence, for use in the United Nations hearings attesting to Hungarian human rights degradations. I argue that legal testimony from hundreds of Hungarians, and the global public discourse resulting from the resettlements, speak to a many-layered discursive resonance of wartime memory of the "Jewish Question" and the Shoah that scholars have yet to fully flesh out.[7] I believe that consideration of this discourse will inspire new ways of thinking about human rights diplomacy in the early Cold War era, the political legitimacy of the Hungarian Communist state, and notions of "Holocaust silence" in the early postwar period. The 1951 dispossession of Budapest's middle class created space for a transatlantic conversation that politicized Holocaust memory at a much earlier stage than scholars on either side of the Atlantic tend to acknowledge.

The "Resettlement/Deportation Operations" and Evocations of the Shoah[8]

Starting in May 1951, as part of a broader "stepping up" of its five-year economic plan, Hungarian authorities forced thousands of people, primarily from Budapest, but also from other larger cities, to the country's eastern hinterlands.[9] According

---

7   András Kovács and Szabó Győri are two of the few to consider the Jewish aspects of the deportations. See Kovács, "Hungarian Jewish Politics from the end of the Second World War until the Collapse of Communism," in Ezra Mendelsohn, ed., *Jews and the State: Dangerous Alliances and the Perils of Privilege* (New York: Oxford University Press/Avraham Harman Institute, 2003), 138–140 and Szabó Róbert Győri, *A kommunizmus és a zsidóság az 1945 utáni Magyarországon [Communism and the Jews in post-1945 Hungary]* (Budapest: Gondolat, 2009), 157–178.

8   Although few individuals or families were actually deported from Hungary, as the essay will show, contemporaries around the world used the term "deportations" because they feared those evicted would be transferred to Soviet gulags, or worse.

9   The deportation campaign came soon after the reintroduction of ration cards for groceries and a resulting wave of strikes. Estimates of numbers expelled in the spring/summer 1951, both contemporary and *ex post facto*, vary widely. A State Security

to officials, this campaign was directed primarily against "lords and counts, representatives of Hungarian feudalism and reaction," meaning retired high-ranking officers and civil servants of the wartime Horthy regime, former aristocracy, shopkeepers, small businessmen, and "socially dangerous" elements.[10] The evictions, preceded by a two-month run-up during which the State Protection Office (ÁVH) "exposed" food hoarding and black marketeering, were meant to "liquidate" the "exploiting class in our towns, particularly Budapest."[11] As Viktor Karády points out, the regime had no need to mobilize explicitly anti-Semitic language since

---

Office report indicates that 17,350 individuals were moved from Budapest, some 12,704 forcibly, and the remainder on their own volition when threatened with deportation. "Zárójelentés a nemkivánatos elemek Budapestről történt kitelepitéséről, /:1951.V.21-1951.VII.18:/ [Final Report on the Expulsion of Undesireable Elements from Budapest, 21 May to 18 July 1951]. Open Society Archive (Budapest) Digital Holdings. These numbers are repeated in Sándor Balogh, et al., *Magyarország a XX.században [Hungary in the 20th Century]* (Budapest: Kossuth Kiadó, 1986), 347–48, apost-1989 investigative committee. A tényfeltáró Bizottság jelentése *Törvénytelen szocializmus [Unlawful Socialism]* (Budapest: Zrínyi Kiadó-Új Magyarság, 1991), 73, and the most recent English language text on the resettlements, Zsuzsa Hantó, *Banished Families* (Budapest: Magyar Ház, 2011), 224. None of these sources specify numbers of Jewish. Most English language works use similar numbers. Paul Lendvai claims 15,000 were deported and tens of thousands more jailed in *The Hungarians. A Thousand Years of Victory in Defeat* (Princeton: Princeton University Press, 2003), 439. His numbers are similar to those cited by László Kontler. Kontler, *A History of Hungary* (London: Palgrave Macmillan, 2002), 413. On the other hand, George Schöpflin estimates that 1951 deportees and internees from Budapest numbered over 100,000. Schöpflin, "Hungary after the Second World War," in György Litván, ed., *The Hungarian Revolution of 1956* (New York: Longman, 1996), 19. In a contemporary estimate, John MacCormac of the *New York Times* calculated that 65,000 were resettled by early August 1951. MacCormac, "Hungary Holds Up Her Deportations," *New York Times*, 3 August 1951, 3. In contrast, James Mark's study of the middle class of Budapest makes no specific mention of the 1951 campaign. James Mark, "Society, Resistance and Revolution: The Budapest Middle Class and the Hungarian Communist State 1948–56," *English Historical Review* 120 (2005): 963–986.

10 "The Resettlements from Budapest," *Szabad Nép*, 17 June 1951, n. pag; Sándor Balogh, et.al, *Magyarország a XX.században*, 347.

11 Ernő Gerő, remarks before the Hungarian Socialist Workers' Party Congress, February 1951, quoted in Gerald Momka (Chargé d'Affaires in Hungary), to Sec State, Budapest #823, 6 June 1951. NARA RG 84, Budapest Legation, Classified General Records, 1946–1963, Box 12, 233 Evacuations. See also György Gyarmati and Tibor Valuch, *Hungary under Soviet Domination 1944–1989*, trans. Sean Lambert (Boulder & New York: Social Science Monographs/Columbia University Press, 2009), 135–36.

its use of terms such as "bourgeois influenced elements" *[polgári hátterű elemek]* were clear enough for domestic audiences.[12] While not disagreeing that both Jews and non-Jews were targeted, many Hungarians, Hungarian-Americans, Jewish aid groups, and Western politicians spoke of these "deportations" using a much more precise vocabulary. Whether they believed these round-ups to be anti-Jewish in character or whether they chose to mobilize the memory of the Shoah for instrumental reasons, many contemporaries who spoke or wrote about the 1951 operations used rhetoric thick with references to the 1944 obliteration of Hungarian Jewry.[13] Even the highest levels of the Hungarian government recognized that their actions had created a general panic among Budapest Jews in particular and revived the specter of genocide.[14]

Many of the Jews who remained in Hungary after the war resided in Budapest. While most were middle class, they were not well off. Many were suffering through the trauma and trials of survival. Some tried to return to village homes, found them "burgled and ravaged," and were forced to return to the safer haven of Budapest. For all Budapest Jews, the prospect of eviction must have been nightmarish,

---

12 Viktor Karády, "Antiszemitizmus és zsidó identitásdilemmák [Antisemitism and Jewish dilemmas of identity] János Gadó *et.al.,* eds. *Új antiszemitizmus [New antisemitism]* (Budapest: Mackensen Kft./Magyar Zsidó Kulturális Egyesület/Szombat, 2007), 64.

13 According to the *Virtual Jewish Library/Encyclopedia Judaica,* some 20,000 Jews were deported, primarily from Budapest. The *YIVO Encyclopedia of Jews in Eastern Europe* provides a much lower estimate, claiming only 2–3,000 of Budapest's Jews were deported. Zachary Levine confirms the lower YIVO estimate of approximately 2,500, as do András Kovács, who uses the 2–3,000 range, representing approximately one-fifth of the actual number of deportees, and Szabó Győri, who estimates 15–20 percent of all deportees were Jewish. See "Hungary," *Virtual Jewish Library,* http://www.jewishvirt uallibrary.org/jsource/judaica/ejud_0002_0009_0_09319.html (Accessed 1 December 2016) and "Hungary since 1945," *YIVO Encyclopedia of Jews in Eastern Europe* http:// www.yivoencyclopedia.org/article.aspx/Hungary/Hungary_since_1945 (Accessed 1 December 2016). Levine, "Concealed in the Open: Recipients of International Clandestine Jewish Aid in Early 1950s Hungary," *E-Journal of the American Hungarian Educators' Association,* 5 (2012) http://ahea.pitt.edu/ojs/index.php/ahea/article/view/67/57 (Accessed 1 March 2014); Kovács, "Hungarian Jewish Politics…" 138; Győri, *A kommunizmus és a zsidóság…,* 170–71.

14 Zoltán Vas to Mátyás Rákosi, 8 June 1951. This memorandum recounts a report from the head of the Neology Jewish community and chair of the Israelite National Office Lajos Stöckler, about a "great fear" erupting among Budapest's Jewish community as a result of the expulsions. Stöckler, an ardent anti-Zionist also claimed that the Israeli embassy and Hungarian Zionists were manipulating the situation. Quoted in András Kovács, "Hungarian Jewish Politics…," 153.

particularly because the experience had been made fathomable in 1944.[15] Descriptions of the expulsions smuggled out of Hungary reached TREVI soon after the action began, and they reveal evidence of widespread terror. A 26 May 1951 letter noted that "orders of eviction are usually delivered at dawn…Rumors of eviction fill not only the members of the former middle-class with dread but also the entire country, since nobody knows when a similar fate will befall one of his relatives. Since the mass deportations of the Jews by the Szálasi (Hungarian Nazi) regime, no other event made such a deep impression on the public…." The days of the dreaded *csengőfrász* (doorbell terror) had returned. A 28 May 1951 anonymous letter spoke of a climate of fear, attesting that Hungarians "know that this is but the first station on the way to a Russian Auschwitz…A deadly silence reigns in the capital, everybody is petrified waiting for the fatal end…"[16] "With the experience of Nazi rule behind them," wrote a representative of the American Joint Distribution Committee (AJDC) in Hungary, "these new victims of Communist brutality are not deceived by the apparent 'moderation' or by claims of mere 'resettlement.' They clearly see the final step, extermination, in the very first assault upon their freedom and dignity, the evictions and 'resettlement.'"[17]

Hundreds of letters collected by the Hungarian branch of the Joint Distribution Committee demonstrate just how dumbfounded the Jews of Budapest were when they were labeled "enemies of the state." Some framed their appeals in terms of conversion, asking to be exempted from resettlement as they were no longer Jewish or had served in World War One.[18] Many, however, highlighted the incredible losses they suffered during the recent war because of their backgrounds. How could we not be "inclined toward people's democracy," having seen our families

---

15 Viktor Karády, "On the Sociology of Social Trauma in Relation to the Persecution of Jews in Hungary," in Molnár, ed., *The Holocaust in Hungary*, 552–554.

16 Quoted in "Memorandum" attached to letter from Dr. L. E. Acsay, Director of the Hungarian National Council to Mr. Walter Kotschnigg of the US State Department, 9 July 1951. NARA RG 59, TREVI, 1945–59, Entry 1524, Box 15, "Hungary Deportations: 1951 (II)".

17 AJC report titled "Mass Deportations from Communist Hungary" dated 18 June 1951, p. 3. NARA RG 59, TREVI, 1945–59, Entry 1524, Box 15, "Hungary Deportations: 1951 (II)".

18 Rezső Hadácsy to Lajos Stöckler,13 November 1951. Hungarian Jewish Archive (hereafter MZA), XXXIII-7-b, 16 tétel/1951 – Kítelpítétettek névsora- a Tokaji Szeretetotthonba költöztettek 1951 [Registry of those resettled in the Tokaj home for the elderly, 1951].

"destroyed at Auschwitz" or by "fascist brigands"? asked one deportee.[19] "...I'm 75, and I never was nor could ever be an opponent of the system, because in consequence of the fascist oppression, two of my children were killed in a deportation," wrote Mór Epstein.[20] The widow of Jenő Lukács expressed a similar sentiment: "How is it possible that I am an enemy of the Soviet Union or the People's Democracy? My husband and I hated the pre-fascist and fascist governments, which oppressed us. We both looked forward to the Red Army's triumphant advance and our liberation. My husband publically pronounced this opinion, and the opinion caused his death, as our 'good neighbors' let the Arrow Cross know. They grabbed him and shot him."[21]

These references to religion, Auschwitz, the Arrow Cross, Nazism and extermination were repackaged and reiterated frequently by members of the Hungarian National Council in the US. These majority anti-communist émigrés insisted that the deportations exposed the genocidal, and thus illegitimate, character of the Hungarian Stalinist regime. Some émigrés expressed their opposition in the form of a moral imperative to speak out before their homeland experienced yet another human tragedy. Likening "the methods of Nazism and Communism," Hungarian National Council representatives repeated the mantra that "Auschwitz and Karaganda are based on the same idea."[22] In a 15 June 1951 memorandum submitted to the UN Secretary General (Trygve Lie), the US Secretary of State (Dean Acheson) and the International and American Red Cross, representatives of the Hungarian National Council explicitly referenced the Holocaust. "The civilized

---

19 Letters from Mrs. Ferencz Pásztor, 13 June 1951 and Sándor and Ilona Rosenberg, 29 June 1951.MZA, AJC Hungarian representative, XXXIII-5-b 2.doboz, 23 tétel/ 1951-52– Kítelpítés elleni panaszok, Kítelpítétettek segelyezési ügyei [Appeals against resettlement, Matters concerning resettlement assistance].

20 Appeal from Mór Epstein. MZA, AJC Hungarian representative, XXXIII-5-b 2.doboz, 23 tétel/1951-52.

21 Mrs. Jenő Lukács, 16 July 1951. MZA, AJC Hungarian representative, XXXIII-5-b 2.doboz, 23 tétel/1951-52.

22 15 June 1951 Memorandum of the Hungarian National Council to the Secretary General of the UN, the Secretary of State, and the International Red Cross. NARA RG 59, TREVI, 1945–59, Entry 1524, Box 15, "Hungary Deportations: 1951 (I)". This thought echoed early totalitarian theorists, such as Hannah Arendt. An example of the rhetoric appeared in a 10 July 1951 *New York Times* article titled "Terror in Hungary Charged": "There is no difference whatever between Auschwitz and Karaganda. The freezing cold of the Arctic regions, the unendurable labor in the primeval forests, in the gold mines of Kolyma, the coal mines of Karaganda, or the cotton fields of in the tropical heat of Tashkent and Alma-Ata are as murderous as the gas chambers of Auschwitz."

world learned…the truth about the horrors of Nazi deportations when it was too late to help. This must not happen again. The Western World cannot stand by and look on with indifference to what goes on in Central and Eastern Europe."[23] A 19 June 1951 speech made by Dr. Béla Fábián, a Hungarian National Council Executive Committee Member, made the equation even more clear. "This is the third great massacre in our lifetime. If it is not checked it can surpass its predecessors in frightfulness. The first was Stalin's murders of the Russian Kulaks; the second was Hitler's massacre of the Jews and other so-called 'subhumans'; the third, the elimination in all communist controlled countries of the anticommunist and non-communist elements." Fábián quoted an anonymous source who claimed: "Today the same cattle cars in which the Nazis deported the Jews in 1944 stand ready at Budapest's railway stations awaiting their new victims."[24] He then quoted another Hungarian missive charging, "Seven years after the Nazi deportations the Communists are now deporting the same people who escaped death in the concentration camps of the Nazis."[25] Gábor Görgey, himself a deportee, explained that not only was Hungary transporting the same victims, but they were using the same "sadistic fascist henchmen" whose prior terrorist past was forgiven only because "they accepted terror service in the new system."[26]

Use of Shoah rhetoric and memory to draw attention to the evictions was more than simply a tactic of the Hungarian National Council and other groups of American-Hungarians. Non-Jewish deportees in Hungary appealed for exemptions based on having aided Jews during the war.[27] The AJDC published the account of an informant alleging, "All Jews who are not in the Communist Party and are members of the bourgeois class are being deported."[28] The *Washington Post* added credence to this indictment, noting that by late July, "Various sources estimate the number of these deportees at 47,000 to 70,000. They are from all

23 "Memorandum of the Hungarian National Council, New York," 15 June 1951. NARA RG 59, TREVI, 1945–59, Entry 1524, Box 15, "Hungary Deportations: 1951 (I)"

24 "Statement of Dr. Béla Fábián, Member of the Executive Committee of the Hungarian National Council at a Press Conference in Washington, D.C., June 19, 1951." NARA RG 59, TREVI, 1945–59, Entry 1524, Box 15, "Hungary Deportations: 1951 (I)".

25 Quote from a letter, Ibid.

26 Gábor Görgey, quoted in Hantó, *Banished Families,* 114. See also p. 125.

27 Kinga Széchenyi, *Megbélyegzettek. A kitelepítések tragédiája [Stigmatized. The tragedy of deportation]* (Pomáz: Kráter, 2008), 149–151.

28 Zachariah Shuster (American Jewish Committee European Director) to Dr. Simon Segal, 22 June 1951. NARA RG 59, TREVI, 1945–59, Entry 1524, Box 15, "Hungary Deportations: 1951 (II)".

classes of society, including peasants, workers, intellectuals and other members of the 'middle class.' All sources agree that there was a high proportion of Jews among them, most of whom had been imprisoned or interned for 'offenses against the economic order of the people's democracy,' and including thousands who had been interned at Auschwitz by the Nazis."[29] On July 21, Eleanor Roosevelt interviewed Paul Fabry, the head of Hungarian Section of the National Committee for a Free Europe and a former member of the Hungarian lower house of parliament, on her NBC-broadcast show. The former first lady opened by announcing that:

> The free world thought that when the Nazis were finally defeated...and many of the people who had committed crimes were tried and convicted...that that would end the kind of thing that had been done to [sic] [by] Hitler...[to] the Jews...The mass-deportations, that knock on the door at night...was over. And unfortunately now, behind the Iron Curtain... the mass-deportations are beginning again.[30]

When Roosevelt asked Fabry who was doing the deporting, Fabry answered: "Practically the same people who were in charge of the Nazi deportations in 1944. Those blackguards, who obeyed Nazi orders, are being converted now to Communism and are carrying out instructions from the Kremlin into Hungary."[31] This accusation was reiterated in numerous Hungarian émigré publications during the summer of 1951.[32]

---

29 "Budapest to Oblivion. The Terror at Dawn," *The Washington Post,* 22 July 1951): 5B. State Department estimates in 1952 concluded that possibly as many as few as 30,000 and as many as 81,000 people were deported from Budapest between 21 May and 16 July 1951. This was typical of contemporary numbers, which ballooned in an atmosphere of fright. See Walter Dowling, AmEmbassy Vienna, #1973, "Deportations in Hungary," 4 June 1952 and AmEmbassy Paris, Telegram #67, 29 February 1951. NARA RG 84, Budapest Legation, Classified General Records, 1946–1963, Box 12, 233 Evacuations. See footnote 9 for overall numbers, footnote 13 for Jews.

30 "Spotlight on Mass-Deportations," NBC broadcast, 21 July 1951. Reprinted in RG 59, TREVI, 1945–59, Entry 1524, Box 15, "Hungary Deportations: 1951 (I)". Forward slashes in original.

31 Ibid. Numerous authors discuss this phenomenon in which fascist police were recruited to join the Communist Party. E.g. Hal Lehrman, *Russia's Europe* (New York: D. Appleton Century Co., 1947), 187, esp. Rákosi quote; and Karády, "On the Sociology of Social Trauma...," in Molnár, ed., *The Holocaust in Hungary,* 554.

32 E.g. "Some of the executioners of the 1944/45 /Nazi/ terror are serving today in the Communists [sic] Terror-detachments." Excerpt from a letter in *Az Ember [New York Hungarian weekly],* (23 June 1951). Reprinted in RG 59, TREVI, 1945–59, Entry 1524, Box 15, "Hungary Deportations: 1951 (I)".

Tens, if not hundreds, of reports, articles and speeches conveyed similar sentiments: the 1951 expulsions utilized the same trains, trunk lines, policemen and procedures as did those carried out by the Nazis and they implicitly, if not overtly, targeted the only Hungarian Jews who had survived the Shoah in large numbers, the Jews of Budapest.[33] "Has the Western world become so apathetic," asked another Hungarian, "that they have no understanding for our second tragedy? Seven years after the Nazi deportations the Communists are now deporting the same people who escaped death in the concentration camps of the Nazis."[34] In an awful irony, reports emerged that hundreds of Jews who had obtained permission to emigrate but were denied that privilege by the Hungarian State Security apparatus chose to "fasten the yellow star to their clothes" as a desperate and symbolic reference to the recent past.[35] The situation became so dire that the following example of black humor began to circulate in Budapest:

> One morning Mr. Kohn receives the order of expulsion. By 6 am the next day he has packed everything. The policeman who comes to fetch him, after proceeding only a few steps with him, announces, "Well, Mr. Kohn, you limp just as you did seven years ago ..."[36]

International Reaction and the Hungarian Response

Voices around the world, not only in America, expressed fear of a recurrence of the Shoah. The *London Jewish Chronicle* reported in an article titled "Many Budapest Jews Evicted" that although the expulsions were not "actuated by religious or racial reasons...the proportion of Jews involved is very high, because the Government eviction orders are directed primarily against former industrialists and middle-class business men—two groups in which Jews predominated."[37] The

33 American Jewish Committee to Seymour Rubin, forwarded to Sam Klaus, 11 July 1951. NARA RG 59, TREVI, 1945–59, Entry 1524, Box 15, "Hungary Deportations: 1951 (II)".
34 Quote from anonymous letter, Ibid.
35 Jacob Beam (Belgrade) to Department of State, #117, 11 August 1951. "Evacuation of 'Undesirables' from Budapest." NARA RG 84, Budapest Legation, Classified General Records, 1946–1963, Box 12, 233 Evacuations. See also "Letter forwarded to the Hungarian National Council, NY," from Budapest, June 1951. Reprinted in NARA RG 59, TREVI, 1945–59, Entry 1524, Box 15, "Hungary Deportations: 1951 (I)".
36 Imre Neufeld to Béla Fabian, 9 June 1951. NARA RG 59, TREVI, 1945–59, Entry 1524, Box 15, "Hungary Deportations: 1951 (II)".
37 "Many Budapest Jews Evicted," *The London Jewish Chronicle* (18 Sivan 5711 [17 June 1951]), 1. When AJDC representative Charles Jordan met with Minister of State Zoltán Vas to discuss the anti-Jewish tinge of the deportations, Vas callously answered rationalized the state's actions by declaring "Can we help it if we only need 3000 of the

French papers *Le Monde, Courier de l'Occident [Nyugati Hirnök], Le Figaro,* and several other Paris papers printed articles discussing repetition of the "days of the reign of the Gestapo," and deportations "analogous to those of the Jews in 1944... based on precisely the same decree to which the Nazis referred." All noted that these threats produced huge jumps in suicide rates and police raids on hotels in search of those seeking to avoid arrest and banishment east.[38] Depositions taken by American officials specifically mention suicides in Lípotváros, a well-known Jewish section of Budapest.[39] These brutal incidents were unalloyed references to all who were familiar with the 1944 destruction of Hungarian Jewry. Taken as a whole, the emerging narratives left no doubt: the darkest clouds of history were reforming.

Through June and July 1951, the British House of Lords, the US Congress, and various organizations within the United Nations held hearings and issued resolutions condemning the Hungarian depredations. Governors, such as John D. Lodge of Connecticut,[40] senators, diplomats, clergy, metropolitan city councils and leading American figures all spoke out decrying Hungary's actions, and they too made direct connections with the Shoah. In Senate hearings, William Benton of Connecticut read a letter from the editor/publisher of the Connecticut-based newspaper, *American Hungarian,* asserting that there were many Jews among the current expellees and the "recklessness and brutality of the current expulsions

---

10,000 retail stores in the city of Budapest?" Memorandum, dated 11 July 1951, written by Charles H. Jordan of the Joint Distribution Committee. In RG 59, TREVI, 1945–59, Entry 1524, Box 12, "Mr. Klaus' instructions."

38 Quotes, in order of appearance, from "Autorités de Budapest deportment en masse les éléments <<déclassé>> de la population," *Le Monde,* 17–18 June 1951; "Facts on deportation in Hungary as reported in the *Courier de l'Occident* of June 15 [1951]," reprinted in NARA RG 59, TREVI, 1945–59, Entry 1524, Box 15, "Hungary Deportations: 1951 (II)"; "Les deportations en Hongrie rappellent l'époque le plus funeste de la terreur nazie [The deportations in Hungary recall the most grievous era of the Nazi terror]," *Le Figaro,* 19 June 1951. Agudas Israel representatives also observed spikes in suicide rates among Jews and attributed this to the deportations. Levine, "Concealed in the Open…"

39 Deputy High Commissioner Walter Dowling to State, Vienna 1759, 24 April 1952, 2. NARA RG 84, Budapest Legation, Classified General Records, 1946–1963, Box 12, Folder 233: Evacuations 1952.

40 "Laws conceived in the depths of Nazi depravity have apparently been resurrected to give the semblance of legality to the present heartless dispersal of certain groups" in Hungary. "Gov. Lodge Warns of New Soviet Evil," *New York Times,* 8 July 1951, 13.

'outdoes even what the Nazis did against the Jews.'"[41] Senator Herbert Lehman referenced President Roosevelt's warnings to the Hungarian government in 1944 and promised that the perpetrators of 1951 would also be held to account.[42] Dr. Isaac Lewin, head of the Agudath Israel World Organization, testified before the UN's Economic and Social Council's Committee on Non-Governmental Organizations and ominously warned that "present conditions in Hungary and Romania [were comparable to] the gas chamber action established by the Nazis," and that "after concentration camps, the next step to be expected was 'extermination.'"[43] The American Federation of Labor, Congress of Industrial Organizations, and United Mine Workers passed a joint resolution at the World Congress of the International Confederation of Free Trade Unions meeting in Milan on 10 July 1951. Calling on the US government to "take immediate action" to halt the Hungarian expulsions, they noted that "an especially high percentage of Jews are among those now being deported, including many who barely escaped death as a result of similar deportations."[44] The International League for Human Rights lodged official complaints with the Hungarian government around the same time using similar language. Tens of thousands of Hungarian Jews living in Israel gathered to voice solidarity with their former compatriots in Tel Aviv rallies in July 1951, while American-Hungarians stood vigil outside of the Soviet Embassy in New York in parallel protests.

In late July 1951, the din of protest reached its loudest point. President Truman condemned Hungary's "infamous conduct," "brutal acts," and "wanton disregard

---

41 László Bóros to Senator William Benton, 17 June 1951. Benton read the letter in the Senate on 19 June 1951. US Congress, Senate. 1951. 82nd Cong, 1st session, *Congressional Record,* Vol 97, part 5 (Washington, DC: Government Printing Office, 1951), 6711.

42 See US Congress, Senate. 1951. "The Hungarian Reign of Terror," 29 August 1951. 82nd Cong, 1st session, *Congressional Record,* Vol 97, part 8, 10785–10789.

43 United Nations' Department of Public Information, Press and Publication Bureau, 5 July 1951 press release "ECOSOC'S [Economic and Social Council's Committee on Non-Governmental Organizations] NGO Committee Hears Charges of Mass Deportations in Hungary and Rumania." At the same meeting, the Soviet delegate to the Committee dismissed the charges as "inventions and unfounded" which provoked a colleague of Lewin to respond that "we kept hearing those reports from Germany under Hitler…After the war we found 6,000,000 Jews dead to prove the reports were neither inventions nor unfounded." "Russia Clashes with US over Hungarian Jews," *The Chicago Daily Tribune,* 6 July 1951, 7.

44 "Unions Urge Truman Action to Halt Mass Deporting in Hungary," *The Evening Star,* 10 July 1951, n. pag.

of every principle of right and decency" in a 27 July statement.[45] Four days later, Secretary of State Dean Acheson charged that the West believed the resettlements would lead to "slow but inevitable death by exhaustion, disease, forced labor," starvation and other causes. Promising, as President Roosevelt had in 1944, that individual leaders would be held responsible for "wholesale persecution," Acheson insisted on a UN investigation. He further demanded the Hungarian government halt its actions and either return and restitute expellees or allow them to "depart freely from Hungary and accept such safe haven as may be offered them by the governments of other lands."[46] While neither Truman nor Acheson explicitly mentioned the plight of Hungarian Jews, allusions were clear and immediately recognized by American Jewish organizations, which lauded the administration's stand.[47]

Western charges of Shoah-like potentialities were bolstered by a somewhat unlikely source. A month prior to the Truman and Acheson speeches, the mouth-piece of the Communist Party of Yugoslavia condemned Hungary in much harsher terms: "...[T]he internment of the 'unreliable' population from Bucha-rest, Budapest, and some other cities, are but part of the aggressive tactics of the Soviet Government and its mercenaries in this part of Europe, who are capable of perpetrating any crime, even genocide..."[48] This charge of genocide was echoed across the ocean two months later by Edward M. O'Connor, Commissioner of the US Displaced Persons Commission, in a September 1951 speech in New York.[49]

Public discourse, even when it included grave accusations of genocide, was but one site where memory of the Shoah materialized in response to the Hungarian terror campaign. In addition to police practices and eviction procedures, other scripts and behaviors developed during the Shoah were repeated or mimicked. Between late-April and mid-July, over 30,000 Jews applied for permission to flee

---

45 "International & Hungarian National Statutes on Human Rights—Statement by the President of the United States, July 27, 1951." NARA RG 59, TREVI, 1945–59, Entry 1524, Box 15, "Hungary Deportations: 1951 (I)".

46 Dean Acheson, "Mass Deportations in Hungary," 1 August 1951. NARA RG 59, TREVI, 1945–59, Entry 1524, Box 15, "Hungary Deportations: 1951 (I)"

47 "Jewish Leaders Praise President's Stand on Hungary," The Hartford Courant, 6 August 1951, 7.

48 "Yugoslav daily 'Borba' on forced displacements in Hungary," 9 July 1951. Reprinted in RG 59, TREVI, 1945–59, Entry 1524, Box 15, "Hungary Deportations: 1951 (I)". Late June and early July deportations from Szeged and Pécs, relatively close to the Yugoslav border, likely prompted this allegation.

49 O'Connor, speech commemorating 950th anniversary of the crowning of St. Stephen, 3 September 1951.

to Israel, and the American Legation expected that number to at least double by August.[50] These are stunning statistics, a palpable demonstration of the fear of a possible Holocaust redux, particularly when compared to the fact that only 50,000 Jews left Hungary between 1945 and 1956 *in total*.[51] The Israeli government vehemently protested the expulsions and its embassy personnel frantically purchased visas from other countries.[52] In a frightening replication of the 1944 Wallenberg mission in Nazi occupied Hungary, Israeli personnel created "letters of protection" for Jewish Hungarians in the hopes of rescue.[53] The Netherlands offered asylum to deportees regardless of age in July 1951, and the Hungarian National Council proposed the US follow suit a month later. Even the wartime activities of the AJDC seemed to be reprised. The Joint, long an active diplomatic force in Hungary, attempted to ransom some three thousand Hungarian Jews during the summer of 1951.[54] The World Jewish Congress and other organizations hatched

---

50 Gerald Momka, Telegram #29 to Sec State, 11 July 1951. NARA RG 84, Budapest Legation, Classified General Records, 1946–1963, Box 12, 233 Evacuations. Gerald A. Mokma, "Jewish Emigration from Hungary to Israel," 17 July 1951. NARA RG 84, Budapest Legation, Classified General Records, 1946–1963, Folder 570.1: Jews 1951.

51 For emigration numbers, see Tamás Stark, *Hungarian Jews during the Holocaust and after the Second World War, 1939–1949*, trans. Christina Rozsnyai, (Boulder, CO & New York: East European Monographs, 2000), 148–156, esp.156; András Kovács, "Hungarian Jewish Politics," in Mendelsohn, ed., *Jews and the State*, 130; Viktor Karády, "Szociológiai kísérlet a Magyar zsidóság 1945 és 1956 közötti helyezetének elezésére (A sociological attempt to analyze the fundamental situation of Hungarian Jewry between 1945 and 1956) in Péter Kende, ed. *Zsidóság az 1945 utáni Magyarországon [Jewry in Hungary after 1945]* (Paris: Magyar Füzetek, 1984), 100–103; Attila Novák, *Átmentben. A Magyar cionist mozgalom négy éve Magyarországon, 1945–1945 [In transition: Four years of the Zionist movement in Hungary]* (Budapest: Múlt és Jövő Könyvkiadó, 2000), 38; Tamás Stark, "Kísérlet a zsidó népesség számának határólására 1945 és 1995 között [An attempt to determine numbers of Jews in Hungary between 1945 and 1995]," in András Kovács, ed., *Zsidók a mai Magyarországon [Jews in Contemporary Hungary]* (Budapest: Múlt és Jövő Könyvkiadó, 2002), 101–128.

52 Győri, *A kommunizmus és a zsidóság...*, 176; Gerald Mokma to State, 16 July 1952, Desp 33. NARA RG 84, Budapest Legation, Classified General Records, 1946–1963, Box 20, "Memoranda of Conversation"-1951.

53 NARA RG 59, TREVI, 1945–59, Entry 1524, Box 15, Deport (I)–AHF_UN Book, 117.

54 Dr. L. E. Acsay, Director of the Hungarian National Council to Mr. Walter Kotschnigg of the US State Department, 9 July 1951. NARA RG 59, TREVI, 1945–59, Entry 1524, Box 15, "Hungary Deportations: 1951 (II)". Acsay aserts that the "Joint" ransomed 3000 Hungarian Jews for $1.2 million.

schemes to smuggle Hungarian Jews out of the country.[55] These covert activities were not only eerily reminiscent of the Kasztner effort of 1944, but of attempts to revive schemes to "purchase" Hungarian Jews that had failed between 1946 and 1949.[56] The Hungarian government rejected all entreaties, arguing that population movements were an internal matter. However, fearing further diplomatic black eyes, Hungarian Secret Police (ÁVH) took preemptive action, specifically targeting citizens who had engaged in Holocaust-era protection activities. For example, Élek Nagy, former Hungarian Minister to the Vatican, who during the Nazi occupation had saved hundreds of Jews by giving them "papal letters of safe conduct," was one of the first "Horthyites" driven out of Budapest.[57]

Stung by the rhetorical and diplomatic barrage launched by Americans, Western Europeans, Yugoslavs and Israelis, and worried about "Western sympathy for the plight of Jews in Hungary today," Hungary adopted an aggressive stance.[58] Beginning in the early summer, Communist leaders chose to fight for, rather than cede, memory of the Shoah, and utilize it to legitimate their social engineering. In an article in Új Élet [New Life], the government-sponsored official weekly of the Hungarian Neolog Jewish community, a self-identified Jewish author justified the banishments and expropriations by arguing "that the masses of our patriotic co-religionists approve that the apartments of the harmful elements should belong to the best workers, to the best office clerks, to the most excellent writers and artists, to the most prominent engineers, to the most zealous pedagogues..." Further, he insisted that, "the memory of six million killed co-religionists obligates the working public of our religious community, not to get—not even by chance—in the

---

55 Walter Dowling, AmEmbassy Vienna, #610, 3 October 1952. NARA RG 84, Budapest Legation, Classified General Records, 1946–1963, Box 32, 570.1 Jews. Levine, draft of NYU dissertation, "Restarting Relief to Eastern Europe One Parcel at a Time (1953–55)," ch. 3.

56 Kinga Frojimovics, "The Role of the American Joint Distribution Committee and the World Jewish Congress in the Reconstruction of Jewish Life in Hungary in the Aftermath of the Shoah (1945–1953), in Randolph Braham, ed., The Treatment of the Holocaust in Hungary and Romania during the Post-Communist Era (Boulder, CO: Social Science Monographs/Columbia University Press, 2004), 169. The prices for Jews varied between $800 and $2000/person.

57 "Comment" by The National Committee for a Free Europe issued by the Research and Information Center, Hungarian Section, NY, 18 June 1951 to 12 June Hungarian Radio broadcast about deportations. Reprinted in RG 59, TREVI, 1945–59, Entry 1524, Box 15, "Hungary Deportations: 1951 (I)".

58 Gerald Momka, Telegram #54 to Sec State, 18 July 1951. NARA RG 84, Budapest Legation, Classified General Records, 1946–1963, Box 12, 233 Evacuations.

camp with the knights of fascism!"[59] Budapest Radio aired a joint statement from the Hungarian Council of Rabbis and the National Executive Committee of Hungarian Israelites denying that anyone was deported because they were Jewish, but rather because they were part of the oppressing class which had cooperated with the Horthy regime whose "persecution of the Jews is known all over the world."[60] Put differently, the evictions were not oppression of Jews, but an opportunity to avenge Jewish loss. The fact of the Shoah, by this reading, required these actions.

Conclusions

In light of the TREVI and public evidence, how should we frame the historical significance of the 1951 expulsions? Most texts on the history of communist Hungary ignore these events, see them as a minor component of the Stalinist reign of terror, or attribute them to Hungary's agricultural and economic crisis brought on by collectivization. I propose that these events are much more significant.

In a concrete sense, the eviction episode reveals how varied actors mobilized Holocaust rhetoric and memory in a global argument about human rights and state legitimacy.[61] This instrumentalization itself conditioned responses and formed narratives of expectation, of extermination and genocide, of the moral imperative to act, or of existential justification. While extermination did not prove to be the fate for most of the evacuees, in Western minds it did create an equation. Scholars and politicians spoke of Nazism and Communism as two sides of the same coin, and the idea that Auschwitz was no different than the gulag gave the American public a tangible frame of reference not only to understand the terror of early Communist rule, but also to denounce communism's violation of the social contract. Hungary's leaders, on the other hand, also used the Shoah and the legacy

---

59 "A kitelepítések ügyét [The matter of relocations]" *Új Élet*, 21 June 1951, 3. This article, ironically, came almost exactly five years after an *Új Élet* article lauding the overturning of the Jewish laws and the restitution of Jewish property. See *Új Élet* (2 May 1946).

60 Transcript of "Statement of Representatives of Hungarian Jewry," Budapest Radio, Hungarian Home Service, 16 July 1951. Reprinted in RG 59, TREVI, 1945–59, Entry 1524, Box 15, "Hungary Deportations: 1951 (I)". The statement was signed by Lajos Stöckler, István Földes, Leo Csengeri, Menyhért Spiegel, and Dr. Schwartz, some of whom (Spiegel for certain) were themselves later deported. According to the Israeli Legation, this statement was coerced under threat of deportation. See Momka, Telegram #54 to Sec State, 18 July 1951.

61 The late Mark Pittaway reminds of how important legitimacy was for the leaders of postwar Hungary. Mark Pittaway, "The Politics of Legitimacy and Hungary's Postwar Transition," *Contemporary European History* 13 (2004): 456.

of the "Jewish question," but did so in an entirely different manner. Reports from émigrés during the summer of 1951 indicated that the atmosphere of antisemitism was pervasive, "even greater than in the days of Hitler."[62] Hungarian-Jewish émigrés in Israel believed that this antisemitism became manifest in the expulsions in perverse and contradictory ways. The country was in economic crisis, and since many of Hungary's communist leaders were of Jewish birth, these leaders made special efforts to target Jews to insulate themselves from and appeal to popular anti-Semitic sentiment. Conversely, by targeting Horthyites, they were exacting a measure of revenge for the Holocaust.[63] Both attest to the continuing power of anti-Semitic feeling in immediate post-war Hungary as well as its multivalent function as a rationale for state existence and action.[64]

From the perspective of American responses, the public discussion of the Hungarian resettlements allows us to reassess some Cold War and Shoah-related orthodoxies. First, the expulsions provide evidence that under Truman, the United

---

62 Oliver L. Trexal, Jr., "Hungarian Deportations in the Tel Aviv Hungarian-Language Press," 3 Tel Aviv 221, dated 20 September 1951. NARA RG 84, Budapest Legation, Classified General Records, 1946–1963, Box 12, 233 Evacuations. This is significant, since the 1946 wave of pogroms, with Miskolc and Kunmadaras as the worst examples, created a widespread trepidation among Jews. János Kovács, "Neo-Antisemitism in Hungary," *Jewish Social Studies* 8 (1946): 157–160.

63 See Enclosure Tel Aviv 750, 6/15/51. "Relocation of Jewish Population in Hungary," translation from *Uj Kelet [New East]*, Hungarian-Jewish journal in Tel Aviv. In NARA RG 84, Budapest Legation, Classified General Records, 1946–1963, Box 12, 233 Evacuations. For a broader explication of this phenomenon, see Charles Gati's chapter "A Note on Communists and the Jewish Question," in *Hungary and the Soviet Union* (Durham: Duke University Press, 1986), 100–107.

64 A similar argument was made by Peter Meyer in 1953, but most scholars have since rejected this approach. Peter Meyer, Bernard D. Weinryb, Eugene Duschinsky & Nicolas Sylvain, *The Jews in the Soviet Satellites* (Syracuse: Syracuse University Press, 1953), 40. András Kovács argues "repressive policies employed by the party-state against the Jewish denomination were no different from policies pursued against other religious denominations, Jews were affected by forms of repression that in the case of the other churches were clearly absent. Such repression was inflicted on real or perceived manifestations of secular Jewish identity or Jewish descent was used merely as a pretext for political repression." I would argue that the use of antisemitism varied, and that the variant mobilized in the expulsions was qualitatively different than the anti-Zionism of the show trials beginning in 1949 and the antisemitism of the doctors' plot trials of 1952–53. András Kovács, "Jews and Jewishness in Post-war Hungary," *Quest. Issues in Contemporary Jewish History* 1 (2010): http://www.quest-cdecjournal.it/focus.php?issue=1&id=192.

States genuinely believed a human rights-based diplomacy towards the Soviet bloc was legitimate and could be persuasive.[65] It demonstrates not just idealism, but a belief that targeted global pressure, particularly if exerted through the United Nations, could undermine state legitimacy and potentially avert human catastrophes. That numerous parties publicly utilized the term genocide—from Hungarian émigrés to Yugoslav communists—perhaps indicates the existence of an early faith in the 1948 Convention on the Prevention and Punishment of the Crime of Genocide that deserves further examination.

Second, the example of the 1951 terror demonstrates that the school of thought asserting that "between the end of the war and the 1960s...the Holocaust made scarcely any appearance in American public discourse and hardly more in Jewish public discourse," most prominently represented by Peter Novick, is incorrect.[66] Rather the Hungarian events bolster Hasia Diner's argument that American Jews were not only conversant about the Holocaust, but utilized Holocaust memory in support of political agendas quite soon after World War II.[67] The politicized responses to what much of the world purposely described as "deportations," from Hungarian-American, American-Jewish, and world Jewish communities mark a convergence of anti-Communist and Holocaust-related thought, not the self-censorship normally attributed to American Jewish communities during this period. In a related sense, we may also want to consider the psychological impact of the 1951 events on Hungarian Jews. György Vikár writes of the "sack of sand" carried by Hungary's postwar Jewish generation, survivors' post-Holocaust experiences which suppressed Jewish identity, fostered marginalization, and silenced discussion of the Shoah.[68] Considering the horror experienced by Hungarian Jews in 1951, we must include the evictions and expropriations in the sack.[69]

---

65 Sarah-Jane Corke indicates that around the time of the deportations, the US was reconsidering its stance towards the entire Soviet bloc, and Hungary in particular. Corke, *US Covert Operations and Cold War Strategy* (London & New York: Routledge, 2008), 111.

66 Peter Novick, *The Holocaust in American Life* (Boston: Houghton Mifflin, 1999), 103. For a description of this school, see Hasia Diner, *We Remember with Reverence and Love* (New York: NYU Press, 2009), 6–9.

67 Diner, *We Remember*, ibid.

68 Vikár, quoted in Ferenc Erős, "The Long Term Psychological Consequences," in Molnár, ed., *The Holocaust in Hungary*, 539.

69 Silence may have been required in order for underground Jewish aid programs to exist. In light of the 1951 resettlements and expropriations, and the winding down of overt AJDC activities in Hungary, global Jewish aid agencies resorted to secret smuggling programs to provide for the neediest Jews, particularly those dispossessed and

Hungarian-American relations, marked by tension since the Communist take-over, aggravated by the 1949 banishment from Hungary of Selden Chapin, the American Chargé, and the show trial and 15 month internment of the American Robert Vogeler, were on the brink of improving with Vogeler's release in April 1951.[70] With the wave of resettlements, relations again spiraled downward. Hungary lost its most favored nation trade status. Using information gathered by TREVI, the US continued to block Hungarian admission to the UN. It also unilaterally abrogated the two countries' 1925 Treaty of Friendship, further evidence of how deeply the expulsions had delegitimized Hungary's government in the eyes of US officials. However, as in 1944, the US and its allies found themselves with little leverage to prevent the resettlements themselves. Although Hungary halted its Budapest expulsions in early August, it did so, it appears, neither because its government perceived a crisis of legitimacy nor because of Western pressure. Rather, the trucks and trains used in the resettlements were required instead for the harvest and for population transfers from other Hungarian cities.[71]

---

deprived of work as a result of the deportations. Levine, "Concealed in the Open…" and draft of NYU dissertation, "Restarting Relief to Eastern Europe One Parcel at a Time (1953–55)," ch.3.

70 The US was also reconsidering the notion of rollback and beginning serious negotiations over Korea.

71 "Jews Criticize Hungary," *New York Times*, 25 August 1951, 3. By August, Debrecen became the main target of the eviction effort, and Jews there were also targeted.

Viktoria Sukovata

The Holocaust Response in American and Soviet Cultures as a Reflection of the Different War Experiences and Cold War Politics[1]

Abstract: *This essay explains why the US and the USSR were worlds apart in defining the nature of the Holocaust. The American experience of the Holocaust was largely indirect, based on the stories of survivors who immigrated to start new lives, which made, the Jews the center of the Nazi horrors. The fate of the Soviet Prisoners of War was directly noticed and resembled the gloomy fate of Jews in ghettos, and Slavic civilians who were discovered hiding Jews. The Cold War conditioned these competing perspectives.*

The tragedy of the Holocaust changed post-war thinking in all European societies as it threw into disorder Enlightenment values and the idealism and rationalism associated with the nineteenth century. The Holocaust served to deconstruct moral concepts such as good and evil, spirituality, the value of life and the meaning of death. Civilians who died during World War II were 65 percent of the total victims, compared to five percent in World War I.[2] This enormous increase in civilian deaths meant that millions of civilians had experienced firsthand the cruelties and traumas of war including repression, humiliation, horrification, random violence, torture, unbearable pain, starvation, and death. Yet, reflection on these experiences differed greatly in the East and the West.

---

1   The material for this paper was collected thanks to fellowships at the Netherlands In-
    stitute for War Documentation and Amsterdam University (2006–2007), the Virginia
    Foundation for the Humanity, USA (2008), and the Netherlands Institute for Advanced
    Study in Humanities and Social Sciences at the Royal Netherlands Academy of Arts and
    Science (2009). I express my sincere gratitude to professors who discussed some my
    ideas: Karel Berkhoff (University of Amsterdam), the Netherlands), Wim Blockmans
    (Leiden University, the Netherlands), Gabriel Findler (University of Virginia, USA),
    Yuri Slezkine (California University in Berkeley, USA), Aron Shneer (the International
    Institute for Holocaust Research Yad Vashem, Israel). No organizations or persons are
    responsible for the text. All conclusions and mistakes which might remain are only my
    own ones.
2   Israel Charny, ed., *Encyclopedia of Genocide*, 2 vols. (Santa Barbara, CA: ABC-CLIO,
    1999), 2:555.

A comparison of American and Soviet trajectories in responding to the Holocaust reveals the key components of the reflection process. At first sight the US and the USSR were worlds apart in the way they defined the Holocaust, but a more detailed look shows many similarities there were–in media attention, news coverage, and in the literary world. The interpretations differed on whether the Jews were at the center of the Nazi horrors, or whether they constituted only a part of a much larger spectrum of victims. External features accentuated the differences in these interpretations. Circumstances such as a population's direct encounter with the Nazi policies, the number of victims as a percent of a local population, proximity to, or the mere fact of the location of the camps in the East, grand narratives, collective emotions, and especially Cold War political priorities played a large role in the formulation of the interpretations in East and West. The elaboration of the events in academic circles served to widen the horizons of post-war interpretations even as their articulation of the issues bridged the gaps.

Especially in Eastern Europe the Nazi occupation laid bare its cruel character, mainly due to the many Jewish ghettos and Nazi concentration camps. These camps cannot be understood within the normal bounds of experience nor can they be described with common language. They were a kind of "inhuman utopia" where all human values were overturned.[3] The Holocaust and Nazi concentration camps forced Western intellectuals to problematize not only traditional liberal values, but also Christian doctrines such as the superiority of the spirit over the flesh. Nazi victims were killed solely on the basis of belonging to a certain race or nation.

Immediately after the war, Western European and American historians, philosophers and survivors, such as Jean-Paul Sartre, Karl Jaspers, Viktor Klemperer, and Hannah Arendt tried to comprehend the causes of a racist and totalitarian state in the heart of Europe. Karl Jaspers postulated several basic principles that shaped post-war philosophy and ethics: 1) acknowledgment of the universal guilt of European Christians for their anti-Semitism, and for the promulgation of anti-Jewish laws which made possible the exclusion of Jews from fully legitimate citizenship; 2) acknowledgment of the political responsibility of the whole German nation i.e., including children, for the genocide committed by the Nazis against the Jews; 3) understanding that the fate of all nations is intertwined and creates a global integrity, and that changing of any part of a nation's diversity can disorganize the history of other nations; 4) seeing every innocent victim as unique and

3   Eric D. Weitz, *A Century of Genocide: Utopias of Race and Nation* (Princeton, NJ: Princeton University Press, 2003).

5) accepting responsibility for non-action in the face of a humanitarian catastrophe, when the murder of a nation or race is at stake.[4] One can say that Jaspers founded a new direction in humanitarian and social thought, which came to be known as "Ethics-after-Auschwitz." These philosophical and ethical considerations created an innovative trans-disciplinary field encompassing Social Anthropology, History, Aesthetics and Political Science, all aimed at changing mass-consciousness lest tragedies of the type under study take place again.

Horror about the Holocaust and feelings of guilt towards the Jewish people were so profound that they prompted the creation of special foundations, research centers, educational programs, and university courses in the US and Western Europe a few decades after the war.

Memoires and testimonies of Holocaust survivors, and emotional images of horror, vulnerability, helplessness, and dependence found expression in poetry, drama, diaries, and paintings by eyewitnesses to the Holocaust. This emotional response to the Holocaust in the immediate post-war period was the basic element that would eventually lead to the formation of Holocaust studies decades later: artists, poets, and writers who had survived the Holocaust—Elie Wiesel, Paul Celan, Nelly Sax, Bruno Bettelheim, Primo Levi, Jean Amery—were the first to formulate Western Holocaust studies as early as the 1950s and 1960s.

The first movies on Holocaust issues—which caused much public discussion—were filmed in the 1950s and 1960s. Many were based on real stories of Holocaust survivors. To name a few, *The Stranger*, Orson Welles, USA, 1946; *The Search*, Fred Zinnemann, USA-Sweden, 1948, *The Diary of Anne Frank*, George Stevens, USA, 1959, created a wide sympathy for the victims of Nazism.

A second stage of commemoration began in the 1970s when scholars such as Omer Bartov, Christopher Browning, Saul Friedländer, Michael Berenbaum, and others endeavored to create a conceptual framework for Holocaust studies. They expanded the interest in the Holocaust beyond the historical and moral levels to include cultural and psychological aspects.

Examples of the new explorations include Christopher Browning who dealt with the correlation of fault and responsibility among ordinary people and Emil Fackenheim who examined the Judeo-Christian dialogue and religious anti-Semitism.[5] There was Paul Marcus who studied the history of the Nazi concentration camps and victims' lives there, Miriam Novitch who investigated resistance in the

---

4   Karl Jaspers, *The Question of German Guilt* (New York: The Dial Press, 1947).
5   Ch. Browning, *Ordinary Men: Reserve Police Battalion 101 and the Final Solution in Poland* (New York: Harper Collins, 1992); Emil Fackenheim, "Jewish Faith and the Holocaust. A Fragment," *Commentary* 46:2 (1968).

Jewish ghettos and the concentration camps, and Robert Eaglestone who examined the impact of the Holocaust on modern culture and values.[6] Michael Mack explored the commemoration of the Holocaust, while Klaus Theweleit examined the Nazi unconscious, and Samuel Totten probed Holocaust studies as a way to pursue genocide phenomena. German historian Christian Striet was the first in Western academia to expose the tragic fate of Soviet POWs in German captivity. His research set off a cultural bomb in the context of Genocide studies. Some scholars paid attention to the non-Jewish victims of the Holocaust in its wide context and fates of the Jewish rescuers.[7]

A third stage in the development of Holocaust studies can be indicated in the late 1970s when Holocaust survivors' memories were taken seriously and recorded, often with support of money from American foundations. The concept of the individual as witness giving valued testimony is particularly situated within American representation and study of the Holocaust and has found a place in the many Holocaust museums of the 1990s that were modeled on the first one, the Los Angeles Museum of the Holocaust, established in 1961.[8]

Since the mid-1990s, blockbuster films such as *Schindler's List* (1993), *Jakob the Liar* (1999), *The Pianist* (2002), and others created a kind of "visual anthropology," or "visual memory," or "public history" of the Holocaust. As a result, this type of

---

6 P. Marcus, *Autonomy in the Extreme Situation: Bruno Bettelheim, the Nazi Concentration Camps and the Mass Society* (New York: Praeger, 1999); M. Novitch, *Sobibor: Martyrdom and Revolt* (New York: Holocaust Library, 1980); R. Eaglestone, *The Holocaust and the Postmodern* (New York: Oxford University Press, 2004).

7 M. Mack, *Anthropology as Memory: Elias Canetti's and Franz Baermann Steiner's Responses to the Shoah* (Tübingen: Max Niemezer Verlag, 2001); K. Theweleit, *Male fantasies*, Vol.1, transl. from German (Minneapolis: University of Minnesota Press, 1987); S. Totten, W. Parsons, I. Charny, eds., *Century of Genocide: Eyewitness Accounts and Critical Views* (New York, NY: Garland Publishing, Inc., 1998); C. Streit, "The Fate of the Soviet Prisoners of War," in M. Berenbaum, ed., *A Mosaic of Victims: Non-Jews Persecuted and Murdered by Nazis* (New York: New York University Press, 1990), 142–149; L. Altman, *The Forgotten Victims of the Holocaust* (Berkeley Heights, NJ: Enslow, 2003); G. Block and M. Drucker, *Rescuers: Portraits of Moral Courage in the Holocaust* (Ann Arbor, MI: Ergo, 1992).

8 New American museums dedicated to the Holocaust memory include the United States Holocaust Memorial Museum (1993), the William Breman Jewish Heritage Museum (1996), the Holocaust Museum Houston (1996), the Florida Holocaust Museum (1999), the Virginia Holocaust Museum in Richmond (2003), the Dallas Holocaust Museum (2005), and the El Paso Holocaust Museum and Study Center (2005) among others.

work has become an independent subject located at the intersection of Holocaust and aesthetic and commemoration studies.[9]

The broadening attention paid to the Holocaust was the result of linking academic and popular interests, and incorporating the emotionally charged coping of survivors with the historically dynamic expression of the artistic community. These developments broadened the initial historical description to include a wide trans-disciplinary investigation that attracted new public and scholarly interest to the field. Postmodernist thinkers in the 1990s and beyond connected the Holocaust to the theory of the "other," and to disability and minority studies. Zygmunt Bauman proclaimed that the Holocaust was not "simply a Jewish problem" nor solely an event in Jewish history. He believed the Holocaust grew out of a modern rational society, with a high degree of civilization and, "for this reason it is a problem of that society, civilization and culture," and not a problem for Jews alone. Bauman was among those who pointed to two intellectual paradigms in research and recognition of the Holocaust, they are "Jewish centric" and "common cultural."[10]

There are two ways to conceptualize contemporary approaches to the Holocaust, with either a wider or a narrower lens. Elie Wiesel's conception restricts the term Holocaust to Jews only, carrying out a Judeo centric approach. Simon Wiesenthal's positions connected the 6 million Jews and 5 million gentile victims together. From this point of view the Holocaust includes Polish political prisoners, Soviet prisoners of war, homosexuals, Gypsies, the handicapped, Jehovah's Witness, and the mentally ill, and many others. Michael Berenbaum identified Simon Wiesenthal and Elie Wiesel as representatives of the wider or the narrower position. Wiesenthal, a secular Jew, was incarcerated in Mauthausen camp, where Jews constituted only a minority of inmates. Wiesel was deported by Nazis and incarcerated in a Jewish camp and thus emphasized the Jewish tragedy, constituting a "Judeo centric" position.[11] These two approaches are neither mutually exclusive nor competing in academic significance because they are complementary, in our opinion: A wide panorama that studies Nazi victims does not contradict the uniqueness of the Holocaust, but clarifies it. The scholars in Genocide studies accent the multiply character of the Holocaust as the mass murder of several

---

9   For example: J.E. Doneson, *The Holocaust in American Film* (Syracuse, NY: Syracuse University Press, 2001); Anne-Marie Baron, *The Shoah on Screen: Representing Crimes against Humanity* (Strasbourg: Council of Europe Publications, 2006).

10 Z. Bauman, *Modernity and the Holocaust* (Cambridge, UK: Polity Press, 1991).

11 M. Berenbaum, "The Uniqueness and Universality of the Holocaust," in Berenbaum, ed., *Mosaic of Victims*, 20–22.

groups of victims: "From historical perspective, it is now accepted that Nazi policy towards the Romanies was in many ways similar to that directed at the Jews... the policy of the genocide was not unique in the sense of being directed only ever once and against one people...Shoah studies can and should contribute to our understanding of other genocidal regimes."[12] The analysis of American and Soviet approaches to the Holocaust offers evidence for this argument, as does the distinction between Holocaust studies and Genocide studies.

America's internal debate on the Holocaust should not, however, obscure the different cultural and academic responses to the Holocaust in Soviet and American societies. The goal of the remainder of this article is to present the Soviet's political argumentation and cultural response to the Holocaust. This examination is carried out in the context of the history of the Nazi occupation of Soviet land, and the post-war ideological system developed in the Soviet Union to deal with the Holocaust. These responses are contrasted to American developments of the same time.

For a significant part of American society, feelings of guilt grew out of having to face the thousands of refugees from post-Holocaust Europe and hear their countless stories about Nazi murders and humiliation at the same time as the Americans were trying to forget the US pre-war insensitivity to Jewish persecution. It had been the Americans, after all, who had refused to allow the passengers of the transatlantic liner from Hamburg, the *St. Louis*, to disembark. All the passengers were Jews fleeing the Nazis and the majority perished after the ship sailed back to Europe.[13]

The fact that the US had not directly experienced the German occupation nor had it fought the battles of World War II on its own soil, colored the way citizens and scholars perceived the Holocaust. Without experiencing the direct trauma of occupation, the majority of academic and artistic works concentrated on the fate of the Jews.

The Soviet Union, on the other hand, suffered both Nazi occupation and intensely bloody battles on its own soil during the war. The United States entered World War II on December 7, 1941, but the Western Front in Europe did not open until June 6, 1944. By that time the Red Army had liberated almost all of Russia, Byelorussia and the Left-Bank of Ukraine. The losses of the United States in the

---

12 Hunter A.G. "Intruding on Private Grief," in H.J. Cargas, ed., *Problem Unique to the Holocaust* (Lexington: University Press of Kentucky, 1999), 129–130.

13 United States Holocaust Memorial Museum, "Holocaust Encyclopedia: Voyage of the St. Louis", n.d., http://www.ushmm.org/wlc/en/article.php?ModuleId=10005267 (accessed 1 December 2016).

war amounted to about 418,000 dead soldiers and about 3,000 civilians; while the Soviet Union's military losses amounted to 28,476,700 people in addition to 17,931,600 civilians. Among the victims of the Holocaust were about 2.9 million Soviet Jews.[14] In the Soviet Union interest in the Holocaust had already begun during the war, initially connected to eyewitness accounts, and soon followed by artistic works.

The first records and papers of the Holocaust was published in the Soviet Union in 1943–1944, just days after the liberation of the Soviet territories by the Red army. Jewish Soviet writers and journalists, Ilya Ehrenburg and Vasily Grossman who served as war reporters for the Red Army reported their findings in *The Black Book of the Holocaust* (since 1943). The authors had actively collected eyewitness accounts of the Nazi crimes against Jews in Ukraine and Poland as part of their activities for the Jewish Anti-Fascist Committee in the SU.[15] Grossman visited the Treblinka death camp right after its liberation by the Red Army and published his article "The Treblinka Hell" (1944) as a documentary account of what he saw there. Grossman's paper was used by the prosecution at the Nuremberg Trials as documentary proof of what had taken place. An early report about the tragic fate of the Jews in Soviet Ukrainian Kharkiv was published in a famous Soviet journal *Znamya* in 1944.[16]

Other Soviet military correspondents, writers, and poets operated on their own when collecting materials about the Nazi genocide against Jews. The Soviet Ukrainian writer and war correspondent, Boris Gorbatov published his novel *The Unvanquished* in 1943. This book contained scenes of the execution of Jews in the small Ukrainian town of Donbass and was turned into a movie in 1945. In the next year the book won the Stalin Prize, the Soviet's highest award for artists and writers. Jewish photojournalists in the Soviet Union were able to keep Nazi atrocities on the front pages and they continually emphasized the Jewish aspect of Nazi violence.[17] Jewish Soviet journalists, photographers, writers were

---

14 According to data from the Statistic military research collection: G. Krivosheev, *Soviet Casualities and Combat Losses in the Twentieth Century* (Barnsley, UK: Greenhill Books, 1997).

15 I. Ehrenburg and V. Grossman, *The Complete Black Book of Russian Jewry*, transl. from Russian (New Brunswick, NJ: Transaction Publishers, 2002).

16 K. Berkhoff, "Ukraine under Nazi Rule (1941–1944). Sources and Finding Aids," *Jahrbücher für Geschichte Osteuropas* 45 (1997): 298.

17 D. Shneer, *Through Soviet Jewish Eyes: Photography, War and the Holocaust* (New Brunswick, NJ: Rutgers University Press, 2012).

the first witnesses of the Nazi atrocities—three years before Americans arrived at Buchenwald and Dachau.

After this initial wave of publications on the Holocaust, however, the post-war Soviet academy blocked further art works and academic publications on the Holocaust. It was stipulated by several political and ideological reasons of the post-war time: Stalin's fears of rising Jewish nationalism (and any other nationalism), which could stimulate the post-war disintegration of the multinational Soviet empire. Stalin initiated the campaign against "rootless cosmopolitanism" (1946–1953) and the "Doctors' Plot" (1948–1953) which were directed against Soviet doctors, scientists, writers, and journalists, a great number of whom were Jews. A significant part of the post-war Stalinist repressions became members of the Jewish Anti-Fascist Committee which was established in early 1942, and a goal of which was the Soviet Anti-Fascist propaganda abroad. This committee include prominent Jewish writers, poets, directors and the activity of the Committee during the war has been extremely successful: it collected massive financial sums to the needs of the Red Army, among the Jewish communities abroad. However, after the war, Stalin had not seen the necessity in the Jewish Anti-Fascist Committee's activities. Besides it the Committee tried to protect Jewish citizens inside the Soviet country and Stalin seen a particular danger for own power in international connections of the Jewish Anti-Fascist Committee. Many contemporary scholars believe that repressions against "rootless cosmopolitanism" and "Doctors' Plot" campaign were the beginning of the "semi-official" anti-Semitism in USSR in the post-war years.[18]

The "rootless cosmopolitanism" and the "Doctors' Plot" campaigns were quite obviously an anti-Semitic campaign but it also had the feature of opposing different nationalist efforts including the movement for Zionism. Indeed, the victims of NKVD repressions in these campaigns and plots had constituted not only the Soviet Jewish intelligentsia, but also a large representative section of the Soviet secret service and the counterespionage agency. Stalin feared that the Soviet people and especially Soviet officers who were winners Nazism will require more public recognition and more political freedom after they saw life in Europe. This period of Stalinism's "spy-phobia" can be partly comparable to the anti-communist panic during the McCarthy era of Cold War America.

One more reason of the Soviet silence about Holocaust and the Nazi terror against Jews in the late 1930s was the obvious parallel between Nazi and Stalin's

---

18 G. Kosturnichenko, "The Genesis of Establishment Anti-Semitism in the USSR: the Black Years, 1948–1953," in Z. Gitelman and Ya. Ro'I, eds., *Revolution, Repression, and Revival: The Soviet Jewish Experience* (Lanham, MD: Rowman & Littlefield Publishers, 2007), 179–192.

totalitarian regimes. For example, Vasily Grossman's greatest work, his novel *Life and Fate*, which was written in the 1950s and contained the parallel scenes from Nazi concentration camps and Stalinist camps, was arrested by the People's Commissariat for Internal Affairs, (the NKVD—predecessor to the KGB),[19] and was not published till 1989. This position of the Soviet state blocked the process of academic study of the Holocaust for many years and the survivors' gathering evidence but the emotional and artistic reflection in Soviet society existed throughout the Soviet period. Soviet artists found ways to inform Soviet readers and spectators about the Holocaust through allusions, hidden motives, and plot lines. Soviet scholars did not create academic Holocaust studies between 1950 and 1970, but Soviet artists, writers and directors created a kind of a "visual anthropology" and a "literary anthropology" of the Holocaust to the extent to which this was legally possible in the democratic period known as *Ottepel*, or Thaw. The prominent Soviet poet of the *Ottepel*, Evgeny Evtushenko published the poem *Babi Yar* in 1961, which was devoted to the massacre of Ukrainian Jews near Kiev by the Nazis in 1941. *Babi Yar* was the symbolic break with what had become in the USSR, a twenty-year silence about the Jewish tragedy. The poem was translated from Russian into seventy-two languages. Also images of Holocaust was reflected in the Thirteen Symphony of the great Russian composer Dmitri Shostakovich called "Babi Yar" (1962).

Soviet writer Anatoly Kuznetzov published a documentary novel also titled *Babi Yar* in 1966. The novel was based on the author's childhood impressions of pre-war life in Kiev and detailed of the killing of Ukrainian Jews under the Nazi occupation.

A prominent Soviet film with references to the Holocaust was *The Commissar* directed by Aleksandr Askoldov. The movie was based on the short story by Vasily Grossman, *In the Town of Berdichev*, and was filmed in 1967. It was the story of a Jewish family in a small, provincial Ukrainian town that shelters a female Commissar near the end of her pregnancy and agrees to keep the baby when she returns to the front in the face of the advancing White Army. One of the central sequences of the film envisions the future fate of the Jews in the Second World war, showing a long procession of Jews being marched into the gates of a concentration camp. In this scene the Russian baby shares the fate of the Jewish

---

19 Russian abbreviation from a title of the "People Commissariat for Internal Affairs of USSR," the Soviet Ministry which during 1934–1946 has controlled the Soviet traffic police, firefighting, border guards, system of GULAG, political police, secret service and the counter-intelligence espionage during the World War II.

people, and the message is one that equalizes the Russian and Jewish vulnerability during the Nazi genocide.

A popular Soviet writer and veteran of the war, Vasily Bukov published a story *Sotnikov* (1970), about a Soviet partisan and a comrade who betrays him to the Nazis. One of the characters in the story is a Jewish female teenager Basya, who is caught by the Nazis in a Byelorussian village and handed over to the Gestapo for questioning. The motif in this story is the significance of the Holocaust in Byelorussia, the fate of the Soviet Jews and their Slavic rescuers.

The main explanation for silence on the issue of the Jews in the Holocaust was the desire of the state apparatus to keep "international solidarity" alive inside the multinational post-war Soviet society. In fact, the initial work on *The Black Book of the Holocaust* carried more than 200 eyewitness accounts of the crimes against Jews carried out not only by the Nazis but also by their collaborators on Soviet lands. These reports were drawn from, and divided into several sections: the Ukraine, Byelorussia, the Russian Federation, Lithuania, Latvia, "the camps of destruction" and "Executioners." Nonetheless Soviet authorities decided in 1948 that publishing *The Black Book of the Holocaust* would be counter-productive because it contained incriminating testimony pointing to the guilt of local collaborators in the destruction of the Jewish population. Soviet authorities thought that publishing and promoting the book would break the Soviet ideological myth of the friendship of the Soviet peoples, which they considered necessary to maintain the multinational Soviet state. This is not unlike Enlightenment myths of equality and fraternity utilized for the unification of early bourgeois France or those employed in the US in the present day to offset the racist reality.

All of Soviet officialdom knew that local nationalists in Western Ukraine and the Baltic countries, for example, had taken an active part in the Holocaust.[20] In the Western Ukrainian region there was a strong nationalist influence and a history of anti-Jewish pogroms during World War II. It was commonly recognized that non-Jewish neighbors took part not only in rescuing Jews, but also in betraying them. When the war was over, the Soviet authorities tried to preserve the mood of national reconciliation in Soviet society. They felt that disseminating information exclusively dealing with the Nazi genocide against the Jews might provoke nationalistic feelings in the country. To speak or write mainly about the Jews would clearly require uncovering and revealing the role of the local residents in the anti-Jewish pogroms. The post-war Soviet administration feared that the

20 T. Snyder, *The Reconstruction of Nations: Poland, Ukraine, Lithuania, Byelorussia, 1569–1999* (New Haven, CT: Yale University Press, 2003), 170–200.

opposition on a national basis—Jews as victims and representatives of local ethnic groups as perpetrators, can provoke spite and a social explosion of anti-Semitism in the post-war Soviet society. Thus the majority of Soviet historians did not emphasize the Nazi racial policy against the Jews. Instead they concentrated on the Nazi genocide against the Soviet people.

A prominent political reason for silence about the Holocaust in the 1950–1970s was connected to Soviet history itself. Study of the Holocaust style of repression against a certain groups of citizens was bound to stimulate questions about similar situations in the Soviet past. There were several incidents with which to be concerned: The Stalinist *Holodomor* or Big Famine in Eastern Ukraine and Russian Volga region during 1932–1933, and the violent resettlement of Ukrainian and Russian peasants to Siberia.[21] Then there was the "Great Terror" of 1937–1938 that included reprisals against the intelligentsia and members of the party, but also against ordinary people. There was the deportation of Crimean Tartars and Chechen people during the war, the ethnic cleansing in Western Ukraine after the war, repression against former prisoners of war, and other crimes linked to Stalin's totalitarian state. Not only was the Holocaust a prohibited issue during the Soviet era, it was also impossible to speak of the fate of Soviet prisoners of war that had been held in Nazi concentration camps, the Red Army retreat of 1941–1942, the Penal Battalions inside the Red Army, NKVD repressions against Red Army soldiers and Soviet citizens even during the war, and finally the collaboration of Ukrainian, Tatar, and Caucasian nationalists with the Nazis.

One more reason was that in contrast to the Western European and American societies, post-war Soviet society felt no guilt for any passivity they may have shown toward the annihilation of the Jews during the war. After all, the entire Soviet society had struggled mightily against German Nazism, both in far distant battles and on the home front. The first years after the Victory were a time of collective euphoria, common optimism and high hopes for a bright future. Millions of people in the Nazi-occupied territories and those who languished in the Nazi concentration camps were liberated thanks to the Red Army. The status of the Red Army and its veterans among the Soviet masses was incredibly high in the post-war decades. Furthermore, Soviet propaganda created an image of the Soviet people as a common body, the great mythological hero who had won against the most treacherous of enemies, who was wounded but still alive after the battle. This image of the great Soviet people and their Red Army was posed

---

21 J. Dietsch, *Making Sense of Suffering: Holocaust and Holodomor in Ukrainian Culture* (Lund: Lund University Press, 2006).

against the image of the "Nazi hydra"—the absolute evil. The war had been a time when millions of Soviet people had gone through great hardships and intense suffering while displaying selfless heroism. Pain during the war was universal for majority of Soviet people, but it was a collective pain and not that of a single ethnic group like it had been in Europe. That is why if American Holocaust studies have mainly used the recorded memories of eyewitnesses to relate the experiences of Jewish minority in Western European nations, in contrast, the Soviet approach has been to look at how "the Holocaust was incorporated into the epic suffering of the entire Soviet population, ignoring any uniqueness of the Jewish experience," as Johan Dietsch has noted.[22]

The American response to the Holocaust is based on the fact that the Holocaust grew out of World War II and could be viewed as having roots in entrenched anti-Semitism and not just in the war. But the Holocaust in Soviet territories was one and the same thing as the German invasion and the German occupation. All were a part of Nazi war crimes against Soviet citizens. If Jews in Western and Central Europe were vulnerable and oppressed, if they occupied the lowest place in the racial hierarchy of the Nazis and could be destroyed, so could any Ukrainian, or Russian no less than any Jew be killed at any time, for any reason, or for no reason at all.[23] Such were Nazi racial politics. The Germanic (Nordic) peoples, such as the Dutch, Swedes or Danes were considered in the Nazi ideology as "racially close." As a result, they had significant opportunities to survive in Nazi occupied territories unless they were Communists or members of the anti-Nazi underground.

An impressive illustration of the differences in Nazi racial policies in Western Europe and the Soviet Union is the well-known story of Anne Frank. After betraying the Frank family, the family's rescuers, Victor Kugler and Johannes Kleiman, were arrested and sent to a concentration camp considered enemies of the Nazi regime occupying Holland. Kleiman was released after several weeks, and Kugler was held in various work camps until the war's end. The Dutch women, Miep Gies and Bep Voskuijl who took a significant part in the rescue of the Frank family, were questioned by the Security Police but not detained. Such an outcome would have been absolutely impossible on Soviet lands occupied by the Nazis. Nazi policy demanded that the Slavic families who hid Jews and were found out, be killed by the Gestapo, or burnt or hanged by the Sonderkommandos, together with their

22 J. Dietsch, "Holocaust in Ukrainian Historical Culture," in M. Davies and C.-C. Szejnmann, eds., *How the Holocaust Looks Now: International Perspectives* (Basingstoke, UK: Palgrave Macmillan, 2007), 107–115.

23 K. Berkhoff, *Harvest of Despair: Life and Death in Ukraine Under Nazi Rule* (Cambridge, MA: Belknap Press of Harvard University Press, 2004).

own children, and the Jews that they hid. On Soviet territory, the victims of the Holocaust were not only Jews, but also people of different nationalities. It is difficult to divide the Jewish and non-Jewish victims of the Holocaust in Ukraine, Russia, and Byelorussia. The majority of non-Jewish people in the Soviet Union shared a "Jewish fate" during the Holocaust. Slavic rescuers of Jews risked their own life and the lives of their relatives, in a distinctly different scenario from that faced by rescuers in the Netherlands, Germany, or Denmark. In particular, German or Dutch Jews could avoid being sent to a concentration camp if they had a German/Aryan spouse. This was the case of Viktor Klemperer who was married to a German woman who supported him all during war and the Holocaust. German philosopher Karl Jaspers helped his Jewish wife to survive. And German businessman Otto Weidt, the owner of a small factory in Berlin which employed mostly blind and deaf Jews—in Nazis terms: *racial aliens* and the *unfit*—was able to protect most of his Jewish employees against deportation by claiming that they were valuable workers for the Reich.

One of the most tragic examples of the Nazi genocide towards the Slavs is found in the Byelorussian village of Khatyn in which Nazi troops and their collaborators intended to burn alive all of the habitants on March 22, 1943. The trapped people in the village managed to break down the doors, but in running out to escape, they were killed by machine gun fire.[24] 147 people, including 75 children under 16 years of age were either burned, shot or died by suffocation in the fire. The village was then looted and burned to the ground. Only eight inhabitants of the village survived, of whom six were recognized as witnesses to the tragedy. They were five children and a single adult. The official reason given for this atrocity was the need to punish the locals because they had helped the partisans when the Nazis engaged in a "struggle with the Red partisans." In reality, the German losses in that territory were small and isolated; there were almost no fights with the Red partisans. The Nazi action had a target pure and simple: the mass murder of Byelorussian civilians of Slavic origin. During what is known as the Spring Extermination in Byelorussia, more than 600 villages were destroyed and 3,500 locals burned alive. Two thousand Byelorussian children were sent to German concentration camps and more than 1,000 children were sent to the Salaspils death camp in Latvia. Unfortunately the truth of this vast loss of innocent Byelorussian lives in Khatyn is less well known in European historical memory than the shooting death of Polish officers in a town with a similar name—Katyn.

---

24 A. Rudling, "The Khatyn Massacre in Belorussia: A Historical Controversy Revisited," *Holocaust and Genocide Studies* 26 (2012): 129–158.

Soviet Ukraine held a special place in the political plans of the Third Reich. The entire Eastern Ukraine according to the plans of Nazi ideologues, was to be turned into the "breadbasket" of the Third Reich, and all native inhabitants—Ukrainians, Russians, and Byelorussians—were forced to work as slaves. The Slavic and Ukrainian populations would be allowed to survive only in this capacity. For example, one of the largest industrial and scientific centers of the Soviet Union and the first capital of Soviet Ukraine, Kharkiv, was in Nazi opinion, the source of Bolshevik ideology. As such, the Kharkiv population had to be eliminated and a harsh occupation regime installed. The famous Ukrainian historian A. Skorobogatov in his book *Kharkiv in German occupation* wrote that Kharkiv was given to plunder the first few days after the German occupation, many locals were shooting or hanging, and sometimes Germans raped mother and daughter in the same room.[25] Starvation was one of the policies of Nazi genocide against the Soviet Slavic population, especially, against those in the big Soviet cities.[26] Kiev and Kharkiv were starved by the German occupation in a manner comparable to the famine in the big Jewish ghettos.

Soviet POWs and some Polish officers were the first victims of the Auschwitz gas chambers.[27] The fate of the Soviet POWs in German captivity was an unspoken issue for a long time in both American and Soviet social sciences. Jonathan North calls Soviet POWs the "Forgotten Nazi Victims." He emphasizes that of the more than 5.7 million Soviet soldiers captured between 1941 and 1945, 3.5 million died in German captivity.[28] This means that about 57 percent of those taken prisoner, were dead by the end of the war. By comparison, about 8,300, or 3.6 percent of American, British, or Canadian POWs died in German custody. These facts and these numbers have had a profound influence on the different perceptions of the Holocaust and on the post-war response in both the American and Soviet societies. Russians citizens do not see the Holocaust as having solely to do with the Jewish population.

---

25 A. Skorobogatov, *Kharkiv y chasu nimazkoj okupazii (1941–1943)* (Kharkiv, 2006), 80 (Translation: A. Skorobogatov, *Kharkiv during the German occupation (1941–1943)* (Kharkiv, 2006).

26 Berkhoff, *Harvest of Despair*, 164–174.

27 R. Lukas, "The Polish Experience during the Holocaust," in Berenbaum, ed., *A Mosaic of Victims*, 88–95.

28 J. North, "Soviet Prisoners of War: Forgotten Nazi Victims of World War II", 12 June 2006, http://www.historynet.com/soviet-prisoners-of-war-forgotten-nazi-victims-of-world-war-ii.htm. (visited 1 December 2016).

A prisoner of the Riga Ghetto remembered how one of his ghetto neighbors had come to know his brother who was among the Soviet POWs in the Nazi concentration camp—*staatlag*—near Riga. That the brother could not possibly survive the camp was obvious to the man because living conditions in the camp were even worse than they were in the ghetto. It was a story of paradox and irony: A resistance group from the ghetto organized the escape of the brother from the POW camp…to the Jewish ghetto! The brother survived the war and the ghetto, but all his comrades from the Red Army who remained in the POW camp died in the first months of captivity.[29] This sample illustrates that the fate of Russian prisoners of war was sometimes more hopeless than the fate of Jewish victims in the ghettos, although this topic was not taken up in American Holocaust studies.

As A. Jones wrote, "next to the Jews in Europe…the biggest German crime was undoubtedly the extermination by hunger, exposure and in other ways of Russian war prisoners…and the murder of at least 3,3 million Soviet POWs is one of the least-known of modern genocides…It was one of the most intensive genocide of all times."[30] The most horrible fate could wait for the Soviet women who served in the Red Army as doctors, nurses, communication personnel, and other spe-cialties. Israeli historian A. Shneer in his fundamental monograph *Capture* has described a case in the camp Stutthoff when female POWs were burnt alive in a fireplace for corpses.[31] Some of the Soviet women who served in the army and were captured by Germans, in first were sexually abused and then shot. The status of Soviet prisoners of war when compared to the situation of Jews in the ghetto had many obvious analogies, all of which allow us to state that the attitude of the Nazis toward Russian POWs also had a genocidal character.

The Nazi occupation of Soviet lands was so brutal that some people preferred *any* regime to the Nazi occupation and so, even while remembering Stalin's repres-sions, the Red Army was greeted as deliverer when it defeated the Germans. The triumph of the Red Army and its promise of liberation from Nazism, fixed in the people a type of Soviet identity that was maintained in the post-war generation. As

---

29 Smirin G. "Chto s nami slucholos'" memuaru yznika Rizgskogo getto Georga Frid-mana" In Materialu Desyatoj egegodnoj konferenzii po iydaike. Chast' 1. – Moskva, 2003, c. 291–308 (Translation: Smirin G. "What happened with us": memoirs of Riga ghetto inmate") In *Materials of the 10th Anniversary International Conference on Judaic Studies* (Moscow, 2003): 291–308.

30 A. Jones, *Genocide: A Comprehensive Introduction* (New York: Routledge, 2006), 175.

31 A. Shneer, *Plen* ("Captivity") 2 vols. (Jerusalem, 2003), 1:312.

Nina Tumarkin has posited, the cult narrative of the Great Patriotic War and the twenty millions wartime losses have a *messianic* character in the Soviet Union.[32]

Western scholars have asserted that German racial policy toward the Soviet people resulted in the people feeling a general unification—a unity cemented in the years-long period before and after liberation.[33] The fact of the Holocaust overall no doubt influenced the self-consciousness of Jews who served in the Red Army or who struggled against the Nazi in the Soviet partisans. But the prevailing majority of Jewish battlefront veterans, who were born and educated in the Soviet Union, felt a Soviet identity over a Jewish one. As the American scholar Zvi Gitelman notes, for a majority of Soviet Jewish veterans, the idea of struggling against Nazis for the Soviet homeland had greater importance than the idea of struggling to defend the Jews only.[34]

Post-war memory has generally produced three types of commemorations devoted to heroes, martyrs, and victims. These are meant to stand in stark contrast to enemies, collaborators, and traitors. The Soviet mass media actively pursued a discussion of heroism and the heroic archetype they presented was associated with soldiers and officers of the Red Army, and with the Soviet partisan movement in the anti-Nazi resistance. Everyday life and survival during the occupation were cast in a positive light only if they were connected to the resistance. The unspoken idea in Soviet mass consciousness was that all those taken to the Jewish ghettos and Nazi concentration camps carried the stigma of "victim;" they had somehow been passive in their acceptance of a tragic fate. *Not* fighting against the Nazi enemy was decided less popular in the war and the post-war Soviet society and it would even arouse contempt among Soviet war veterans and members of the underground. As a result, many Jewish and non-Jewish survivors, who had experienced ghettos and concentration camps, were demoralized in the first decades after the war. Their painful experiences could not find a cultural matrix from which they could engage in public and cultural expression.

The big combat actions—the Battle of Stalingrad, the defense of Moscow, Odessa and Sevastopol, and the Soviet partisans' movement—were reflected in many Soviet films, novels, and songs of the 1960s through the 1980s. What had

---

32 N. Tumarkin, "The War of Remembrance," in R. Stites, ed., *Culture and Entertainment in Wartime Russia* (Bloomington: Indiana University Press, 1995), 197.

33 A. Weiner, *Making Sense of War: The Second World War and the Fate of the Bolshevik Revolution* (Princeton, NJ: Princeton University Press, 2001).

34 Z. Gitelman, "Internationalism, Patriotism and Disillusion," in *The Holocaust in the Soviet Union: Symposium presentations* (Washington DC: Center for Advance Holocaust Studies, 2005), 95–125.

happened to the Jews, or to the Soviet POWs inside the concentration camps was not a popular topic for the Soviet cinema, neither was it for monuments and sculptures. The history of Aleksandr Pechersky, a Jewish lieutenant in the Red Army who was sent by Germans to Sobibor, Poland, is a case in point. Pechersky organized a successful uprising in Sobibor in October of 1943. Despite the fact that this uprising was the only successful uprising in any Nazi death camp, and had been organized by a Soviet military officer, the Soviet propaganda machine never publicized this story during the Cold War. In the eyes of official Soviet propaganda, the fact that Pechersky had been captured and, as it were, showed passivity in relation to the enemy, cancelled out his heroic actions. No film or novel about Pechersky's feat was ever created in the USSR during the Soviet time, and only when the heroism of the Sobibor rebels received international attention in the British film *Escape from Sobibor*, 1987, did it become known to post-Soviet audiences. Coming at history that way meant that the brave and controversial figure of Pechersky was seen mostly as a vestige of the European anti-Nazi resistance rather than as a heroic part of the Soviet Jewish struggle against Nazism.

If the Holocaust took up a sacred place of ontological trauma in Western European and American cultures, in the USSR it occupied a place of eternal pain but pain that was finalized in the "glorious victory" of the Soviet people in the Great Patriotic War of 1941–1945. Known as the Great Patriotic War in Russian, it was called the Eastern front in Germany, or "Ivan's war" in American scholarship.[35] Soviet public culture focused on this theater of war as the cruelest and bloodiest part of World War II. Since 1945 Soviet social sciences have published thousands of volumes devoted to the Great Patriotic War and all its aspects. Soviet cinema has filmed thousands of reels of both brilliant and ordinary motion pictures dedicated to the Soviet-Nazi struggle, to the Soviet underground resistance, and to the Red Army's heroic liberation of Soviet and Eastern European territories from Nazi occupation. In comparison with the Soviet historical and artistic response, the fighting in Europe did not drum up such significant reflection in American literature and art. Only a few well-known American writers such as Irwin Shaw, Norman Mailer, Kurt Vonnegut, and James Jones included the motif of World War II in their works. But many more both famous and little known artists paid attention to the Holocaust in their works. The way the Soviet Union commemorated the Great Patriotic War—their cultural response to it—had many analogous to the way the Americans held the Holocaust in a sacred place.

---

35 C. Merridale, *Ivan's War: Life and Death in the Red Army, 1939–1945* (New York: Metropolitan Books, Henry Holt and Company, 2006).

The Cold War between the Communist Soviet Union and the anti-Communist West developed just after the war and lasted until 1991. It insured that any new academic, historic or public initiative that emerged in Western countries would be considered suspect by Soviet authorities and seen as directed against Soviet ideology. Holocaust studies were established as an academic field in the US in the 1960s and 1970s. These studies concentrated on Jewish suffering, and were interpreted in the Soviet Union as America's attempt to disregard the suffering of all Soviet peoples during the Nazi occupation and to supersede that suffering with the suffering of only one ethnic group. It was perceived as disrespectful to the memory of the Soviet victims of Nazism; in American studies of the Holocaust of the 1970–1980s, Slavs and other non-Jewish victims had been given second place.

In order to accept a wider approach to the Holocaust, one needed to look at the research done outside the Judeo-centric premise. Studies of the Nazi crimes against Soviet citizens including different nationalities in addition to Jews certainly existed. Most of it was set within the Soviet theme of glorification and a general heroic recounting of the Soviet victory in the war. If the Judeo-centric (national) conception of the Holocaust inspired American scholarship, then the "Soviet-centric" (ideological) tendency dominated Soviet historiography. Decades of Cold War and anti-Soviet (anti-Russian) propaganda fueled a situation where the American and Western European public and scholars did not know, and did not want to know that Soviet Slavs and POWs were Nazi victims *almost* at similar level as the Soviet Jews.

Likewise, Soviet approaches to the Holocaust did not spread in American scholarship between the 1950s and the 1980s due to Cold War ideology. The contradictory relationship of Soviet Union with Israel in 1960–1980, did not promote the studies of the Holocaust in the period as well. If Soviet Holocaust films and other academic work never made it into the public memory in the West it was because of the Cold War rise of anti-Sovietism and Russian-phobia in the United States. Here one needs to cite the words by American scholar James Young: "Motives of memory are never pure."[36] He is referring to national traditions and political meanings used in selecting and commemorating events. It was not only the Soviet and American cultures that had different responses to the Holocaust and World War II, all European countries more or less concurred with America, a fact which is evident in the museum exhibits they devoted to World War II

---

36 J. Young, *The Texture of Memory: Holocaust Memorials and Meaning* (London: Yale University Press, 1993).

and the Holocaust.[37] The different national memories chose different events to commemorate as the most significant. This was true for both tragic and glorious events. As a result, in Russia, memorials, museum and exhibits marked battles like the defeat of the German Armies near Moscow and the blockade of Leningrad. In Germany the Allied bombing of Dresden was singled out. In Poland, the Warsaw Uprising was given prominence. For the British, Canadian and American veterans, the Normandy invasion held and still holds a most celebrated position.

Decisions made in assigning the moral dividends of victory over Nazism only served to increase the mutual distrust and suspicion between the Soviet Union and the US–countries that of course had been allies during the war. The majority of American scholars during the Cold War tended to ignore the enormous sacrifices that the Soviet Union had brought to the "Altar of Victory" over Nazism and to discount the personal heroism of the Soviet people. Contemporary American scholar A. Jones wrote, for the Slavs of Ukraine, Russia, and other parts of the Soviet Union their suffering and heroism during the war was legendary: "Titanic Russian sacrifices and, eventually, crushing military force were the key to Nazi Germany's defeat, with the other Allies playing supporting role. Between the Germany invasion of the USSR in June 1941 and the D-Day invasion of France in June 1944, some 80 percent of German forces were deployed in the East."[38]

Similarly, until the end of the Cold War, Soviet historiography paid little attention to the Holocaust issue, or to the theme of the Jewish anti-Nazi resistance in the ghettos. They minified the importance of the American Lend-Lease Act for Soviet survival in war years when starvation was a real threat, and the courage of the American, Scottish, and British sailors in the Arctic convoys was not widespread in Soviet culture. The Soviet propaganda during the Cold War, 1960–1980s, accused standard American post-war history of downgrading the battles on the Eastern front into mere episodes in the background of the Allied combat in Europe. It was difficult for both parties to recognize the moral and physical merits of their opponent in the defeat of Nazism.

That political atmosphere inevitably affects historical research and positions scholars as representatives of a particular national or religious culture. This became clear as the tragedy of the GULAG unfolded. The Stalin regime sent thousands of Nazi ex-prisoners to concentration camps in Siberia or Kolyma after

---

37 A. Whitmarsh, "We Will Remember Them: Memory and Commemoration in War Museums," *Journal of Conservation and Museum Studies* 7 (2001): 11–15.

38 Jones, *Genocide*, 175.

their liberation from Nazi captivity.[39] The GULAG and the Stalinist repressions remained a deep and inexhaustible trauma of Soviet and post-Soviet society. The GULAG caused feelings of guilt based on the fact that in order to stop the Holocaust, the Soviet Army did everything what was possible and impossible, fought and perished, to overcome the Nazis—but could not protect their own heroes against the NKVD repressions. Acknowledging the Stalinist crimes was the first step Soviet scholars took in creating a conceptual framework for genocide studies. They delved into studies of "victim status" and the "complex of cultural guilt," for example. The Soviet scholars of the late 1980s tried to create the conceptual framework for "Ethics after the GULAG" (like Western Ethics after the Holocaust). And along with these studies post-Soviet investigation of the Holocaust gained in prominence, as it made sense in Soviet scholarship in the 1980s and1990s to interweave studies of the Holocaust with studies of the GULAG.

Since the mid-1990s the theme of the Holocaust as a national tragedy of European Jews has returned to public culture and academic discussions in post-Soviet countries, as the collapse of a Soviet identity has created space for national identities and the history of minorities to reemerge. The post-Soviet (principally Russian) cinema has produced many films with motifs and plots growing out of the Holocaust. Contemporary studies and debates on the Holocaust in post-Soviet countries include points of views that incorporate and adapt American academic methods and themes into any examination of World War II and the Holocaust.

---

39 R. Otto, "The Fate of Soviet Soldiers in German Captivity," in *The Holocaust in the Soviet Union*, 127–138.

Emiliano Perra

Intermittently Americanized? Italian Debates on Holocaust Cultural Products

Abstract: *The essay argues that the political situation in the country in which miniseries and films are shown, determines whether they are severely criticized for being Americanized. Four Italian case studies show how the transatlantic political relations were a defining factor in framing cultural products as Americanization of the Holocaust for domestic purposes.*

For many years, the Americanization of the Holocaust has been a major subject of debate in the field of Holocaust Studies, often being used as a shorthand criticism for crass and vulgar trivializations of the event. Although the debate originated in the United States, it has reverberated in Europe, frequently producing significant—and country-specific—theses independent from American discussions.

This essay explores the discussion of the Americanization of the Holocaust in Italy. The Italian case is significant because the country witnessed a massive penetration of American capital, culture and attitudes in the immediate post-war period. This American presence played a fundamental role in the modernization and secularization of the country even if it did not always sit comfortably with pre-existing social structures. Perhaps even more importantly for this article, the fact is that this penetration occurred in a country that was firmly situated in the Atlantic sphere yet was also home to the strongest Communist party in Western Europe.[1] As the essay shows, this international context strongly influenced not only the general debate about the Americanization of Italian culture; it also influenced the more specific one about how to remember the Holocaust. The paper analyzes successful popular films and television miniseries such as *Holocaust* (Marvin J. Chomsky, NBC, 1978), *Schindler's List* (Steven Spielberg, 1993), *Life Is Beautiful* (La vita è bella, Roberto Benigni, 1997), and *Perlasca: The Courage of a Just Man* (Perlasca: un eroe italiano, Alberto Negrin, 2002). By looking at the specific cultural products that helped generate public debates before and after the collapse of the Eastern Bloc, this paper will show that Italian debates on the Americanization of the Holocaust shed light on complex issues of Italy's historical consciousness and self-perception in the world. And

---

1   David W. Ellwood, *The Shock of America: Europe and the Challenge of the Century* (Oxford, UK: Oxford University Press, 2012), 259–263.

even though Benigni's and Negrin's are not American products, they fit into the category of "Americanized" representations, with their happy endings and narrative constructions that tend to "individualize, heroize, moralize, idealize, and universalize" the Holocaust.[2]

The category of Americanization applied to Holocaust representations has often been used in Italy with negative connotations. Often, but not always. For Holocaust representations to be negatively perceived as Americanized, other factors needed to be mobilized. These included pre-existing and non-Holocaust-related sources of resentment against the United States, and/or a social and political climate that made it politically convenient to stir anti-American resentment by bringing up the subject of the Americanization of the Holocaust. Without these factors, the Americanization of the Holocaust does not become an issue. This is seen most clearly by the reception of *Schindler's List* (especially if compared with that of *Holocaust*), or in the discussion of the miniseries *Perlasca*. The four cases discussed here show that the Americanization of the Holocaust is always used selectively in the Italian context. Its use is never purely descriptive nor value-free. On the contrary, it is quite loaded. It is often used in the Italian context as interchangeable with "banalization" and "trivialization." In other words, whether American (or Americanized) Holocaust representations are criticized as trivial and banal (i.e. "Americanized" as a negative term) depends on a number of domestic and international factors that are as much about Italy's relationship with its own past and its self-perception in the present, as they are about the Holocaust or American culture. While this article principally investigates the Italian case, brief mention of French and German responses to the same cultural products shows that this analysis can be applied more widely.

The Americanization of the Holocaust is a subset of the more general phenomenon of Americanization, a term fraught with political baggage, but only *prima facie* self-evident.[3] In fact, the first problem to be addressed is to define what qualifies as Americanization. In this article, Americanization is not necessarily synonymous with originating in the United States. Drawing on the work of Joel Hodson and George Ritzer, this article sees Americanization as a dialogic concept that in order to exist requires the receiving context to identify products,

---

2   Alvin H. Rosenfeld, *The End of the Holocaust* (Bloomington, IN: Indiana University Press, 2011), 60.

3   Heide Fehrenbach and Uta G. Poiger, "Introduction: Americanization Reconsidered," in Heide Fehrenbach and Uta G. Poiger, eds., *Transactions, Transgressions, Transformations: American Culture in Western Europe and Japan* (New York: Berghahn, 2000), xiii.

concepts, and practices as Americanized.[4] Indeed, the influence of the United States is so extensive that sociologists have identified instances of Americanization without America, for example, in the spread of consumer capitalism in countries that are not directly affected by the United States.[5] The same applies to cultural consumption, where, for example, cinematic themes, approaches, and narrative modes perceived to be American have a quasi-global reach. These cultural exports are adopted and adapted in a variety of ways in different contexts.[6] As some of the productions discussed in this essay show, it is quite possible to have Americanization with very little active American involvement. In other words, Americanization hybridizes and blends with local cultures.[7] Determining when and on what terms the notion of Americanization comes into play in any particular country is dependent on a number of political and cultural factors. For all these reasons, an investigation into different receiving contexts' responses to Americanization gives rise to a fruitful comparative study.[8]

American influence in Europe—and Europe's often-suspicious response to it—is an old phenomenon, and Italy poses no exception.[9] In the late nineteenth-century, the popular myth of America as the land of opportunity was countered by an intellectual anti-Americanism circulating within reactionary Catholic and conservative nationalist cliques, as well as among genuine republicans.[10] The year

---

4 Joel Hodson, "'Intercourse in Every Direction': America as Global Phenomenon," *Global Networks* 1 (2001): 79–87; George Ritzer, *Globalization: A Basic Text* (Chichester, UK: Wiley-Blackwell, 2010), 90.

5 Gerard Delanty, "Consumption, Modernity and Japanese Cultural Identity: The Limits of Americanization?" in Ulrich Beck, Natan Sznaider, and Rainer Winter, eds., *Global America? The Cultural Consequences of Globalization* (Liverpool, UK: Liverpool University Press, 2003), 117.

6 See Robert W. Rydell and Rob Kroes, *Buffalo Bill in Bologna: The Americanization of the World, 1869–1922* (Chicago, IL: The University of Chicago Press, 2005), 4–6.

7 Martin Albrow, *The Global Age* (Stanford, CA: Stanford University Press, 2006); Jan Nederveen Pieterse, "Globalization as Hybridization," in Mike Featherstone, Scott Lash, and Roland Robertson, eds., *Global Modernities* (London: Sage, 1995), 45–68; John Tomlinson, *Globalization and Culture* (Cambridge, UK: Polity Press, 1999).

8 Fehrenbach and Poiger, "Introduction: Americanization Reconsidered," xiv.

9 Andrei S. Markovits, *Uncouth Nation: Why Europe Dislikes America* (Princeton, NJ: Princeton University Press, 2007), ch. 2.; Rydell and Kroes, *Buffalo Bill in Bologna*, 149–63.

10 Pier Paolo D'Attorre, "Sogno americano e mito sovietico nell'Italia contemporanea," in Pier Paolo D'Attorre, ed., *Nemici per la pelle: Sogno americano e mito sovietico nell'Italia contemporanea* (Milan: Franco Angeli, 1991), 16.

1905 saw the publication of *L'America e l'avvenire* by Ugo Ojetti, an important text that anticipated the interwar period of European anti-Americanism. The anti-American themes proposed by Ojetti and others at the journal *La Voce* were pushed to an extreme by the fascist regime in the 1930s, combining reactionary populism, nationalism, emerging racism, and conservative Catholicism. But the picture was more complex than that, and fascist fear of America's challenge to established values coexisted alongside an admiration for its technology and vitality. A large strata of the cultural elite absorbed American literature, while popular culture idolized stars like Primo Carnera and Rudolph Valentino in a syncretism of fascist and American heroism.[11]

Americanization reached its apogee in Western Europe in the second half of the twentieth century, when the "rise of a great imperium with the outlook of a great emporium"[12] established the American way of life as a familiar set of values for Europeans. Washington's role after World War II became a powerful new influence spurring on anti-Americanism, but expressions of antipathy for the United States never really endangered local elites' established bonds with it.[13]

Postwar Italy proved particularly receptive to American influence, and the consumerist model embedded in the American style of modernization had a real impact in the country.[14] A classic example of American penetration is the Hollywood films which flooded the market with the intent of promoting American production and consumption as the gateway to democratic progress.[15] With their basic secularism, liberalism, and championing of individual values, these films generated a significant negative reaction from intellectuals, opinion formers, and members of the Catholic and communist elite, the two main forces to emerge after World War II.[16] While the Christian Democrats and the Church oscillated between political support

---

11 Ibid., 18–23.

12 Victoria De Grazia, *Irresistible Empire: America's Advance through Twentieth-Century Europe* (Cambridge, MA: The Belknap Press of Harvard University Press, 2005), 3.

13 Fehrenbach and Poiger, "Introduction: Americanization Reconsidered," xix–xx.

14 Stephen Gundle, "L'americanizzazione del quotidiano: Televisione e consumismo nell'Italia degli anni Cinquanta," *Quaderni storici* 21:2 (1986): 563; David W. Ellwood, "Containing Modernity, Domesticating America in Italy," in Alexander Stephan, ed., *The Americanization of Europe: Culture, Diplomacy, and Anti-Americanism after 1945* (New York: Berghahn, 2006), 254–262; David Forgacs, "Americanisation: The Italian Case 1938–1954," *Borderlines: Studies in American Culture* 1 (1993): 157–169; Daniela Treveri Gennari, *Post-War Italian Cinema: American Interventions, Vatican Interests* (New York: Routledge, 2009), 6.

15 Ellwood, *Shock of America*, 368.

16 D'Attorre, "Sogno americano e mito sovietico nell'Italia contemporanea," 30–33.

of US influence in Italy and concern about its undermining of traditional rural and Catholic values,[17] the Italian Communist Party (PCI) was particularly taken aback by America's appeal among workers. Communist response too often drew on the nostalgic humanism and rejection of machine-made modernity that had been the stock-in-trade of interwar conservative anti-Americanism.[18] As a result, while the communist left rejected Americanism, large sections of the younger generation from all political orientations saw American culture as a source of liberation from the mores of traditional authoritarian culture.[19]

A reassessment of American cultural diffusion emerged in the years between the Vietnam War and the Euro-missile crisis, when the United States lost some of its appeal as a political role model. Nevertheless, its impact on Western popular culture remained largely intact, and even anti-authoritarian cultures in Europe incorporated large numbers of products and symbols that came from the "other" United States.[20] In the 1990s, a part-real, part-imagined United States served as a counterpoint against which some Western European societies, for example France, sought to define their sense of themselves and their future. Contrary to this trend, disputes over the impact of Americanization ebbed in post-Cold War Italy.[21] This relatively recent, relaxed approach to American culture in Italy does not contradict the fact that for many people and for many years, Americaniza-tion had posed a challenge to established norms, models and values, and had an impact on memory culture.

The Americanization of the Holocaust

Americanization also applies to the specific case of the Holocaust, with the impor-tant difference being that the discussion of the Americanization of the Holocaust originated in the United States. There, it has been a major subject of debate in the field of Holocaust Studies for decades, dating back to NBC's miniseries *Holo-caust* in 1978. Spearheaded by Elie Wiesel's claim that *Holocaust* transformed

---

17 David W. Ellwood, "Comparative Anti-Americanism in Western Europe," in Fehren-bach and Poiger, eds., *Transactions, Transgressions, Transformations*, 31.

18 Ellwood, "Containing Modernity," 255–257.

19 Rosario Forlenza, "Sacrificial Memory and Political Legitimacy in Postwar Italy: Reliv-ing and Remembering World War II," *History & Memory* 24 (2012): 93.

20 Ellwood, "Containing Modernity," 264; Ellwood, "Comparative Anti-Americanism," 32.

21 Markovits, *Uncouth Nation,* ch. 6; Ellwood, "Comparative Anti-Americanism," 39; Ellwood, "Containing Modernity," 268.

"an ontological event into soap-opera,"[22] a number of American scholars and intellectuals have bemoaned what they see as the trivialization of the Holocaust caused by the miniseries.[23] From that moment on, Americanization as the byword for trivialization became central in scholarly discussions of Holocaust memory, mirroring the rise of Holocaust memory itself into the center of memory culture and representation. It is a well-known debate, rehashed time and again with every milestone in America's relationship with the Holocaust, such as with the release of *Schindler's List*, the opening of the United States Holocaust Memorial Museum, or the use of Holocaust imagery to raise public awareness about the crimes perpetrated in the former Yugoslavia.[24]

Not all American scholars who have intervened in the discussion of the Americanization of the Holocaust have dismissed it; some deem it necessary in order to allow this European event to resonate with the American public, even if it means partially distorting the historical record in the process.[25] However, many others saw it as a manifestation of America at its crass and vulgar worst, the source of "banalization" and "trivialization" of the Holocaust.[26] Still others, like Peter

22 Elie Wiesel, "Trivializing the Holocaust: Semi-Fact and Semi-Fiction," *New York Times*, 16 April 1978.
23 Jeffrey Shandler, *While America Watches: Televising the Holocaust* (New York: Oxford University Press, 1999), 167–175.
24 Tim Cole, *Selling the Holocaust: From Auschwitz to Schindler: How History Is Bought, Packaged, and Sold* (New York, Routledge, 1999); Miriam Bratu Hansen, "'Schindler's List' Is Not 'Shoah': The Second Commandment, Popular Modernism, and Public Memory," *Critical Inquiry* 22 (1996): 292–312; Alan E. Steinweis, "The Auschwitz Analogy: Holocaust Memory and American Debates over Intervention in Bosnia and Kosovo in the 1990s," *Holocaust and Genocide Studies* 19 (2005): 276–289.
25 Hilene Flanzbaum, "'But Wasn't It Terrific?': A Defense of Liking *Life Is Beautiful*," *The Yale Journal of Criticism* 14:1 (2001): 273–286; Hilene Flanzbaum, "Introduction," in Hilene Flanzbaum, ed., *The Americanization of the Holocaust* (Baltimore, MD: The Johns Hopkins University Press, 1999), 1–17; Michael Berenbaum, *After Tragedy and Triumph: Essays in Modern Jewish Thought and the American Experience* (Cambridge: Cambridge University Press, 1990), 8–13; Michael Berenbaum, *The World Must Know: The History of the Holocaust as Told in the United States Holocaust Memorial Museum* (Boston, MA: Little, Brown & Company, 1993); Judith E. Doneson, "Holocaust Revisited: A Catalyst for Memory or Trivialization?," *Annals of the American Academy of Political and Social Science* (The Holocaust: Remembering for the Future) 548 (1996): 70–77; Judith E. Doneson, *The Holocaust in American Film*, 2nd ed. (Syracuse, NY: Syracuse University Press, 2002).
26 Cole, *Selling the Holocaust*; Lawrence L. Langer, *Admitting the Holocaust: Collected Essays* (New York: Oxford University Press, 1995), 157–178; Alvin H. Rosenfeld,

Novick and especially Norman Finkelstein, have seen the cultural phenomenon of the general emergence of Holocaust memory in the United States as politically orchestrated to bolster the strategic alliance with Israel.[27] Many opinion makers in Italy perceived the Americanization of the Holocaust, brought about by the miniseries *Holocaust*, as equally morally inadequate and politically suspicious, although the reasons for this mistrust were different from the ones formulated in the United States.

The Americanization of the Holocaust in Italian Reviews of "Holocaust" and "Schindler's List"

When Italian television aired *Holocaust* in 1979, commentators often saw it as "hammy," overdramatic, and replete with Hollywood clichés. These negative voices compared *Holocaust*'s representation of history with that of the quintessential American historical drama *Gone with the Wind*.[28] Bathos was not the only

---

"Popularization and Memory: The Case of Anne Frank," in Peter Hayes, ed., *Lessons and Legacies: The Meaning of the Holocaust in a Changing World* (Evanston, IL: Northwestern University Press, 1991), 243–278; Alvin H. Rosenfeld, *A Double Dying: Reflections on Holocaust Literature* (Bloomington, IN: Indiana University Press, 1980); Alvin H. Rosenfeld, "Holocaust, Popular Culture, and Memory," in Paolo Amodio, Romeo De Maio, and Giuseppe Lissa, eds., *La Shoàah tra interpretazione e memoria* (Naples: Vivarium, 1998), 239–254; Alvin H. Rosenfeld, "The Americanization of the Holocaust," in Alvin H. Rosenfeld, ed., *Thinking About the Holocaust after Half a Century* (Bloomington, IN: Indiana University Press, 1997), 119–150; Alvin H. Rosenfeld, "The Holocaust in American Popular Culture," *Midstream* 29 (1983): 53–59.

27 Norman Finkelstein, *The Holocaust Industry: Reflections on the Exploitation of Jewish Suffering*, 2nd ed. (London: Verso, 2003); Peter Novick, *The Holocaust in American Life* (Boston, MA: Houghton-Mifflin, 1999).

28 See as examples Domenico Bartoli, "Quando un polpettone è utile," *Il Giornale Nuovo* 23 June 1979; Giovanni Cesareo, "L'"operazione" Olocausto," *l'Unità*, 18 June 1979; Rina Goren, "Olocausto. La massa non si sente coinvolta," *Il Messaggero*, 20 June 1979; Goffredo Parise, "Un telefilm troppo "normale" per contenere la tragedia del genocidio?," *Corriere della Sera*, 19 May 1979; R.L., "Tv. Inizia l'operazione Olocausto. È un telefilm antinazista o un pamphlet filoisraeliano?," *il manifesto*, 20 May 1979; Alberto Bevilacqua, "'Olocausto' Perchè la coscienza ricordi," *Corriere della Sera*, 20 May 1979; Enrico Ghezzi, "Come un olocausto divenne spettacolo," *il manifesto*, 23 May 1979; Fausto Pozzato, "Un'opera mediocre colpita da mediocrità," *il Resto del Carlino*, 18 May 1979; Edoardo Sanguineti, "Un "Holocaust" con tanto Sue," *Paese Sera*, 17 May 1979. See also Giulia Borgese, "Ma quale impressione vi hanno fatto i nazisti vedendo Olocausto in tv?," *Corriere della Sera*, 22 May 1979; Ricciardetto, "Olocausto: Perché

problem, however. Not too unlike their American counterparts (but independent-ly from them), reviewers across the board decried the miniseries' depiction of evil as a problem of deranged individuals and alleged that it fell short of questioning the system's deep structures.[29] They agreed that *Holocaust* appealed almost exclu-sively to viewers' emotions as opposed to their rational understanding.[30] In other words, they saw the miniseries as inherently trivial and unable to convey histori-cal depth.[31] These similarities with contemporary American debates must not be overstated, however. For example, Wiesel's critique of *Holocaust*'s Americanization was based on two claims: that television was an intrinsically trivializing medium and that the Holocaust defied artistic conventions, neither of which was central in Italy. In Italy, on the contrary, commentators saw the trivializing effect not so much in the medium of television, but characteristic of America itself.

In late 1970s Italian culture, the concept of Americanization was politicised for both the left and the right. The right interpreted the miniseries as anti-totalitarian and a rebuttal of anti-Zionism, and in doing so directed its "message" against the PCI and the "new left." The left, in turn, saw Americanization not just as a by-word for trivialization, but also as a troubling example of how the American political-cultural establishment was able to set the agenda in European debates.[32] In this regard, the Italian left found itself in the same situation as its German counterpart, which had to carefully balance approval of an explicitly anti-Nazi product against a wariness of the American culture industry.[33]

Concerns about the trivialization of history and American cultural coloniza-tion dovetailed with traditional anti-American themes and with the more recent suspicions that these products existed to disguise pro-Israel "propaganda." The

---

l'uomo diventa mostro," *Epoca* 1979; Gianni Rondolino, "Il vero Olocausto nei film d'epoca," *La Stampa*, 3 June 1979.

29 Ugo Buzzolan, "Bilancio di Olocausto che termina stasera," *La Stampa*, 19 June 1979.

30 C.R., "Tra tensione e paura precipita la tragedia," *Il Giorno*, 4 June 1979; Cesare Caval-leri, "Un'enfasi che non va alle radici," *Avvenire*, 29 May 1979.

31 Anna Maria Mori, "La violenza: come?," *la Repubblica*, 20–21 May 1979; Alberto Mora-via, "Prodotto privo di arte," *La Stampa*, 20 June 1979; Renato Minore, "Il dolore rap-presentato," *Il Messaggero*, 19 May 1979; Andrea Frullini, "Lo sconvolgente Olocausto resuscita i vecchi fantasmi," *Il Giornale Nuovo*, 20 May 1979; Pier Maria Poletti, "Le immagini della nostra colpa," *Il Giorno*, 9 June 1979; Sergio Surchi, "Olocausto: I limiti e la lezione," *Il Popolo*, 19 June 1979.

32 Sergio S., "Possono i sentimenti generare cambiamenti," *Lotta Continua*, 22 May 1979.

33 Giovanni Giudici, "'Olocausto': Il libro e la memoria," *l'Unità*, 23 April 1979; Jeffrey Herf, "The "Holocaust" Reception in West Germany: Right, Center and Left," *New German Critique* 19 (1980): 30–52.

Italian reception of *Holocaust* shared the same perspective as the French and the Germans in their reception of the television series.[34] The "new left" newspaper *Lotta Continua* read the success of *Holocaust* in Europe as a symptom of the Americanization and "Zionification" of European Jewish culture, while the communist *il manifesto* was so wary of *Holocaust's* supposed pro-Israel message that it seemed to forget that the miniseries was primarily concerned with Nazi crimes.[35]

The left identified *Holocaust's* glib view of history as another fundamental weakness of "Americanization." One element of this critique saw the show's identification of Nazism with anti-Semitism as flawed, since it failed to address in adequate terms the connections between the Third Reich and financial capitalism. The communists in particular criticised these omissions as potentially dangerous because, in their view, such omissions paved the way for presenting the Third Reich as a form of totalitarianism indistinguishable from the Soviet model—a representation of Nazism that could be used to promote anti-communist ideology.[36]

Another leftist critique of the Americanization of the Holocaust, one that questioned the very right of Americans to represent the European genocide, could also be found in Italy, although this reaction was not as strong as was seen in West-Germany.[37] The Socialist party house organ *Avanti!* argued that because Americans had not experienced Nazi occupation, and since their only first-hand knowledge of genocide came from their own experience as perpetrators (most recently in Vietnam), they were not in a position to tell the story of the Holocaust.[38]

---

34 Carlo Scaringi, "Un lieto fine fuori posto per motivi di cassetta," *Avanti!*, 19 June 1979; Herf, "The "Holocaust" Reception in West Germany: Right, Center and Left," 43–46; Moishe Postone, "Anti-Semitism and National Socialism: Notes on the German Reaction to 'Holocaust,'" *New German Critique* 19: Special Issue 1: Germans and Jews (1980): 98; Joan B. Wolf, *Harnessing the Holocaust: The Politics of Memory in France* (Stanford, CA: Stanford University Press, 2004), 73.

35 S. "Possono i sentimenti generare cambiamenti"; "Sbagliando si impara," *il manifesto*, 22 May 1979; Samir Kariuti, "Hitler, sembra dire L'Espresso presentando 'Olocausto', forse era un arabo. E chi condanna oggi Israele puzza di nazismo, anche se nei lager ci vive davvero," *il manifesto*, 20 May 1979; R.L., "Tv. Inizia l'operazione Olocausto. È un telefilm antinazista o un pamphlet filoisraeliano?"

36 Ivano Cipriani, "Questo film che narra il disumano," *Paese Sera* 1979; Giovanni Cesareo, "Discutere per non dimenticare," *l'Unità*, 20 May 1979; S. "Possono i sentimenti generare cambiamenti."

37 Thomas Elsaesser, *European Cinema: Face to Face with Hollywood* (Amsterdam: Amsterdam University Press, 2005), 384.

38 Carlo Scaringi, "Positivo avvio di 'Olocausto:' Pagina di storia da meditare," *Avanti!*, 22 May 1979.

Suspicious of American culture's investment in an episode of history not directly related to the United States, for many on the left, *Holocaust* only made sense as a prelude to America's military involvement in the Middle East following the Islamic revolution in Iran.[39] A pointed reply to these various leftist critiques came from *il manifesto*'s co-founder Luigi Pintor. Writing in a front-page column, Pintor not only defended *Holocaust* but argued further that if the Holocaust was used for Israeli or American propaganda, it was in part because the left had been unable to fully acknowledge the event as a breach of civilization. If a cultural product that uncompromisingly denounced Nazism was received on the left with hostility rather than approval, then this was a sign of an intrinsic cultural weakness—upon which the left needed to reflect.[40]

The *Holocaust* debate in Italy shows that in a politically intense period like the late 1970s, the theme of the Americanization of the Holocaust acquired political significance. The miniseries, and especially the fact that it was an American product, was interpreted in political terms by most commentators. Fifteen years later, in the less ideologically divided domestic and international post-Cold War political context, the release of *Schindler's List* (March 1994 in Italy) generated very few negative responses, both in general, and with reference to its Americanized rendition of the Holocaust. Although some commentators remarked upon the film's focus on a self-made man and its happy ending, which were seen as befitting American "taste," there was nothing comparable to the range of critiques that had been levelled at *Holocaust*.[41] For example, the house organ of the Democratic Party of the Left (as the Communist Party renamed itself in 1991) *l'Unità*, which fifteen years earlier had been among the most critical of *Holocaust*'s Americanized approach to the Holocaust, was largely supportive of the film and not concerned with its interpretation of the event.[42]

If we compare this response with responses in France and Germany, two other Western European countries that generated intense response to *Holocaust*, we can see that the Italian case is not exceptional. Italy responded in ways similar to Germany, the country in Europe where the Americanization of the Holocaust had always generated the most intense debate, but which had responded to *Schindler's*

39 Parise, "Un telefilm troppo 'normale' per contenere la tragedia del genocidio?."; Roberto Livi, "Gli ebrei di sinistra discutono, sulla difensiva, di Olocausto," *il manifesto*, 27 May 1979.
40 Luigi Pintor, "Olocausto. Storia nostra," *il manifesto*, 1 June 1979.
41 Sion Segre Amar, "Ma non chiamatelo Olocausto," *La Stampa*, 3 May 1994.
42 Alberto Crespi, "Tutti da Schindler," *l'Unità*, 11 March 1994.

List with quasi-monolithic praise.[43] Whereas in 1979 many leftwing intellectuals had rejected *Holocaust* as tantamount to cultural colonialism, *Schindler's List* was described as nothing more than an American contribution to the theme of German "coming to terms with the past."[44] In France, on the contrary, *Schindler's List* was subject to harsh criticism precisely for its being American. However, the debate was as much about economics and hard politics as it was about culture, history, or Holocaust memory. *Schindler's List* was issued around the time of the GATT agreement discussions that pitted France against the United States over free trade for cultural products such as cinema and television.[45] In this context, *Schindler's List* became a symbol of American influence.[46]

Unlike France, Italy in 1993–1994 had no particular qualms about American cultural penetration, neither from the film industry, nor any broader cultural or ideological reasons. Since the end of the Cold War and the morphing of the Communist Party into an openly social-democratic and reform-oriented force that took inspiration from the Clinton administration, the type of opinions that had dominated left-wing responses to *Holocaust* were relegated to the extremes of the political spectrum, and thus enjoyed much less visibility than in the past. However, the Americanization of the Holocaust as a contentious theme had not vanished, and was soon reactivated during the public discussion of *Life Is Beautiful*. This time, the right predominantly brought up the theme. The next section of the paper deals with two cultural products that are not strictly American. Americanized representations of the Holocaust do not necessarily have to be American. What they must do is share the trademark features of a happy ending,

---

43 Scott Denham, "Schindler Returns to Open Arms: *Schindler's List* in Germany and Austria," in Peter Hayes, ed., *Lessons and Legacies III: Memory, Memorialization, and Denial* (Evanston, IL: Northwestern University Press, 1999), 199; Liliane Weissberg, "The Tale of a Good German: Reflections on the German Reception of *Schindler's List*," in Yosefa Loshitzky, ed., *Spielberg's Holocaust: Critical Perspectives on "Schindler's List"* (Bloomington: Indiana University Press, 1997), 177.

44 Ellwood, "Comparative Anti-Americanism in Western Europe," 35.

45 Toby Miller, "The Crime of Monsieur Lang: Gatt, the Screen and the New International Division of Cultural Labour," in Albert Moran, ed., *Film Policy: International, National and Regional Perspectives*, (London: Routledge, 1996), 78; Richard H. Pells, *Not Like Us: How Europeans Have Loved, Hated, and Transformed American Culture since World War II* (New York: Basic Books, 1997), 273–277.

46 Natasha Lehrer, "Between Obsession and Amnesia: Reflections on the French Reception of *Schinler's List*," in Loshitzky, ed., *Spielberg's Holocaust*, 213–225; Michael Rothberg, *Traumatic Realism: The Demands of Holocaust Representation* (Minneapolis, MI: Minnesota University Press, 2000), 243.

a highly dramatic tone throughout, clearly defined distinctions between good and evil, and a relative lack of interest in political motives in favour of emotional and moral commitments so often criticised in the literature. Such was the case in Benigni's film and in *Perlasca*.

Life Is Beautiful and Perlasca

While the theme of the Americanization of the Holocaust had been a minor feature in Italian discussions of *Schindler's List*, the topic hovered above the intense debate generated by *Life Is Beautiful*. In that movie for the first time, the limits of representation became an important aspect of the *Italian* Holocaust debate. In Benigni's film, issues of morality, culture, history, aesthetics, and party politics combined to create a peculiar Italian reception.

Giacomo Lichtner has aptly noted that it is difficult to evaluate the debate generated by the film *Life Is Beautiful*.[47] It aroused portentous discussions both in Italy and abroad among scholars and in the press.[48] The film's astonishing success divided the debate into two opposing camps. On the one hand were those who saw *Life Is Beautiful* as a bowdlerised, sugar-coated, manipulative, and inherently trivial misrepresentation of the Holocaust. This position gained currency among scholars, highbrow film critics, and many second-generation Jewish public figures wary of the power of popular film to misrepresent the Holocaust. On the other hand, there was the view held by much of the press and the public in general, including many survivors, that the film was important to preserve the memory of the event. The main bone of contention lay in *Life Is Beautiful*'s use of comedy to tell a story of persecution and deportation.[49] Despite Benigni's attempt to forestall criticism by declaring that the film did not aim at realism, left-wing intellectual Goffredo Fofi and literary scholar Carlo Ossola attacked the comedic form with the Adornian argument that no fable about the Holocaust could replace naked history.[50]

---

47 Giacomo Lichtner, *Film and the Shoah in France and Italy* (London: Vallentine Mitchell, 2008), 206.

48 Emiliano Perra, *Conflicts of Memory: The Reception of Holocaust Films and Television Programmes in the Italian Press, 1945 to the Present* (Oxford, UK: Peter Lang, 2010), 165–175.

49 On this, see Terrence Des Pres, "Holocaust *Laughter*?," in Berel Lang, ed., *Writing and the Holocaust* (New York: Holmes & Meier, 1988), 216–33; Sander L. Gilman, "Is Life Beautiful? Can the Shoah Be Funny? Some Thoughts on Recent and Older Films," *Critical Inquiry* 26 (2000): 279–308.

50 Goffredo Fofi, "'La vita è bella' è brutto," *Panorama*, 8 January 1998; Goffredo Fofi, "La vita è una furbata," *Panorama*, 15 February 1998; Rosetta Loy, "Un giullare nel

The theme of Americanization of the Holocaust entered the debate within this context and was used as a byword for trivialization. No doubt some presented the idea of Americanization out of pure conviction. More often than not, however, the topic emerged as the result of the extreme politicization of culture in Italy. The editor of the right-wing newspaper *Il Foglio*, Giuliano Ferrara, persistently condemned what he characterized as the film's trivialization of the Holocaust, comparing it to another staple of the Americanization of the Holocaust, the Broadway version of *The Diary of Anne Frank*. He saw them both as Holocaust stories that ultimately deprived the victims of their Jewishness and put forward what Ferrara considered a trite message of naïve faith in humanity.[51] His charges of "Americanization" and "trivialization" against the film were in large part politically motivated. At the time, Italy was governed by the centre-left Olive Tree coalition headed by Prime Minister Romano Prodi, and Benigni was an outspoken supporter of the left. In the hyper-politicized Italian context, criticizing Benigni and *Life Is Beautiful* as an Americanization of the Holocaust, served as a way to attack the government.[52]

Thus, during the eighteen months of debate on *Life Is Beautiful*, *Il Foglio* published dozens of excerpts from negative articles published in the international press. The newspaper also reproduced a cartoon by Art Spiegelman originally published in the *New Yorker*, that was critical of the film. In an interview with *Corriere della Sera*, Spiegelman defined films such as *Life Is Beautiful* and *Schindler's List* as relativizations of the Holocaust.[53] Similar remarks were made by historian Enzo Traverso, whose Frankfurt School-inspired criticism of the film lamented its displacement of the actual event in favour of a sanitized version of the Holocaust that privileged emotional stimulation over critical understanding.[54]

---

sacrario del secolo. La favola audace di Benigni," *L'Indice dei libri del mese* 15:3 (1998); Nico Orengo, "La favola a premi di Benigni cancella il ricordo del male," *La Stampa*, 5 February 1998; Carlo Ossola, "L'enigma di Benigni. Se pronunci il mio nome…," *Il Sole 24 Ore*, 1 February 1998; Carlo Ossola, "Ma il vostro film occulta la realtá," *La Stampa*, 12 February 1998.

51 Giuliano Ferrara, "Olocaustoshow," *Panorama*, 22 January 1998; Giuliano Ferrara, "Ora la vita è un po' meno bella," *Panorama*, 18 March 1999. His view was echoed on the left by Marcello Rossi, "I campi di sterminio e il film di Benigni," *Il Ponte* 55:4 (1999): 5–6.

52 Giuliano Della Pergola, "E' sossibile ridere su Auschwitz?," *Rocca* 58:7 (1999).

53 Ranieri Polese, "Spiegelman, una vignetta per non dimenticare," *Corriere della Sera*, 30 March 1999.

54 Enzo Traverso, "La vita è bella? Roberto Benigni e Auschwitz," *Passato e Presente*:48 (1999).

Traverso's critique that Americanized renditions of the Holocaust depend more on emotion than understanding reveals a set of convictions that are somewhat debatable. This critique says that such representations favor empathic and individual approaches to the Holocaust, as opposed to rational and collective-political ones. In this critique the Americanization of the Holocaust reflects the drive toward depoliticization, as well as the rise of individualism in contemporary society and as such, the more critical one is of this process, the more critical one is likely to be of *Life Is Beautiful* or similar representations. A recent scholarly example of this critique in Italy was made by historian David Bidussa. In his view, there is a clear-cut distinction between "rational" and "emotive" (i.e. "irrational") commemorations of the Holocaust, and the increasing preponderance of the latter prefigures a dire future for Holocaust commemoration.[55] However, rejecting these "Americanized" approaches outright fails to acknowledge that most people experience history in individual and emotional terms, and that this form of engagement is not necessarily passive or escapist. Such engagement can lead to the development of forms of ethical thinking that grow out of the empathic relationship with the "prosthetic memories" provided by mass culture.[56] After all, American melodrama serves as a model through which American culture articulates its desire for justice and democracy. The emphasis here is placed on justice achieved through suffering, sacrifice and victimhood, a scenario that can only become more relevant in large parts of contemporary Europe, where political ideologies and grand narratives have lost much of their appeal.[57]

A final example of the importance of context-specific factors in shaping the Italian debate on the Americanization of the Holocaust (or the lack thereof, as in this case) is offered by the 2002 miniseries *Perlasca: The Courage of a Just Man*. The miniseries presents features that have been intermittently accused of being Americanized. However, like with *Schindler's List*, the specific political-cultural context of its release focused its reception on other points. Specifically, the charge of Americanizing the Holocaust was never made because this story of a fascist-turned-rescuer of over 5,000 Hungarian Jews was praised across the board as a

---

55 David Bidussa, *Dopo l'ultimo testimone* (Turin: Einaudi, 2009), 8.

56 Marnie Hughes-Warrington, *History Goes to the Movies: Studying History on Film* (London: Routledge, 2007), 90–92; Alison Landsberg, *Prosthetic Memory: The Transformation of American Remembrance in the Age of Mass Culture* (New York: Columbia University Press, 2004), 15, 126; Natan Sznaider, "The Americanization of Memory: The Case of the Holocaust," in Beck, Sznaider, and Winter, ed., *Global America*, 185.

57 Linda Williams, *Playing the Race Card: Melodrama of Black and White from Uncle Tom to O.J. Simpson* (Princeton, NJ: Princeton University Press, 2001), 26.

display of specifically Italian virtues.[58] Although particularly congenial to the post-fascist right, the miniseries, with its emphasis on the supposed national qualities of compassion and kindness, attempted to appeal to a much broader political spectrum. In other words, it served an eminently national purpose, and no one discussed it as "Americanized," let alone in the derogatory sense used at other times in the past. For this reason commentators were oblivious to the miniseries' style and shortcomings, and the charge of "Americanization"-"banalization"-"trivialization" failed to materialize. The example of the miniseries *Perlasca* once again demonstrated the importance of context in shaping the degree of intensity in the Italian debate on the Americanization of the Holocaust.

Conclusion

The tone and intensity of debates on the Americanization of the Holocaust depend on social, political and cultural circumstances. The broadcast of *Holocaust* in 1979 met with criticism, especially from the communist and radical left. In this context, marked by the Cold War and the backlash of the Vietnam War, the Americanization of the Holocaust was used with clearly negative connotations, especially in Italy and West Germany. In the radically different political climate of the 1990s, the Americanization of the Holocaust was not an issue of primary importance, as shown by the Italian and German reception of *Schindler's List*. This is especially notable when compared with the French reaction, which was marked by the contingent political frictions between France and the US. In Italy, the discussion of the Americanization of the Holocaust around *Life Is Beautiful*,

---

58 Millicent Marcus, *Italian Film in the Shadow of Auschwitz* (Toronto: University of Toronto Press, 2007), 125–39; Emiliano Perra, "Legitimizing Fascism through the Holocaust? The Reception of the Miniseries *Perlasca: un eroe italiano* in Italy," *Memory Studies* 3:2 (2010). There are different assessments of these themes; see as examples Milly Buonanno, *Italian Tv Drama and Beyond: Stories from the Soil, Stories from the Sea* (Bristol, UK: Intellect, 2012), 201–12; Emiliano Perra, "Between National and Cosmopolitan: 21st-Century Holocaust Television in Britain, France, and Italy," in Axel Bangert, Robert Gordon, and Libby Saxton, eds, *Holocaust Intersections: Genocide and Visual Culture at the New Millennium* (London: Legenda, 2013), 24–45; Emiliano Perra, "Good Catholics, Good Italians: Religion and Rescue in Recent Italian Holocaust Dramas," *The Italianist* 33:2: Film Issue: Televisionisms (2014): 156–169. On Perlasca, see Enrico Deaglio, *The Banality of Goodness: The Story of Giorgio Perlasca* [La banalità del bene: Storia di Giorgio Perlasca], trans. Gregory Conti (Notre Dame, IN: University of Notre Dame Press, 1998); Dalbert Hallenstein and Carlotta Zavattiero, *Giorgio Perlasca: Un italiano scomodo* (Milan: Chiarelettere, 2010).

this time raised by the political Right, and the complete lack of discussion of the same theme with regard to the miniseries *Perlasca*, further proves that debates on the Americanization of the Holocaust outside the United States are not primarily about the cultural products themselves, but about their context of reception. More importantly, often these debates are not even primarily about the Holocaust.

Dana Rufolo

The Creation of Characters That Condemn and Characters That Redeem in American and Austrian Dramas About the Holocaust

Abstract: *American dramas use the Holocaust to comment on American values or invite the audience to identify with the altruism or intelligence of the characters. Since the 1980s, the Austrian public is now prepared to be critical of its own heritage, because the plays do not only portray characters who behave despicably, but also altruistic characters.*

Dramatists are confronted with the expectation that representations of the Holocaust require staging an extreme form of violence to remain truthful to history. When violence is re-invented on stage, the audience has a chance to experience horror directly through pity and fear, as they watch what is happening on stage. The nature of this violence, however, is always tempered by the aesthetic context of the drama. Recently there was a mysterious case at Vienna's Burgtheater where persons unknown removed the actor's prop or stage suicide knife and put an authentic knife in its place.[1] When the moment in the plot came for the character to commit suicide, it was not artificial stage blood that coursed from his neck, but his own. That specific performance might be the perfect dramatization of the horror element in the Holocaust, for it captured the devastating moment of surprise. However, it was a theatrical accident. When violence is acted out in classical Holocaust-themed plays of the 1980s such as the American Joan Schenkar's *The Last of Hitler* (1982) or the British Peter Barnes' *Laughter!* (1978), the violence is staged; the actors feel physically safe as does the audience, even if they are emotionally involved.

Nonetheless, theater helps address the "Why did this happen?" question by pushing the original decisive moment further back into durational time. The audience sees how violence is engendered. Violence is less likely to appear to arrive *ex nihilo*. The story—in this case, the story of violent anti-Semitism—is pushed back to an earlier starting point in human motivation. The audience sees the antecedent formation of attitudes that result in violence in a way that is always more or less self-implicating. This is achieved by permitting the dramatic action to

---

1   Daniel Pearse, "Actor slits his own throat as knife switch turns fiction into reality," *The Guardian*, 11 December 2008.

originate in a character; it takes on a human shape, a human dimension. Because the eruption of uncontrolled and character-engulfing violence is omitted from the stage play, characters drive the action–even if the plot portrays the horrific or the inconceivable. Since the action has not overwhelmed the characters, a character-driven play about the Holocaust will appear to humanize the action. Without a character at the crux of the events–both causative agent and one who is being acted upon–there would be no drama.

Of course in the case of these humanistic dramas, the characters must have consistent attributes if the audience is to identify with them. Character cannot be dominated by plot, nor can the character be fragmented into radically opposing personality traits at war within the person. Such is the case in five dramas considered in this essay: the American plays *Incident at Vichy* (1964) and *Broken Glass* (1994) by Arthur Miller and *A Bright Room Called Day* by Tony Kushner (1987), and the Austrian plays *Heldenplatz* (1988) by Thomas Bernhard and *Jedem das Seine* (produced in several theatres as of 2006 and still unpublished) by Silke Hassler and Peter Turrini. Although the plays reflect the national origin of their playwrights, all of these dramas share the virtue of dissipating conflict through character-controlled resolutions that are verbal rather than physically violent. Significantly, there are startling similarities between these plays, even though the Austrian dramas are decades more recent than the American ones. These later arrivals indicate that the process of casting violence inherent in the Holocaust into a "how come?" character drama that softens the implicit violence, is taking far longer in Austria than it did in America, for obvious historical reasons.[2]

---

2   In her 2013 article "Austria's Post-89: Staging Suppressed Memory in Elfriede Jelinek's and Thomas Bernhard's Plays *Burgtheater* and *Heldenplatz*," *European Studies: A Journal of European Culture, History and Politics* 30:1 (2013): 271–272, Veronika Zangl explains, "Austria's historically and geographically close relationship with countries of the former Eastern bloc may suggest an important shift of its socio-political memory in 1989. However, a crucial caesura did not take place in 1989 but in the years before. Especially the Waldheim affair in 1986 brought about decisive changes. The focal point of the affair was Austria's problematic memory politics concerning National Socialism, which has regularly been dealt with in the cultural sphere but scarcely directly in the political sphere. The years between the 'Anschluss' in 1938 and the foundation of the Second Republic in 1945 not only faded by reasons of international law, sustained by post-war power politics, but the years also disappeared from Austria's historiography. Furthermore, hardly any cultural productions such as novels, plays, poems or operas deal with the Second World War and the Holocaust, which is all the more surprising against the backdrop of Austria's widely accepted status as a cultural nation."

Austrian and American Experiences of the Holocaust

America and Austria are on opposite sides of the Holocaust experience. As Silke Hassler and Peter Turrini wrote in 2010 about their play *Jedem das Seine*, "One of our aims was to take this still-neglected chapter in Austrian history, this specifically Austrian repression of the memory of events that took place in plain sight, and to bring it into the open."[3] Thomas Bernhard had already caustically pointed out this Austrian trait of amnesia in his *Heldenplatz* when the play opened in November 1988 at Vienna's Burgtheater. He hinted that the main characters' depressed moods stemmed from the singular event when the mass of Austrians cheered for Hitler as their country was annexed to Germany, and then conveniently forgot about their enthusiasm after the war ended. How can the authors of *Jedem das Seine* still talk about the lack of performances about the Holocaust as if Bernhard's drama had never existed? It is because the Austrian attitude towards its own history has not yet been culturally fixed. As Veronika Zangl pointed out in her seminal article on staging suppressed memory in Austria, "the consensual memory device is definitely obsolete, instead Austria's cultural memory is divided into reactionary and diversifying memory discourses." There has been a progression from an acceptance of silence in respect to the Holocaust, to viewing the Austrian state and its people as victims, to eventually listening to, if not internalizing, the criticism of Thomas Bernhard and others (Elfriede Jelinek among them) who addressed the issue of Austrians as perpetrators of Holocaust-related crimes. In effect, *Jedem das Seine* suggests that the Austrians have a tendency to let go of guilt culturally by suggesting that the Austrian response was a human response, not a nationally-determined one. This is because the redemptive character is introduced to the Holocaust-depicting stage action, and the redemptive quality of the behavior of many of the characters in *Jedem das Seine* masks the brutality of the Holocaust. It is surprisingly similar to an earlier play with a redemptive nature, *Incident at Vichy*. This was one of the first dramas in the United States to address the subject.

Americans never had to internalize guilt for the unfathomable crime against humanity that is the Holocaust. Instead, they were compelled to either identify the perpetrators of genocidal crimes as in some way human, raising the possibility that such evil is universally infectious or else to classify the crimes of the

---

3   "Irreconcilable Opposites," A translation from the German of publicity about *Jedem das Seine* before its premiere on 25 March 2010 at the Theater in der Josefstadt, Vienna issued by the playwrights' agent Thomas Sessler Verlag GmbH (www.sesslerverlag.at).

Shoah as isolated and having been perpetrated by the non-American "other."[4] In *Incident at Vichy* (1964) Arthur Miller suggests that the Holocaust was an isolated and European historic event but that the fortuitous presence of persons of noble character from time to time means that the potential for a humanistic response to evil is contained within all human beings everywhere.[5] In Kushner's *A Bright Room Called Day*, which was staged before it was published at San Francisco's Eureka Theatre in October of 1987, the position is taken that evil can potentially transfer across national borders. And in *Broken Glass*, Miller suggests that knowledge of the Holocaust provokes illness that invades and installs itself in susceptible characters (in this case, American Jews), leaving them speechless sand helpless.

These five dramas attempt to find a retrospective interpretation of the Holocaust that balances condemnation with redemption. For this reason, they communicate messages about the Holocaust in a dramatic form that eschews staged violence. They do so by focusing on characters who themselves act in ways which condemn or ways which redeem. These plays are character-driven. They dramatize aspects of the Holocaust by converting history into good or bad characters. Rather than replicating acts of violence, these plays use specific types of characters: those who are bad and are condemned by history, and those who are good and who redeem the human condition through noble or humanistic acts.

This essay focuses on the nature of the characters that American and Austrian playwrights have chosen to entrust with their holocaust-grieving or holocaust-warning plays. In a meta-communicative way the characters are the message; they embody the nexus of forgiveness or the absence of forgiveness for a historic act that these playwrights do not reproduce on stage. The characters in these plays are decoys that are used to distract from the impact of the Holocaust. They behave with nobility and are therefore better than most, or they act with self-interest uppermost and are as cowardly as one might expect in the range of human behavior. As such, the characters in these plays are drawn realistically, with some tendency towards idealization.

---

4   To this end, Andrew Furman's observation of an internal American competition for the title of the "most suffering" of tribes, which is between the American of African descent and the American of Jewish affiliation, should not be overlooked. See page 5 in *Contemporary Jewish American Writers and the Multicultural Dilemma, Return of the Exiled* (Syracuse, NY: Syracuse University Press, 2000): "Indeed, it is difficult not to see the inscription on the dedication page of Toni Morrison's *Beloved* (1987), "Sixty Million and More," as the author's self-conscious trumping of Jewish victimhood."
5   3 December 1964 at the ANTA Washington Square Theatre in New York City.

And though all five plays deal with the Holocaust, the fact remains that there is a time delay between the American and the Austrian confrontation of the event. Austrian works on the subject produced in the 2010s correspond to American dramas on the subject from the twentieth century. Miller's *Incident at Vichy* has thematic parallels with Hassler and Turrini's *Jedem das Seine*. Significantly, more than 45 years of history intervene between these two dramas. Miller's dates from 1964 and Hassler and Turrini have no plans to publish theirs, although it has had a rich production history beginning at the Stadttheater in Klagenfurt (March 2006-June 2007) as well as in Vienna (January 2010-June 2011) and at the Theater and Orchester GmbH of Neubrandenburg/Neustrelitz from June 2010 until July 2012. Both plays dramatize how a group of Jews who have been arrested and imprisoned by Nazi officials behave during their captivity. Miller stresses the presence of the exceptional individual who acts according to his own moral standards. Hassler and Turrini stress that even an exceptional group of people (two groups actually— the Austrian peasant group and the Jewish prisoner group) must succumb to historic inevitability.

America: From a Safe Distance

Incident at Vichy is one of two plays by Arthur Miller that focus on the Holocaust. The other, which is slipping into the timeless dramatic corpus judging by its 2010–11 London revival, is *Broken Glass* (1994). There are parallels between *Incident at Vichy* and *Jedem das Seine*. Both have a dependence on humanistic characters that disperse the violent impact of the Holocaust. While, for this reason, *Incident at Vichy* is the obvious Miller play of choice for this discussion, looking at *Broken Glass* will help clarify the point being made in this paper, which is that even with a lag of nearly half a century between the plays, on both sides of the Atlantic the history of the Holocaust is being mined for individual examples of bravery and humanistic behavior.[6] Re-creating the violence of the historic event, for whatever reasons the playwrights might have, no longer seems palatable.

Broken Glass interpolates the European social and historical realities of the how and the why of the Holocaust into American reality by transforming historic facts into abnormal psychology. Unlike *Incident at Vichy*, which is set in Europe, *Broken Glass* is set in New York. The year is 1938. The Jewish Sylvia Gellburg constantly refers to the incidents around the *Kristallnacht*, and becomes acutely disturbed by the photos published in a New York newspaper of grown Jewish men being forced

---

6   When discussing Arthur Miller's opus, I use the terms "humanistic" and "noble" interchangeably.

to clean streets with toothbrushes while being jeered by an Aryan crowd. She is so disturbed that she becomes psychosomatically ill. Her friendly Jewish neighborhood doctor practices psychotherapy on her in a homespun way; he delves with temerity into the psychosomatic connection between Sylvia's "hysterical paralysis" (there are no physical causes) and the fact that her husband, Phillip Gellburg, despises his own Jewishness. The emphasis on the physical dysfunction of this American woman in light of the psychological links back to European Jewry was accentuated in the star-studded revival at the Vaudeville Theatre in London. In that production, Phillip, played by Antony Sher, absent-mindedly sits down in his wife's wheelchair during an intense soul-searching conversation that is emotionally painful to both husband and wife. This action takes place immediately before he collapses, the victim of a heart attack. Although this was an insightful directorial decision, the script calls for his wife Sylvia to try to reach and physically assist Phillip as he expires. In that moment, in order to walk towards him, she overcomes her paralysis. Her mobility is restored.[7] Divided as they had been by their relationship to their own Jewishness, ultimately it is as a loving human being free of the racial identity that had paralyzed her that Sylvia the wife reaches out to her husband Phillip.

In *Broken Glass* Miller suggests that the safe distance of America from European conflicts about Jewish racial identity results in a psychological connection to the original nexus of conflict. The geophysical space in which evil happens in Europe is transmuted into psychological space where evil happens to the very bodies of Jewish people in the United States who are confused about their identity. Conceptually classically Greek in this way, Arthur Miller's *Broken Glass* looks at the contiguity between the body politic and the human body—not a king's body as was the case for Sophocles' self-mutilating Oedipus, but a sensitive Jewish woman's body. Miller is relying on the safety of distance—the safety of the relatively tolerant American state, which is removed from the scene of conflict. The American world that is portrayed is not completely safe, because Sylvia is ill and Phillip believes himself to be a victim of anti-Semitism at his workplace. However, there is sufficient safety of distance to convert the suffering of Jews at the hands of the National Socialists into suffering that issues from a tormented inner consciousness. Miller lessens the impact of the European tragedy by drawing it within the framework of

---

7   *Broken Glass* played at the Tricycle Theatre in Kilburn, London in August/September 2011, before transferring to the Vaudeville Theatre in the West End for a run from 14 September 2011 to 10 December 2011.

a melodrama about marriage and its psychological and—in a parody of Freudian psychoanalysis—sexual complexities.

Europe: Scene of the Crimes

The characters in *Incident at Vichy* and in *Jedem das Seine* are less complex. Neither of these plays confounds historical events with psychological ones. In these two dramas, the action takes place in Nazi-occupied territory inhabited by heroic and morally average characters that die before the play ends, or when the historical timeframe of the play comes to an end. Both plays take place on a stage that represents historic spaces that have been erased. In the case of Miller's play, the space is an interrogation building. In Hassler/Torrini's, it is a barn. These spaces are fully occupied with a vitality generated by a confluence of two types of characters: the evil Nazi and the innocent Jew. In *Incident at Vichy*, the audience knows that when the Nazis lose the war they will be forced to surrender their control of the building in which they have interrogated the Jewish characters in the play. In *Jedem das Seine*, the audience is informed by a film-text projected onto a rear stage screen that the Nazi-controlled barn which served to imprison the Jewish characters will be (historically accurately) burned to the ground, taking to their death all the people within. The similarity between both plays is astonishing, not least for having been written and staged 45-years apart.[8]

The condemning, self-loathing *Heldenplatz* by Thomas Bernhard, predates the redemptive *Jedem das Seine* by 20 years, coming on the Austrian national stage, the Burgtheater, after a period of bitter defensiveness and silence.[9] Only when

---

8   In an email correspondence dated 12 June 2010, Silke Hassler replied to the question of whether *Jedem das Seine* had been modeled on *Incident at Vichy*, she replied in the negative: "Das Stück von Arthur Miller hat mich und Peter Turrini bei unserer Arbeit nicht inspiriert, die Übereinstimmung, die Sie sehen, ist also zufällig." (Peter Turrini and I were not inspired by Arthur Miller's play; any similarities you see are coincidental.)

9   Thomas Bernhard's *Heldenplatz* plays against the Kurt Waldheim affair and expresses Bernhard's loathing of his fellow Austrians at that time. Waldheim was elected President of Austria in 1986, and he remained President until 1992; it was discovered that he had been a Wehrmacht officer in Hitler's army during World War Two. In 1988 when *Heldenplatz* premiered, the Austrians were passing through a period of defiance (Bruno Kreisky, former Chancellor of Austria, advertised that the Austrians wouldn't "allow the Jews... tell us who should be our President") and amnesia concerning their past affiliation with the National Socialists. Bernhard's play was meant to be a wake-up call, and when it outraged the public, he fled from Austria and gave the order that his plays should never be produced in his native country.

Heldenplatz had its world premiere in Vienna in 1988, could Austrian drama begin to address moral issues like evil and passive personality types or good and altruistic ones. And it certainly took that long before it could publically take pride in small acts of heroism on the part of the Austrians.[10] This journey into re-examining history from an idealizing distance took nearly two generations before the reality could be acknowledged in a work of drama. Analysts believe the change occurred around the time of Kurt Waldheim's election to the presidency of Austria in 1986.[11] For the Americans, their earlier treatment of the Holocaust is an indication that as a nation they chose not to go through various soul-searching stages and felt they could re-write the Holocaust into an American drama about noble and needy characters without having to ask the fundamental question of why such horror happened in the first place. One could interpret this dearth of soul-searching as a lacuna. One possible answer as to why this might have been is to be found in Andrew Fruman.[12] But this is a line of inquiry that falls outside the parameters of the present paper.

Incident at Vichy takes place after the French have capitulated to the Nazis in Vichy, France in 1942. Men have been rounded up for a forced examination of their papers. They are suspected of being Jews. One non-Jew in the group is a gypsy. The other non-Jew among them is an Austrian nobleman, von Berg. He imagines he has been detained because he has "a certain standing. My name is a thousand years old, and they know the danger if someone like me is perhaps… not vulgar enough" (23). To von Berg, Nazism is "an outburst of vulgarity" (23). Of them all, von Berg is the most confident character, and furthermore the one who is sufficiently relaxed to be able to listen and learn from Leduc, a Jew and the only other individual presented as exceptional in the incarcerated group. Leduc

---

10 In her "The Future of Holocaust Literature: German Studies Association 2013 Banquet Speech," *German Studies Review* 37:2 (2014), 393, Ruth Klüger captures the contemporary attitude towards 'Holocaust literature' when she writes that "the arts have a special problem…because they promise pleasure, they engender what you might call Holocaust aesthetics. That term is a provocation, since it is an oxymoron and the reader might rightfully ask: What can be aesthetic about the Holocaust?? More than any other literary content, the Holocaust as subject overwhelms the sublime entertainment that we expect of an aesthetic construct." In other words, the nature of the Austrian need for depiction of the brutalizing Holocaust on stage has changed in the direction of a balance between aesthetics and history which resembles a far earlier (historic) American need. This is not a static need, therefore, but a stage in a continually historically evolving attitude to the historic event, (see pages 392–393).

11 See note 2.

12 Quoted in note 3.

is the most educated person in the room; he is a medical doctor. He practices Socratic argumentation on von Burg, leading the nobleman to acknowledge that having an artistic sensibility does not ensure that one will be racially tolerant, even though initially van Burg thinks the contrary. Leduc says to von Berg, "It's astounding you can go on with (your curious idea of human nature) in these times…I know the violence inside these (Nazi) people's heads…all this suffering is so pointless—it can never be a lesson, it can never have a meaning." (61) At the climax of the drama, von Berg saves Leduc by providing him with a pass that will permit him to depart the detention center. Von Berg emerges a hero, and Leduc, who has taught von Berg to retain liberal and noble traits, is a secondary, if lesser, hero in Miller's cosmology.

Although Arthur Miller is famously the common man's playwright, in *Incident at Vichy* he chose a dramatic resolution that is more problematic. The person behaving generously and nobly is a rich nobleman. Character stereotypes have been preserved; there is nothing unexpected or out-of-type in any of these characters' behaviors. The implication is that only von Burg is of sufficient standing to be able to act heroically.[13] The other characters remain frightened and small; even though the playwright had leeway to ennoble them to some extent, he chose not to do so.

In effect, Arthur Miller used the setting of Vichy as an exotic locale—as the non-American "other place"—in order to infuse his own ideas of morality into a setting that would be unfamiliar enough to American audiences so that they could accept the value system he himself holds. One can conclude that Miller is himself an admirer of European nobility and that he carries residual ideas of their class superiority.[14] The play *Incident at Vichy* gives pleasure to American

---

13 In *Remembering and Imagining the Holocaust* (Cambridge, UK: Cambridge University Press, 2006), Christopher Bigsby reveals biographical information about Arthur Miller that perhaps explains that he may have been thinking in para-dramatic terms when creating the character of von Berg. Bigsby informs us that Miller's psychoanalyst, "who had hidden in Vichy before the Germans moved in" told a story about a friend of his wife's, "an Austrian prince called Josef von Schwarzenberg, who had refused to cooperate with the Nazis and spent much of the war in France engaged in menial work." Bigsby suggests that the character von Berg was created in order to honour the courage of Prince von Schwarzenberg. (187). For Miller, here historical facts took precedence over the structural dramatic meaning embedded in the play.

14 Repeatedly, Miller and his morally noble characters are intertwined. As is evident from reading the records and as stated implicitly by Alice Griffin in *Understanding Arthur Miller* (Columbia, SC: University of South Carolina Press, 1996), Miller's honourable behaviour in front of the House Un-American House Activities in 1956 where he refused to "name names" stating that this would be a betrayal of his own self–and so

audiences because they can imagine themselves as altruistic and self-sacrificing as von Burg is, or as clever and convincing as Leduc. It is a play that absolutely fails to confront the moral truths and the universal implications of the Holocaust by having Americans zone out of involvement in the events.

If Miller asserts that America has too many good citizens for anything like the rise of Nazism to ever happen between its shores, Tony Kushner asserts quite the contrary in his play *A Bright Room Called Day*, which premiered in New York in 1989. The kind of Holocaust that Kushner imagines, however, differs significantly from the historical event. It is linked to sexual intolerance and to a malaise at the root of American democracy. It is similar to Thomas Bernhard's *Heldenplatz* in that the play is full of what Gene Plunka calls "cynicism and fatalism."[15] Like Bernhard, Kushner is ashamed of his nation's system of politics. Even democracy is called into question, because voting can result in electing persons who are not fit to govern. However, unlike Bernhard's *Heldenplatz* where the characters are weighed down by their guilt and choose to condemn themselves, Kushner's characters choose to rage against a political system that is said to resemble the early years of the Third Reich. The play calls the audience to political action and change by asking them to look at the existence of evil in German history, and to assume that this same evil can spread out of control in the United States. Kushner believes that "the more we know about history, the more we realize…that it really does return, it never ends…Even after the holocaust the monsters are still among us."[16]

Kushner's drama takes place in a Berlin apartment during 1932 and 1933. The apartment is owned by Agnes, who shares it with a group of friends including two actresses, a cinematographer, a homosexual working for a sex institute, an artist, and an author. Some of them are Communist sympathizers, and two are Communist party members who accept the dictates of the Russian Comintern. Besides

---

being accused of contempt of court–is identical to how John Proctor behaves–and which costs him his life–in *The Crucible*. (Griffin, 7) Director Elia Kazan reports in his diaries that the character Quentin in *After the Fall* was "about Miller personally" because, like Quintin "Arthur Miller was honestly and profoundly committed to notions of virtue." This quote comes from Martin Gottfried's book *Arthur Miller: His Life and Work* (Boston, MA: Da Capo Press, 2003), 352. In his autobiography, Miller claimed that identifying as a writer with the failures of the world was a strategy counterbalanced by "in the real world" him "working day and night to achieve what glory and superiority my art might win me." (Griffin, 8).

15 "The cynicism and fatalism of *Bright Room* derives from several despairing events in Kushner's life during 1984–1985." Gene Plunka, *Holocaust Drama: The Theatre of Atrocity* (Cambridge, UK: Cambridge University Press, 2009), 133.

16 Ibid.

a devil, there is also a ghost character, "Die Alte," a starving resident of Berlin who appears in the contemporary present. Then there is a separate character that does not belong to any other group. She is a contemporary woman of the political left named Zillah whom Kushner has asserted does not represent his opinion, though this is a dubious assertion.[17]

The contemporary character Zillah is deeply dissatisfied with the direction of American politics in the late 1980s. She considers the election of Ronald Reagan as president to be as outrageous as was President Paul von Hindenburg's appointment of Adolf Hitler to the position of German Chancellor. Zillah is also absorbed by a book she has come across, that contains photographs of the Holocaust era. Zillah makes much of the fact that there is a photograph in the book that shows one woman in the crowd who is not giving the *Sieg Heil*. Her arm is lowered. This woman goes unnoticed because of the size of the crowd. Her act of rebellion—as Zillah interprets her action—is enough in itself. It is possible, of course, that there is another reason for this woman not having raised her arm. That is to say, her lowered arm in the photograph may not necessarily be an indication that she is willing to risk life and limb to save a Jewish neighbor. Kushner, however, does not have his character engage in such dialectic. Zillah unquestioningly labels this woman a hero. By doing so, she acquires some of the heroism of that anonymous woman. She is herself heroic to protest against the system within which she lives comfortably.

In Kushner's cosmology it is easy for Zillah to take a stand. She protests from a position of safety. Her sense of security, as well as that of the other characters, is revealed dramatically in the language they all use so playfully. Repartee is a strong presence in the play. Because of the wit they continuously display, the characters are charming. Their willingness to compromise principles for the sake of advancement and sexual gratification—a common theme in the play—is not subject to critical moral scrutiny. On the contrary. Their revelations of human desire and appetite are dramatically upheld as appealing because they are frank and purport to tell the truth.

For example, Zillah considers herself daring when she suggests that the vote for Ronald Reagan is equivalent to tacitly permitting a new Hitler to reach prominence.[18] Indeed, Kushner refers to his inserting the character of Zillah, who is

---

17 Tony Kushner, *Bright Room, Production Notes*, page x: "The impulse to interrupt the Weimar-era play with Zillah Katz's editorializing–and she is not the playwright–came from a curiosity about the necessity of metaphorizing political content in theatre." *A Bright Room Called Day* (New York: Theatre Communications Group, 1994).

18 Ibid., 107–108, 162.

a "contemporary American Jewish woman, 30s, BoHo/East Village New Wave with Anarcho-Punk tendencies" as potentially "dangerous."[19] In his *Weltanschau*, it is radical merely to exercise the right of free speech because in doing so one helps highlight a respected American freedom. One need not really change anything in the comfortable security of 1980s America. It is a safe place to live after all. To rage against a system yet to continue to live within it is the extent of the moral responsibility that Kushner demands of his characters.

Kushner has, in effect, employed what Vivian Patraka calls in her paper a *trope* or "the figurative mode of analogizing, e.g., the displacing and distorting in language of an experience by means of comparison or assimilation to their experience."[20] Analogies between the events in Germany and events in America tell us, according to Hayden White (quoted in Patraka), "what…to look for in our culturally encoded experience in order to determine how we should feel about the thing represented" (70). This is precisely the problem: Kushner's play looks inward culturally. The Holocaust becomes something to use, a weapon of attack against home-grown cultural values.

Austria: Confronting Your Own Heritage

The two Austrian dramas under discussion are realistic and are set in Austria. The Holocaust is not a metaphor, nor is it something that happened in another geopolitical space. Antipathetic Jewish characters already figure in Austrian drama as early as 1800, according to Charlene Lea.[21] After World War II Thomas Bernhard started a trend of self-interrogation concerning the accepted prejudice against the Jews. But it is only recently that major Viennese theaters have showcased dramas that castigate the Austrians as exhibiting serious character flaws connected to their tacit racial prejudice.[22] *Winterreise* by Elfriede Jelinek, which critically examines

---

19 Tony Kushner, *Bright Room*, production notes, page xi: "A third possibility, one not yet attempted in any of the play's productions, is to do the play without *Zillah*. … though I believe it makes the play less difficult and *possibly* less *dangerous*."

20 "Contemporary Drama, Fascism and the Holocaust," 70.

21 Charlene Lea, *Emancipation, Assimilation and Stereotype: The Image of the Jew in German and Austrian Drama, 1800–1850 (Modern German Studies)* (Bonn: Bouvier Verlag, 1978), 1–8.

22 In an email dated 30 November 2010 from the press officer Christiane Huemer-Strobele of the Theater in der Josefstadt, I was informed that this review of the Austrian relationship to World War Two was a policy decided by the theater's director Herbert Föttinger: "yes, it is distinct theater policy to present plays like *Jedem das Seine*, *Heldenplatz*, *Moser*, *Jugend ohne Gott*, *Cabaret* which all deal with Nazy (sic) politics and holocaust."

the Austrian personality, opened at the Burgtheater in 2012. The play *Moser* by Austrian playwright Franzobel premiered at the Theater in der Josefstadt in 2010. *Moser* reflects the continued Austrian ambiguity concerning the Holocaust. In it a Hitler character is presented as a God personage and is arguably, intentionally a seductively attractive character. It is a play that uses fragmented character, linguistically fractured speech and inconclusive geographically located scenography in an attempt to recreate the irrational state of mind characterized by the era of National Socialism. Also, a revival of the play *Professor Bernhardi* (1912) by the Austrian playwright Arthur Schnitzler ran from 2011 until 2013 at the Burgtheater. This 1912 play features a medical doctor, Dr Bernhardi, denying a priest the right to perform extreme unction for a patient who is unaware he is dying and who, in the doctor's opinion, should remain unaware. Because Dr Bernhardi is Jewish, his medically sound decision is interpreted as racist and becomes an excuse for the rampant anti-Semitic feelings sweeping Vienna. A savagely unforgiving production of Thomas Bernhard's damning play associating moral corruption with Austria's worship of Nazi figures of authority, *Vor dem Ruhestand* (1979), opened at the Theater in der Josefstadt in Vienna in September of 2013, and a revival of his *Heldenplatz* opened in 2010. A frank acknowledgement of Elfriede Jelinek and Thomas Bernhard as the voices of the Austrian conscience is very recent. It was recognized in 2013 in Zangl's article on staging suppressed memory in plays by Elfriede Jelinek and Thomas Bernhard."[23] At last the Austrian public is taking stock of how their nation aided and abetted, on Austrian soil, the genocide of the Holocaust.

One reason the Austrian public is now prepared to be critical of their own heritage is because they are being exposed not only to plays with characters who behave despicably but also to plays with characters who are altruistic and who therefore appear to be redemptive. Bernhard's *Heldenplatz* reminds the Austrians of their ambivalent reaction to the Nazi takeover of their country in 1938. It was revived in 2010 by the Theater in der Josefstadt. Likewise Hassler and Turrini's *Jedem das Seine*, entered the repertoire of the Theater in der Josefstadt in 2010. *Jedem Das Seine* translated the Holocaust into a de-traumatized form of experience via a distribution of good and evil characters and by creating trust in language's ability to carry the emotions of these characters.

In some concentration camps, in addition to the motto "*Arbeit macht frei*," in iron letters on the entrance gate, there was another motto that read "*Jedem das Seine*." This expression would ordinarily be translated as "To each his own"

---

23 Zangl, "Austria's Post-89."

but during the Nazi era in Germany it meant more precisely, "To each his due."
The title of Hassler/Turrini's play references this Nazi motto. The play itself is a
dramatization of a historic fact; ironically, prisoners lose their lives after the war
has ended. As the playwrights wrote about *Jedem das Seine*:

"At the end of April 1945, as the Provisional Government of the newly rein-
stated democratic Republic of Austria is being declared in Vienna…a group of
Jewish prisoners on a forced march through the Austrian countryside to the concentration camp Mauthausen are locked inside a barn….Our play *Jedem das Seine*
is concerned with a chapter of Austrian history that no one wants to remember,
even today, namely the death marches of Jewish prisoners through the Austrian
countryside in the spring of 1945. On these marches the prisoners met with vile
treatment from the rural population, but also with the opposite, for there are
testimonies of astonishing willingness to help them in their suffering."[24]

The Jewish prisoners in this play are transferred from a camp in Hungary to
a barn in an Austrian village. They are kept locked in the barn under the watch-
ful eye of a Nazi farmer and his superior. The farmer's wife Traudl Fasching is
presented as a character whose heroism has been engendered by despair. She has
lost her only son on the Russian front and is sick of the "Stalin organ" as she calls
the continuous radio talk about the war. When her Nazi husband Stefan initially
tells her not to take pity on the wretched prisoners of mostly Viennese origin, he
says, "They are Jews, nothing more." Traudl shouts back at him in Austrian dialect, "They're people!"[25] She then feeds them some potatoes and later some soup.
In exchange, the dynamic, naïve Hungarian Jew, Ludwig Gandalf proposes that
they all rehearse and stage an operetta in the barn. No sooner said than done. The
bedraggled, frightened group and their captors start to rehearse, at first without
signs of artistic talent of any kind, but eventually they are a convincing orchestra
of piano, violin, fiddle, and accordion, and a chorus complete with male and female lead singer. The audience is often treated to a rendition of the song "*Wiener
Blut*" accompanied by the violin of a character—an old Jewish professor. We do

---

24 See note 2.

25 The text is taken from the script that I was lent and which is in the possession of the
    playwrights. It reads:
    "Stefan: Ein Jud is er, sonst nix.
    Traudl: Und du bist ein Depp, sonst nix.
    Stefan: Jedem das Seine. Lieber a Depp als a Jod."
    (Stefan: He's a Jew, if anything / Traudl: And you're a dork or nothing. / Stefan: Each to
    his own. Better a dork than a Jew.)
    (Manuscript, 36).

not hear the entire concert because *Jedem das Seine* ends there. A final projection on the black rear wall of the set inserts the events of the drama into the events of history: when the Nazis are defeated, those still in control of the territory on which the barn is located lock its door and set it on fire. There are no survivors.

In *Staging Holocaust Resistance*, Gene Plunka champions the drama of resistance. He advocates for plays which dramatically re-enact moments of heroism when people of the Jewish faith, the Christian faith, or atheists risk their lives to save victims of extermination through rebellion, underground resistance or, in the case of the power elite who had the chance to issue visas or false baptismal records, subterfuge.[26] Plunka admits that there are abysmally few records of resistance to the Final Solution, but points out that failed resistance, almost always inevitable, would not have been recorded.[27] He admires documentary-like dramas that have been produced about acts of resistance, and urges that more such plays see the light of day so as to honor the dead and keep the memory of their struggles and the terrible historic facts alive. *Jedem das Seine* seems to be of this genre: a play recording a rare example of resistance that was historically documented. However, the production and even the multi-media approach belie such a favorable interpretation. By switching to a filmed message at its conclusion, the playwrights ensure that the audience is spared the sight of the final violent conflagration that took the lives of *all* the occupants of the barn. The scenes in the barn include its owners Traudl Fasching and her Nazi-sympathizer husband, as well as their housemaid. Visually, we associate these happy music-loving non-Jewish Austrian people with the community of musicians in the barn, as an integral part of the group. The alternative reading which conforms to the historic facts, in which the Faschings are *not* locked inside the barn when the fire starts, is not something the audience gets to witness.[28] It is even a remote possibility that the Faschings

---

26 Plunka, *Staging Holocaust Resistance*, 3–23.

27 Ibid., 208, 209.

28 This is the text projected onto the screen that ends *Jedem das Seine*: "In der Nacht auf den 2.Mai 1945 wurde der Stadel von betrunkenene Nazioffizieren und einigen Dorf-bewohnern angezündet. Alle jüdischen Häftlinge sind verbrannt, keiner von ihnen hat überlebt." (On the second of May 1945, drunken Nazi officials and some villagers set fire to the barn. All of the Jewish prisoners were burnt to death, none of them survived (Manuscript, 98). The careful wording does not reference Traudl, her Nazi sympathizer husband, or their housemaid. It can be read as an attempt to obfuscate the goings-on during 2 May so as to avoid audience asking what their share of responsibility had been for the fire and the fate of the people inside the barn. Also, by using text the playwrights avoided showing their positions and actions during the conflagration, whereas the

---

themselves were among those who started the fire. Thus, the filmed message at the end of the play works as an artistic strategy to divert the audience from considering the alternative and equally valid reading of the death of the prisoners, as an example of Austrian anti-Semitic inhumanity. Furthermore, in the 2010 production at Vienna's Theater in der Josefstadt directed by Herbert Föttinger, the potatoes which the starving Jewish prisoners are offered are raw and the soup they are fed is watery; initially it is a stinted generosity which they receive. As rehearsals take over and the prisoner/villager group works as a whole preparing the musical, the prisoners are offered beer, as demonstrated on stage by the presence of a collection of beer cases filled with empty bottles. This additional nourishment serves to give the prisoners equal status with the non-Jewish Austrians imprisoning them. This sign of well-being is important, since the actors whom the director chose for the role of the Faschings and their housemaid were not costumed so as to appear fat but neither were they emaciated, implying that there had not been a food shortage in their farmland area of Austria in 1945.[29]

Jedem das Seine veers in the direction of character idealization. As in Miller's *Incident at Vichy*, the characters in the production of *Jedem das Seine* have been created so as to have archetypal dimensions and heroic potential. The drama appears to assert that Austrian folk should accept blame for being passive observers of criminal history, but the blame is mitigated. Although the audience is informed that the Jewish prisoners perish in a conflagration, the switch from staged action to the medium of film projection allows the mixed media method to relieve guilt and responsibility. The violence of senseless fire is never represented on stage. Indeed, the message is that the system (represented by film) is more powerful than the individual prisoners and farm household who feed them and join their rehearsals.

---

staging of this final scene could not have avoided putting Traudl and her entourage on stage.

29 The on-stage action of the prisoner Gandolf, driven by maddening hunger, biting into a raw potato is offset by Traudel's line asking if they did not have a way of cooking the potatoes she offers, because "Um Gottes Willen, die sind ja roh, davon bekommts ihr Durchfall oder noch Schlimmeres." (For God's sake, these potatoes are raw; you'll get diarrhoea or something even worst if you eat them like that.) This line's dramatic function is to show the prisoners' hunger, but it also functions to absolve Traudel from the responsibility of offering them cooked potatoes. Her subsequently offering them beer during the rehearsals does exonerate her dramatically. But the initial introduction of food needs to be examined all the same for the sake of understanding the play's position on citizen responsibility during genocidal actions on Austrian soil.

There is a redemptive objective in staging *Jedem das Seine*. Hassler and Turrini structured the play so as to manipulate the Austrian audience into understanding that the Jewish prisoners were just plain Austrians, no more and no less. Traudl treats the prisoners with rough good humor and a measure of respect, and they are of good will toward her and find her attractive. They are willing to identify with her humanitarian position. They are also flattered to see how Jews and non-Jews can create a beautiful performance by working together. Moreover, the playwrights intentionally have many of the Jewish prisoners speak in the Viennese dialect. As Hassler has confirmed, the theme song *Wiener Blut* is a waltz that every Austrian on and off stage knows and loves. It was chosen as the theme song expressly for this reason. Although the song title translates correctly as "The Spirit of Vienna," it literally means, "Vienna Blood" in the sense of "the race of the Viennese." Persons in charge and prisoners alike, all are Austrian at heart, connected by a modern national identity rather than by the outdated racial identities imposed upon them in the past. This is the message of *Jedem das Seine*.

It is also the message of the 2010 revival of Thomas Bernhard's *Heldenplatz* at the Theater in der Josefstadt. In 1988 Bernhard saw his play as a belated admission of guilt over that fact that Austria permitted annexation to the Third Reich without protest. The Heldenplatz of the title is a large square quite close to the Burgtheater off the Ringstrasse in Vienna where Hitler gave his annexation speech to an enthusiastic, noisy and welcoming crowd in 1938.

Heldenplatz opens shortly after Jewish Herr Professor Josef Schuster has committed suicide. He has jumped from the window of his apartment, where acts one and three of the play take place. The apartment overlooks the landmark Heldenplatz. Presumably Josef Schuster committed suicide because he was obsessed by the sound of the cheering crowds of 1938; the cheers he remembers, even though it is 50 years on. This memory has destabilized him, just as it has deranged his wife, who is under psychiatric treatment for repeatedly claiming to be deafened by these cheers. These raucous cheers saturate the auditorium in the original Burgtheater production of 1988. However, in the 2010 revival at the Theater in der Josefstadt these sounds were played backwards at the close of the play.[30] The wife who hears them during the family dinner after the burial of her husband is

---

30 How the crowd sounds reproducing the enthusiastic reception of Adolf Hitler in Vienna on 15 March 1938 are created is a directorial decision. However, the script clarifies they must be heard by the audience. Before Frau Schuster collapses, a guest Professor Robert speaks "während das Massengeschrei vom Heldenplatz herauf an die Grenze des Erträglichen anschwillt" (while the mass outcry from Heldenplatz swells to nearly intolerable limit of volume), *Heldenplatz*, 165.

drawn back into a distorted, inverted memory of the past, and she dies, presumably of a stroke, with these reversed sounds echoing in her ears. With no husband
to keep her in everyday reality, the Hitler-welcoming voices of the crowd have
finally exterminated her.

The cheers are authentic; the audience hears them as well, so the wife Frau
Professor Schuster cannot be called insane. There is a hint of criticism of the wife
in this production, in that she has permitted the evil sounds of the past to drown
out the potentially more humane melodies of the future represented by the chat-
ter about her at the family dining table. However, we do not see her as insane.
As background noise the cheers are also audible to the audience. This revival of
Heldenplatz wishes to remind contemporary Austrians that they are still affected
by this echo from the past and that even if its full impact is attenuated, the memory
remains traumatic.

No production can alter the script, of course. *Heldenplatz* is constructed so
as to drive home the point that Professor Schuster was primarily Austrian and
only secondarily Jewish. This is the same theme at the heart of *Jedem das Seine*,
although Bernhard's Austrian characters are not peasants, but rather the sophis-
ticated pinnacle of Austrian cultural life. Professor Schuster's behavior is typically
Austrian, the audience is told by the Schuster family's maid in a virtual mono-
logue. The maid recounts how "Herr Professor" constantly criticizes his wife,
even going so far as to say she ought never to have been born. This rebuking of
one's family members, a cultural habit permitted in patriarchal Austrian society
in the mid-twentieth century, is a way of turning on a part of one's social self and
psychologically murdering that detested part.[31] But Bernhard's accurate eye for
the Austrian way of life does not stop there. The character Uncle Robert Schuster,
present at the funeral, tells his nieces and nephew how detestable the Austrian
people are. He offers many details about how the nation has increasingly lost its
identity since the war, claiming that there were more National Socialists in Vienna
in the 1980s than there ever were during World War II and that all that is left of the
country is the church and big business. He even criticizes the local press, saying
that they print lies and stupidities for idiots to read; the day of quality journalism
is over. This line often provokes laughter of recognition from audience members
during performances of the play in revival.

---

31 See, for example, Ritchie Robertson, *The 'Jewish Question' in German Literature, 1749–
    1939: Emancipation and its Discontents* (Oxford, UK: Clarendon Press, 1999) and
    http://www.guardian.co.uk/world/2009/mar/19/josef-fritzl-austria-society (accessed
    24 January 2017).

Conclusion

To conclude, the American plays discussed in this paper interpret the Holocaust as a warning that evil exists and that it is perpetual, although sterling good men and women can occasionally thwart it through noble acts of sacrifice or love, or by means of opposition. Those sterling individuals are Americans by default. Arthur Miller and Tony Kushner have failed to imagine the Holocaust as a direct assault on their faith in humanity. Kushner's dramatization of the Fascists' win over the Communists is mired in the American realities surrounding him. He does not perform the act of imagination that would, as it were, place him on the European continent experiencing the unfolding tragedy of the European experience, or, conversely, enable him to translate the scope of the European tragedy into an imagined American experience. Between America and Europe there is a great divide that is not even imagined as traversable. To Kushner, America is a chosen place, gifted by an unquestioned supreme power to be exempt from the taint of insane negative emotions that, when acted upon, lead to frenzy and murder. His is an American rather than an international sense of responsibility.

Miller, on the other hand, has taken offense at the baser instincts of the universal man. His Austrian nobleman must be generous, because generosity is a trait of noblemen. The human condition is to reveal what one is made of, and so the characters in *Incident at Vichy* progressively manifest themselves on stage. By the conclusion of the play, each character has become what he or she is destined to be. The end is, in fact, stasis: a fixed and unmovable core of character as essence. Miller has made a plea bargain. He reduces the criminal aspect of the Nazis, because their barbarity gives a noble character the chance to shine forth. In his play, acts of kindness are inevitable. The good man will always be found, even in a heap of those who are hollow with self-interest and can be perverted through example.

The Austrian plays interpret the genocide of the Holocaust as a warning that their society is capable of turning upon its own members. Hassler and Torrini warn that Austrians committed violent acts on a part of themselves that they had declared repulsive in order to sustain a feeling of inclusiveness and community. Through the representation of a musical drama on stage in the barn (which is itself the stage in the theatre), the playwrights stage a community united in the love of the musical arts which is just as vital as any potentially race-separating Austrian geopolitical community. The audience sees a fabricated community that is inclusive instead of exclusive. Their play *Jedem das Seine* is a character-based drama. The characters have been idealized so as to provide examples of what is to be condemned in the national identity when in fact each and every citizen has a common language, even common dialects, and a common cultural heritage—the

love of joyful songs and music. They even share dietary customs. Both the Austrian and the Jewish Austrians in *Jedem das Seine* eat potatoes. However, some
eat them cooked, and others eat them raw depending on circumstances. Since
it is not inspiring to portray the resistance in condemnatory terms, even those
Austrians who did help out their persecuted neighbors, the heroes and heroines
like Traudl and her entourage, are idealized so as to underline that redemption
is also possible. And by the obfuscation of detail, the overwhelming message of
the production is that national character includes those with personality traits in
which every Austrian can take pride.

Thomas Bernhard comes the closest to offering an imaginative dramatic literature that permits an understanding of the horror couched in the violence of
the Holocaust, because his characters dramatize the complexities of memory as
guilt-laden. *Heldenplatz* has nothing but opinionated characters that condemn
their own culture, but the only path to redemption for these characters is through
self-destruction. Turned inwards upon themselves and their Austrian cultural
rituals, the characters fail to disassociate themselves from the course of history.
Their failure is, ultimately, the necessary failure of human understanding of human actions. And yet, though ignorant of their motives, the characters in these
Austrian plays are at least restrained in their search for a way forward. They do
not trust in dialogue nor do they reject the need to re-create violence in order
to keep the impact of the Holocaust culturally viable. By opening up the stage to
redemptive characters, it is now possible to confront the condemning character
without feeling the force of overwhelming violence. Previously, the condemning
character was alone on stage. Without any counterbalance, the audience experienced this character as so brutalizing that it was unbearable. The only recourse
had been to bury this character behind walls of silence. In present day Holocaust
drama in Austria, the redeeming character and his/her counterpart, the condemning character, are inextricably linked.[32]

---

32 Marie Louise Seeberg, Irene Levin and Claudia Lenz, the authors of *The Holocaust
    as Active Memory* (Farnham, UK: Ashgate Publishing, 2013) point out that "(t)he
    atrocities of the Holocaust are so enormous and the sufferings so deep that words may
    seem inadequate. This feeling may in turn contribute to the silencing of memories....
    Klüger suspects parts of the Holocaust commemoration that builds on notions of the
    'unspeakable' of contributing to a mystification and sacrilization which in the end
    fits the perpetrator's interest in obscuring what 'really happened'." (6) In agreement
    with this statement, it can be argued that the invention of the redemptive character
    sooner or later, depending on which side of the Atlantic one is referring to, advances

This move towards creating characters that represent a spectrum of human responses is perhaps the most significant antidote to James Young's warning that "Holocaust memory (can become) a substitute for real action against contemporary genocide, instead of its inspiration."[33] If, as he suggests, "memory cannot be divorced from the actions taken in its behalf,"[34] then nestling the possibility of identification with the redemptive character within the Holocaust drama is perhaps the best way at the present time in history of ensuring an active commitment to the prevention of genocide, wherever it may occur.

---

the meaning of Holocaust studies and its relevance to a contemporary society which contains a rapidly diminishing population of persons bodily harmed by the Holocaust.

33 James E. Young, "America's Holocaust. Memory and the Politics of Identity," in Hilene Flanzbaum, ed., *The Americanization of the Holocaust* (Baltimore, MD: Johns Hopkins University Press, 1999), 82.

34 Ibid.

Małgorzata Pakier

Between Memory and Post-memory: Once More on the Awkward Marriage of the Holocaust and the American Mass Media

Abstract: *This essay explores the transition from individual experience to collective memory mediated by the mass media. It uses the example of the 1953 broadcast of Hanna Kohner's story which was the first instance of televising the Holocaust experience.*

The problem of the mediation of meanings and the character of the media's influence on the shape of our collective remembering, including Holocaust memory, is broader than just the mass-medialization, i.e., popularization and trivialization, of memory. The relation between historical or biographical experience and its cultural representation and memory is both dynamic and interactive. These relations transcend the simple questions of whether a particular cultural text on the Holocaust is an accurate representation of authentic historical events, or whether there are greater aims that could justify possible misuses. In order to rightfully assess the role of mass media in shaping memory culture, one needs to move away from seeing the media in a static and passive way and take note of their active role in the creation of meanings of the past. This means that media are not merely containers for memories, nor are they merely vehicles ready to carry historical content. Media aren't just tools in the hands of those who remember, negotiate, revive, and annihilate pasts. Media can become active agents in memory processes.[1] Media establish discursive frames, provide or impose narrative styles and formulas of expression, and create and promote particular memory tropes. Thus media not only distribute meanings, they actively participate in their creation and organization.

The 1953 episode of the popular American weekly TV show *This Is Your Life!* carried on the NBC network, casting a Czech-born Holocaust survivor offers insight into the role of mass media in shaping the processes of both cultural and individual memory. The story of Hanna Kohner became a well-known culturally

---

1   It is sufficient to recall here the role the TV series "Holocaust" had played in the German process of coming to terms with the Nazi past. See, for example, Andreas Huyssen, "The Politics of Identification: Holocaust and West Germany," *New German Critique* 19 (1980): 117–136.

transmitted theme since then.[2] Typically the show presented stories of Hollywood celebrities, music legends, Olympic athletes, but more often told of the lives of ordinary unknowns who had experienced major events, including World War II. Hanna Kohner survived Theresienstadt, Auschwitz, and Mauthausen, and subsequently migrated to the United States, becoming the wife of a film producer. Her studio appearance on May 27th, 1953 is believed to be the first postwar instance where the Holocaust was discussed in the context of popular entertainment on TV. As such, it marks a historical moment: the origination point for the dynamic between the mass media, the Holocaust, and memory building.

Hanna Kohner's *This Is Your Life!* segment aired in a social climate still largely insensitive to the historical significance of the Jewish extermination which had not yet become *the Holocaust*. This was a period lacking firm cultural memory frames for these events. The survivors themselves were caught between the past and the present, often conflicted about speaking up or keeping silent. Jeffrey Shandler discusses in detail the challenge presented by Hanna's segment.[3] Here was a televised episode coping with a history that was both so close and so vague at the same time. In Shandler's convincing analysis, he shows that despite the show's stylistic awkwardness viewed from the present day's perspective, the producers did worthwhile memory work in preparing Hanna Kohner's story for presentation to an American audience. After the show Hanna became a prominent figure of cultural memory. In this essay I am interested in the reception her episode has received within the changing context of Holocaust memory discourse since that time. As well, I look at the role that the episode subsequently played in Hanna's and her family's biography. My analysis will be situated within the broader debate about the role the mass media plays in the social and cultural process of referencing the past, or, to use the popular metaphor—in collective remembering.

The Holocaust in a TV show

While *This Is Your Life!* presented the Holocaust in a way that appears inappropriate from today's perspective, the show is nevertheless, an important cultural text in that it was the first treatment of the Holocaust in an entertainment genre. It marks the beginning of the genre of Holocaust representations that is situated on the frontier where seriousness meets entertainment. Notable examples that would

---

2   The article was prepared during the Charles H. Revson Foundation Fellowship at the Center for Advanced Holocaust Studies, USHMM, Washington D.C.

3   Jeffrey Shandler, *While America Watches: Televising the Holocaust* (New York: Oxford University Press, 1999), 27–40.

follow were the TV series *Holocaust* by Marvin J. Chomsky, *Schindler's List*, by Steven Spielberg, or the comedy *Life is Beautiful* by Roberto Benigni. The *This Is Your Life!* episode with Hanna Kohner has been mostly overlooked by memory and media scholars, with the exception of Jeffrey Shandler who discusses it in his book *While America Watches*.

The format for *This Is Your Life!* had the featured guest arrive at the studio unaware that they were chosen to star. The host, Ralph Edwards, would spring the surprise as the camera captured the guest's reaction amidst resounding fanfare and audience applause. The show's promotional materials concede that the producers deemed the authenticity of that first reaction so important that they would cancel an already elaborated theme if the guest happened to learn about the intended surprise.[4] Onstage, the suspense was maintained by the sequential appearance on screen of long-lost relatives and friends of the program's star.

Edwards exploited the technique of heightening anxiety and anticipation for the viewers. "Looking at you, Hanna it is hard to believe that during the seven years of your still short life, you lived a lifetime of fear, terror, and tragedy. You look like a young American girl, just out of college, not at all like a survivor of Hitler's cruel purge of German Jews." When in a later scene a voice of Hanna's wartime friend is heard, the host dramatically announces the appearance of a new guest, "Do you recognize this voice, Hanna? It belongs to a woman who was your friend in four concentration camps." Edwards then recounts how the two arrived at Auschwitz, "You were sent to the so-called showers. Even this was a doubtful procedure because some showers had regular water, others had liquid gas. And you never knew which one you were being sent to."

The narrative about Hanna's wartime experience was constructed in such a way as to balance the moments of pain, like the loss of close relatives, with stories of happy reunions, and the story of romantic love for her second husband with whom she shared a happy life in America.[5] *This Is Your Life!* developed its story line around the theme of a love that began during childhood in Teplice, Czechoslovakia, and was then renewed after years of separation. In the summation that was a part of every episode, the host imparted a message. To Hanna he said, "The never to be forgotten tragic events you experienced have been tempered by the happiness you found here in America." Romantic love and immigration to the United States are two dominant motifs structuring the experience of Hanna Kohner as remade for TV.

---

4   www.thisisyourlife.com (accessed 24 January 2017).
5   Shandler, *While America Watches*, 36.

Setting Memory Frames

This Is Your Life! with Hanna Kohner shows how, within a decade of the war's end, the experience of a survivor could become interactively entangled in the processes of mass cultural production. Biography and media were mutually dependent. Exclusively focusing on either aspect would obscure their complex relationship. The episode with Hanna Kohner can on the one hand be seen as a classic entertainment genre. On the other hand, as Jeffrey Shandler insightfully observes, the preparation of the program required a lot of effort from both the scriptwriters and Hanna's relatives.[6] Retelling Hanna's wartime fate, searching for witnesses, documents, and places, can all be understood as active memory work, set in motion in order to produce the TV show. *This Is Your Life!* is important too, because it established the discursive frame for Holocaust memory in this early stage. The genre-characteristic features of the TV show set a pattern for narrating the Holocaust.

In this context it should be noted that Hanna was not yet presented as a "Holocaust survivor" according to the notion that term would later acquire. Ralph Edwards introduced her as having lived through "Hitler's cruel purge of German Jews." Decades would pass before the idea of the Holocaust assumed the status of a recognizable symbol in American culture. Only with the passage of time would European Jews be perceived as a group that had suffered enormously during World War Two. By focusing on one individual and reconstructing Hanna's story from childhood through the war, then to the early postwar years, the program does nevertheless draw the portrait of a victim. There is an attempt to convey the character's wartime trauma, albeit framed within a happy-ending story; the narrative leads the audience to the liberation of the concentration camp and Hanna's subsequent arrival in the United States. The story is also propelled by Hanna's love story, thereby satisfying the audience desire for harmony and closure. A smug American postwar triumphalism combined here with a classic narrative.

But mere facts incorporated into a narrative are not sufficient on their own to create the image of a victim as outlined in the show. The program writers insisted that Hanna relate intimate details of her wartime experience. The script punctuated certain moments of Hanna's story in expectation of her emotional response. "You were practically passing through your own hometown, weren't you Hanna?" observes Ralph Edwards, the host of the show, while recalling Hanna's transportation to the camp Theresienstadt. On another occasion, he reveals facts about her physical condition, "You were down to 73 pounds. Ill with a fever of 103 degree." It was a moment at which this medium anticipated, in one glimpse, the power of

---

6   Ibid., 34.

reality TV. *This Is Your Life!* was not alone in focusing on private stories. Other American TV shows invited their viewers to discover voyeurism.[7] The subjective, intimate experience, which only witnesses are capable of relating would, in later years, become the crucially substantive feature of cultural narratives of 20th century history. *This Is Your Life!* stood in stark contrast to the dominant treatment of Nazi crimes presented in newsreels of the day. *This Is Your Life!* invited viewers to look beyond anonymous pictures and statistics, and glance through the lens of a single person who experienced the persecution. A similar approach would be adopted later and vigorously developed by the historians of everyday life and by researchers collecting oral histories.

At the end of the half hour that featured Hanna Kohner, the episode is dedicated to all former prisoners of the Nazi camps. An account number was provided where viewers could make donations for the survivors. Ralph Edwards' TV show thus pioneered in celebrating the memory of Nazi victims, with Hanna Kohner as their emblematic representative.[8] At the popular level, for the American mass audience, she preceded Anne Frank, Elie Wiesel, or Primo Levi in that regard.

The Holocaust as a Media Discourse

Hanna's 1953 TV appearance was recalled on April, 3rd, 2011 by the popular radio broadcast, *This American Life.*[9] In an episode titled "Oh, You Shouldn't Have," the journalist Alison Silverman went back to the Ralph Edwards program and picked up the story of Hanna Kohner. Silverman criticized the show for not informing Hanna in advance about being cast in the show, and for the crass, even trivial (by today's standards) manner in which her story was presented, embedded in postwar American optimism. "If I was surprising someone and sharing the murder of her parents and husband on national television I would do it differently," reports Silverman. "I wouldn't do it." A moment later she comments in a similarly critical and rhetorical way, "Less than a month before the execution of the Rosenbergs, calling a Jewish emigrant from Czechoslovakia, a communist country, a patriot is one of the best presents she can get." Silverman's commentary is another voice in the media's discourse on the Holocaust. As such it exemplifies certain characteristics of the current state of that discourse: its self-reflexivity and its inner diversity. The *This American Life* broadcast indicates a media self-aware of the problem of

---

7   Ibid., 38.
8   Ibid., 40.
9   http://www.thisamericanlife.org/ (accessed 24 January 2017).

representation, and conscious of the political complications of commemorative processes—both topics of considerable debate over the last few decades.

An historical distance of more than half a century provides a perspective from which to better see the question of Holocaust representation. Today we are beyond the postwar conceptualization of the Holocaust as an event impossible to represent in any traditional genre or narrative. We are past the postwar pessimism of Theodor Adorno, and have gone through the dissections of Claude Lanzmann's documentary *Shoah*, and the debates about the TV-series *Holocaust*. Today we are in the midst of a dialogue on the concept of a global culture of Holocaust memory. The role of mass media in shaping public memories has been approached by scholars of Holocaust representations in two contrasting ways: The first, found in the works of Susan Sontag or Geoffrey Hartmanfor example, maintains that media create passive observers, desensitizing viewers to the violence they witness.[10] As well, this school of thought holds that media trivialize the Holocaust by creating the sense of a safe distance from it, or by putting it into genre frames inappropriate for such serious and difficult content. The second approach emphasizes the positive role the mass media plays in shaping cultural memory. Media democratize memory, according to this argument, by opening up the possibility that various groups will identify with a history that is not their own. Media can therefore create broader communities of remembrance, or communities of moral awareness. This second approach can be found in various works of post-memory, for example in Alison Landsberg theory of a prosthetic memory or in the idea of a globalized memory as understood by Natan Sznaider and Daniel Levy.[11] The latter have proclaimed the emergence of an ethical community of Holocaust remembrance on a global scale, for which mass media representations have prepared the ground. Here the role of mass culture is seen as taking away Holocaust memory from exclusive elite circles claiming the right to legitimize the ways one may or may

---

10 Susan Sontag, *Illness as Metaphor* (New York: Farrar, Straus & Giroux, 1978); Susan Sontag, *Regarding the Pain of Others* (New York: Farrar, Straus, Giroux, 2003); Geoffrey H. Hartman, *Scars of the Spirit: The Struggle Against Inauthenticity* (Basingstoke, UK: Palgrave MacMillan, 2002).

11 Alison Landsberg, *Prosthetic Memory: The Transformation of American Remembrance in the Age of Mass Culture* (New York: Columbia University Press, 2004); Daniel Levy and Natan Sznaider, "Memory Unbound: The Holocaust and the Formation of Cosmopolitan Memory," *European Journal of Social Theory* 5:1 (2002): 87–106; Daniel Levy and Natan Sznaider, *The Holocaust and Memory in the Global Age* (Philadelphia, PA: Temple University Press, 2006).

not represent and commemorate the Holocaust.[12] Similarly, Landsberg claims that popular culture allows for the potential development of progressive political thought and civic responsibility.

In both paradigms, representation—the difference between the reality of historical experience and its cultural images—remains the dominant approach. In an attempt to overcome this modernist contradiction between the truth of history and its representation, historian and filmmaker Robert Rosenstone researches historical cinema as an autonomous discourse, and as an alternative to the work of historians.[13] He does not only question how to accurately put history on the screen. Instead, Rosenstone introduces the question: what other images of the past are being created by the audiovisual media? In general, however, historical experience especially of the Holocaust, has been treated in the literature on the subject, as something substantially different from its cultural representations. Both critical approaches to the mass media, as well as those finding other reasons to value the media's role in shaping public memories, posit an essential difference between the truth of history or biography on the one hand, and culturally constructed meanings of the past on the other.

A similar understanding also characterizes general narratives about how the memory of the Holocaust developed in the postwar period. Here, public memories and official commemorations are often juxtaposed to the truth of private memories. This kind of rhetoric is present in theses on postwar silence in Europe, the United States, or Israel, according to which the survivors' memories were not represented, and were only publicly discovered at the end of the 1960s.[14] Such a narrative still dominates, although more and more attention has been paid recently to the variety and complexity of postwar commemorative practices, thereby modifying the theory of a postwar silence.[15]

---

12 Levy and Sznaider, *Holocaust and Memory*, 157.
13 Robert A. Rosenstone, *Mirror in the Shrine: American Encounters in Meiji Japan* (Cambridge, MA: Harvard University Press, 1988); Robert A. Rosenstone, ed., *Revisioning History: Filmmakers and the Construction of the Past* (Princeton, NJ: Princeton University, 1995).
14 Peter Novick, *The Holocaust in American Life* (Boston, MA: Houghton Mifflin, 1999); Bernhard Giesen, *Triumph and Trauma* (Boulder: Paradigm, 2004); Tony Judt, *Postwar: A History of Europe after 1945* (London: Penguin, 2006); Aleida Assmann, *Der lange Schatten der Vergangenheit. Erinnerungskultur und Geschichtspolitik* (München: C.H. Beck, 2006).
15 For example, Hasia R. Diner,, *We Remember with Reverence and Love: American Jews and the Myth of Silence after the Holocaust, 1945–62* (New York: New York University Press, 2010).

Biography, Culture, and Post-memory

Jan Assmann's classic notion of memory distinguishes two aspects of socially framed remembrances: communicative memory and cultural memory.[16] The two differ according to the communities from which they emerge, the medium used in communication, and the distance in time to the historical event that is remembered. Communicative memory belongs to the generation that has personally experienced the past. It is transmitted orally above all, and usually within the narrow circle of family or friends. It usually lasts no longer than three or four generations. With the passing of time, as historical witnesses age and disappear from the scene, a need for the institutionalization of the oral memories arises, developing into cultural objects and commonly accessible forms of memory such as books, archives, and commemorative rites. In this way recorded history becomes the content of what Assmann calls "cultural memory." Assmann's understanding of the processes involved in memory creation suggests a certain threshold between private and cultural forms of memory, where cultural memory is the process of storing and archiving something that is already shaped and ready—the communicative memories.

The various concepts of post-memory, prosthetic memory, or cultural trauma, formulated by other memory scholars, nonetheless negate the tight ontological relation between experience and memory, suggesting that it is possible to remember events not personally experienced, and to appropriate others' stories.[17] The concept of post-memory by Marianne Hirsch comprehensively discusses this fluid border between memory and cultural representation.[18] According to Hirsch, generations born after the Holocaust are capable of bonding with the past in a manner resembling the traumatic, genuine memories of their parents—the actual survivors. What differentiates the post-memory of the children from that

---

16 Jan Assmann, *Moses the Egyptian: The Memory of Egypt in Western Monotheism* (Cambridge, MA: Harvard University Press, 1997).

17 Celia Lury, *Prosthetic Culture: Photography, Memory, Identity* (London: Routledge, 1998); Van Alphen, Ernst, "Second-Generation Testimony, the Transmission of Trauma, and Postmemory," *Poetics Today* 27 (2006): 473–488.

18 Marianne Hirsch, *Family Frames: Photography, Narrative, and Postmemory* (Cambridge, MA: Harvard University Press, 1997); Marianne Hirsch, "Surviving Images Holocaust Photographs and the Work of Postmemory," in Barbie Zelizer, ed., *Visual Culture and the Holocaust* (New Brunswick, NJ: Rutgers UP 2001), 215–246; Marianne Hirsch, "The Generation of Postmemory," *Poetics Today* 29 (2008): 103–128; Alison Landsberg, *Prosthetic Memory: The Transformation of American Remembrance in the Age of Mass Culture* (New York: Columbia University Press, 2004).

of their parents is that they borrow narrative tools from other sources. Searching for comprehension, meanings, and continuity, the second generation reaches for available cultural images and narratives—to fill the gaps in the (non)memories transmitted to them by their parents. Post-memory is thus a kind of relation with the past in which the subject of memory is not constituted by recall of the past, but is evoked through an investment of imagination and creativity on the part of the remembering person. It is precisely the narrative quality, as noted by Mieke Bal that becomes the added value.[19] The transformation of trauma into memory, a cultural artifact in itself, necessitates entering into social relationships. Hirsch describes a characteristic relationship with the past among children of the survivors, and there is a broader perspective here too, which draws attention to the porosity of the frontier between remembering and imagining the past. These activities cannot be seen as separate, and for both societies and individuals, remembering and imagining are what makes space for the past in the present.

Post-memory of a Survivor

In light of Marianne Hirsch's work one could also ask about the relation between individual and cultural memory for survivors themselves. Do they too, in the course of their lives, develop forms of memory of their own experience that are structurally similar to the work of post-memory? In a paper devoted to the problems of "recovered memory," Marita Sturken points to an important aspect of the relationship between traumatic experience and narration.[20] She writes that it is in the process of cultural communication—the act of "confession" of a recovered memory, where one constructs the content of the memory. The postwar story of Hanna Kohner invites us to consider this aspect of memory work. The *This Is Your Life!* episode from 1953 was an early example of the relation between private memory and media culture, but perhaps more significantly, the episode went on to become a formative event in the postwar biography of Hanna.

This Is Your Life! positioned Hanna's story in narrative and stylistic frames typical of its genre. It proposed a narrative formula focused on intimate experiences of the character and drew her as an emblematic victim. The role of a victim, however, was not something the person, Hanna, easily identified with, which was

---

19 Mieke Bal, Jonathan Crewe, and Leo Spitzer, eds., *Acts of Memory: Cultural Recall in the Present* (Hanover, NH: University Press of New England, 1999).

20 Marita Sturken, "The Image as Memorial: Personal Photographs in Cultural Memory," in Marianne Hirsch, ed., *The Familial Gaze* (Hanover, NH: University Press of New England, 1999).

evident from her reactions and behavior during the show. The gender and social identity of Hanna, a young immigrant from Eastern Europe with aspirations to the American upper middle class, seemed to overtake the role of victim into which the show's producers had cast her. While Hanna did not, in that moment, adopt the convention of telling a moving and dramatic story as its heroine, some three decades later she did just that. In 1984 she selected a popular, literary genre, and together with her husband published a memoir titled *Hanna and Walter: A Love Story*.[21] This time the interpretive context for the story of the Kohners was a new rhetoric shaping American culture in the 1980s, a context which accorded special status to the victims of historical oppression, idealizing them and bestowing full dignity and unquestioned moral authority on them.

As an author, Hanna developed threads similar to those presented on *This Is Your Life!* thirty years before. The threads were woven in a more polished language, and she lingered on details that had not been graphically described in the TV broadcast. The rampant disease in the camps, the hunger, the feelings of humiliation and fear that she suffered during the 1940s assumed an explicit part in her recorded narrative memory. On TV she described her look at Auschwitz as "impossible." In the memoir she speaks of her appearance with literary eloquence. "…in Auschwitz one never could tell a person's age. There were girls in their twenties who looked like wilted old women.… I stood there, almost nude, with no hair on my skull, and started to cry."[22] As a writer Hanna also disrupts the narrative imposed by the show, where her case was closed and she enjoyed a happy-ending: "The nightmare that lasted seven years," Ralph Edwards reported, "is at an end as the American army truck roll to a stop before the prison gates." Hanna replaced this idea with a description of the trauma she and her friend experienced in post-liberation life and what that meant to the whole camp experience. "On one of the first afternoons in Brussels, Eva and I decided to go to a movie. We picked *Les Enfants du Paradis*. It was beautiful. But halfway through the film we got fidgety, crouching miserably in our seats. In the darkness we looked at each other. We nodded and left the ornate old movie theater feeling lost and out of touch with the world."[23]

Upon publishing her memoir in the 1980s Hanna adopted a narrative style that allowed her to fully identify herself as a victim, a role she had not been ready to adopt in 1953. But it was the TV show that had established her public identity and

---

21 Hanna Kohner, Walter Kohner, and Frederick Kohner, eds., *Hanna and Walter: A Love Story* (New York: Grand Central, 1984).

22 Ibid, 157.

23 Ibid., 189.

paved the way for her to be known by popular audiences in the United States. The show thus stands at a dynamic moment in the formation of Hanna's fundamental narrative as a heroine. Her appearance on the program was specifically cited in the epilogue to the book as an important biographical event. Years later, Hanna's daughter Julie Kohner, a Holocaust educator, would harken back to her mother's past and retell the story through media. Julie launched "Voices of the Generations," a non-profit organization as well as an educational program inspired by the *This Is Your Life!* episode and the subsequent written biography.[24] Julie's assessment of the episode from 1953 remained positive overall: "It was a groundbreaking effort to tell a very difficult story to the American people who were used to television as pure entertainment. It was a bold move and one that needed to be done, and I believe Ralph Edwards did it as appropriately as anyone could for the time and place we were in history. It was eight years after the war, people were not talking about the Holocaust in their homes, let alone on national television. People criticized him for his glossy overtones but as the daughter of a survivor and one who makes her life mission at keeping her mother's memory alive I can only say I am glad he chose to take this bold step and put the first survivor on television, and that it happened to be my mother."[25]

The blurred distinction between biographical and cultural memory, as posed by Marianne Hirsch and others, invites us to consider media and culture not only as archives or transmitters of meanings passed on to us by the witnesses to historical events. Media and culture according to Hirsch, are also the space within which meanings and frameworks are created, and from whence individual and social-memory work draws inspiration. Julie Kohner recalled the role the episode played in the Kohners family life: "We watched the episode on Passovers with our entire family at our home. It was always a way of looking back at the past and what happened to our family."[26]

Looking back at the 1953 *This Is Your Life!* episode with Hanna Kohner, a Holocaust survivor and star of the program, highlights the fluidity of the boundaries between media representational framework, working memory, and biographical experience. Using the premises of voyeuristic-sensational mass entertainment, the show's host, Ralph Edwards also took time to celebrate the memory of all victims of Nazi concentration camps. The program shows the dynamic interaction between individual biography and its public airing. As of 1953, Hanna Kohner

---

24 http://VOGCharity.org (accessed 24 January 2017).
25 Interview with Julie Kohner via e-mail, September – November 2011.
26 Ibid.

was not simply a subject of a survival narrative. She partly resisted the story developed about her during the program, and demurred at being positioned solely in the role of victim. Nevertheless, years later she would refer to her appearance in the show and use the accessible narrative style of the 1980s, which had not been available to her three decades earlier. Her published autobiographical narrative ultimately appeared after three decades as a culture artifact in an altered memory environment. Her own earlier TV appearance had played a role in setting those changes in motion.

Could this example only have happened in America? Did it set the tone for other mass-media productions of the holocaust experience in other parts of the world? These are questions of interest not only to Holocaust studies, but also to the ongoing efforts to research and debate memory and representation.

Acknowledgments

This book grew out of an international conference organized by the Netherlands American Studies Associations, the Belgium and Luxembourg American Studies Association, the Institute of Jewish Studies at the University of Antwerp, Belgium, the Roosevelt Study Center in Middelburg, the Netherlands, and the Netherlands Institute for War Documentation and Holocaust and Genocide Studies. The editors are grateful for the harmonious cooperation with Vivian Liska and Gert Buelens, the valuable feedback by the reviewer of Peter Lang Publishing, the indispensable editorial work of Ms. Michael Strange, and the indexing skills of Jasper Collette.

The editors

Notes on Contributors

Jeffrey Demsky is a historian of politics and culture. He is currently an Assistant Professor of History at San Bernardino Valley College. Recent publications include: "A Duty to Remember, A Duty to Forget: Examining Americans' Unequal Memories of the War on Armenians and War on Jews" in *War Memories: Commemoration, Recollections, and Writings on War* (McGill-Queens University Press, 2017); "Not Buying It: Reconsidering American Consumer Opposition to Nazi Anti-Semitism," in *Shopping for Change: Consumer Activism and the Possibilities of Purchasing Power* (Cornell University Press, 2017); "Searching for the Humor in Dehumanization: American Sitcoms, the Internet, and the Globalization of Holocaust Parodies," in *Analyzing Humor in Online Discourse* (IGI Global Press, 2016).

Hasia Diner is the Paul S. and Sylvia Steinberg Professor of American Jewish History; Professor of Hebrew and Judaic Studies, History; and Director of the Goldstein-Goren Center for American Jewish History at New York University. She received her Ph.D., 1976, University of Illinois at Chicago. She work is located at the intersection of American and Jewish history. She is currently completing a book on global Jewish migrations and the history of Jewish peddling. Her recent work includes: *We Remember with Reverence and Love: American Jews and the Myth of Silence after the Holocaust, 1945–1962* (New York University Press, 2009); *From Arrival to Incorporation: Migrants to the U.S. in a Global Age*, with Elliott Barkan and Alan Kraut (New York University Press, 2007); *The Jews of the United States, 1654 to 2000* (University of California Press, 2004).

Laura Hobson Faure is an Associate Professor of American Studies at the Sorbonne Nouvelle University in Paris. Her research focuses on French and American Jewish life, during and after the Holocaust. In addition to scholarly articles, her publications include (with Katy Hazan, Catherine Nicault and Mathias Gardet) *L'Œuvre de Secours aux Enfants et les populations juives au XXᵉ siècle, Prévenir et guérir dans un siècle de violences* (Paris: Éditions Armand Colin, 2014); *Un "Plan Marshall juif": la présence juive américaine en France après la Shoah, 1944–1954* (Éditions Armand Colin, 2013) and "Le travail social en milieu juif après la Seconde Guerre mondiale," *Archives juives. Revue d'histoire des Juifs de France* 45/1 (March 2012).

David Frey is an Associate Professor of History and the Director of the Center for Holocaust and Genocide Studies at the United States Military Academy at West Point, USA. He has spearheaded efforts to increase the Academy's and US

Armed Forces' awareness and understanding of the phenomenon of genocide, its history, and means of prevention. With the support of Fulbright-Hays, DAAD, Mellon Foundation, Harriman Foundation, and ACLS fellowships, he earned his Ph.D. in Central European History at Columbia University in 2003. I.B. Tauris will publish his book *Jews, Nazis, and the Cinema of Hungary: The Tragedy of Success, 1929–44,* in early 2017. His current research involves human rights, espionage, deportations, show trials and the rhetoric and memory of the Holocaust using newly declassified records of the State Department's post-World War Two Treaty Violations [TREVI] Program, a previously classified spy ring known as "the Pond," and Hungarian National and State Security Archives.

Hans Krabbendam was Assistant Director of the Roosevelt Study Center in Middelburg, the Netherlands, until January 2017, when he became Director of the Catholic Documentation Center in Nijmegen. He published *Freedom on the Horizon: Dutch Immigrants in America, 1840–1920* (Eerdmans, 2009) and edited twenty volumes on European (Dutch)-American relations, among them, with Michael Boyden and Liselotte Vandenbussche, *Tales of Transit: Narrative Migrant Spaces in Atlantic Perspective, 1850–1950* (Amsterdam University Press, 2013). He recently wrote about the reception of Etty Hillesum's work in the United States. He is working on a monograph *From Confrontation to Cooperation: American Protestants in Western Europe, 1940–1980.*

Jan Láníček studied at the Palacký University, Czech Republic (2006, History) and the University of Southampton (2007, Jewish History and Culture). He received his Ph.D. from the University of Southampton in Britain and in 2011–12 had a postdoctoral fellowship at the Center for Jewish History in New York. He currently works as a Lecturer in Jewish History at the University of New South Wales in Sydney, Australia. He published *Czechs, Slovaks and the Jews, 1938–1948: Beyond Idealisation and Condemnation* (Palgrave, 2013), and also co-edited a volume on *Governments-in-Exile and the Jews during the Second World War* (Vallentine Mitchell, 2013). His most recent book, *Arnošt Frischer and the Jewish Politics of Early 20th-Century Europe,* was published by Bloomsbury Academic in November 2016.

Małgorzata Pakier is Head of the Research and Publications Department at the Museum of the History of Polish Jews. She is a member of the Social Memory Laboratory at the Institute of Sociology, University of Warsaw. She received her PhD degree from the European University Institute, Florence, History and Civilization Department. Her thesis 'The Construction of European Holocaust Memory: German and Polish Cinema after 1989' was published with Peter Lang in 2013. In 2010, she was a Research Fellow at the Center for Advanced Holocaust Studies at the US Holocaust Memorial Museum, Washington, DC. Together with Bo Stråth she co-edited the volume *A European Memory? Contested Histories and Politics of Remembrance* (New York: Berghahn Books, 2012). Her other publications include articles in English and Polish on Holocaust memory, film and mass media, Europeanization of memory, and memory studies in Eastern Europe.

Emiliano Perra is Senior Lecturer in Modern European History at the University of Winchester. His research interests are in the area of Holocaust and genocide memory and representation, with a primary focus on Italy and on visual culture. He is author of *Conflicts of Memory: The Reception of Holocaust Films and Television Programmes in Italy: 1945 to the Present* (Peter Lang, 2010). He has published articles in, among others, *Holocaust and Genocide Studies*, *Memory Studies*, *The Italianist*, and *Cinema e Storia*, as well as in a number of edited volumes. He is currently working on a monograph on genocide representation.

Derek Rubin taught in the English Department and the American Studies program at Utrecht University until his retirement in 2016 and lectured widely on Jewish American writing both in the Netherlands and in the United States. He has published articles about Saul Bellow, Philip Roth, Paul Auster, and the younger generation of Jewish American fiction writers. He was coeditor of American Studies, a series published by Amsterdam University Press, and of the essay collections *Religion in America: European and American Perspectives* (VU University Press, 2004) and *American Multiculturalism after 9/11: Transatlantic Perspectives* (Amsterdam University Press, 2009). Rubin is editor of the anthology *Who We Are: On Being (and Not Being) a Jewish American Writer* (Schocken Books/Random House, 2005), which won the National Jewish Book Award, and of *Promised Lands: New Jewish American Fiction on Longing and Belonging* (Brandeis University Press, 2010), which was a finalist for the National Jewish Book Award.

Dana Rufolo is the editor-in-chief of the theatre magazine *Plays International & Europe*. She is the founding director of the Theater Research Institute of Europe which has engaged in—among other activities—street performances for Amnesty International and peace and conflict resolution drama workshops. She has a doctorate in Theater Studies from the University of Wisconsin-Madison and a diploma from Luxembourg University in association with the University of Paris V in art therapy, specializing in drama therapy. Her publications include: "Collective Playwriting in the Language Classroom" in *Imagination* (New Jersey City University, 2011); "Psychodrama Strategies that Protect Tennessee Williams' Late-play Characters from a Violent World" in *Essays On Violence in American*

Drama (McFarland Publishing House, 2011); "Correspondence between the inner and outer voice by means of intercepting objects in Arthur Miller's Death of a Salesman and Sam Shepard's Fool for Love," in *Journal de la littérature générale et comparée* (Luxembourg, 2011).

Zohar Segev is professor of Jewish History at the University of Haifa, Israel. His research areas are American Zionism and American Modern Jewish History. Currently he is Head of The Department of Jewish History at the University of Haifa, Israel. He co-edited with Danny Ben Moshe, *Israel in Diaspora Jewish Identity* (Sussex Academic Press, 2007) and published *From Ethnic Politicians to National Leaders, American Zionist Leadership, the Holocaust and the Establishment of Israel*(Ben Gurion University Press, 2007) and *The World Jewish Congress during the Holocaust: Between Activism and Restraint* (De Gruyter Oldenbourgh, 2014).

Viktoria Sukovata defended her Ph.D. thesis in Theory of Culture in 1997 and her Habilitation dissertation in 2009 at Karazin Kharkiv National University in Ukraine. She is professor in the Theory of Culture and Philosophy of Science Department, in Karazin Kharkiv National University, Ukraine. Her publications include *Face of Other* (Kharkiv National Karazin University Publishing House 2008) and more than 120 articles in the domain of Holocaust Studies and Jewish Studies, Cinema and Soviet Identity Studies in Ukrainian, Russian, Byelorussian, Polish, Serbian, Romanian, and American journals. Recent ones include "The Holocaust in South-Eastern Europe: The Case of the Ukrainian Kharkiv Region," *Holocaust: Studies and Cercetari* 7 (2015) 137–156 and "Teaching Holocaust and Genocide Studies in Modern Ukraine: Problems and Perspectives," in *The Holocaust in Ukraine: New Sources and Perspectives* (United States Holocaust Memorial Museum, 2013), 199–211.

Index

INTERAMERICANA

Inter-American Literary History and Culture
Historia literaria interamericana y sus contextos culturales
Histoire littéraire et culture interaméricaines

The new series continues, in substance, series C, "Inter-American Literary Studies" published by Wallstein-Verlag for the Göttingen Center for Advanced Studies in the Internationality of National Literatures (1997-2001).

Publications in the former series:

Frank, Armin Paul, & Helga Eßmann, eds. *The Internationality of National Literatures in Either America: Transfer and Transformation 1. Cases and Problems* (1999 – vol. 1:1).
Frank, Armin Paul, & Kurt Mueller-Vollmer. *The Internationality of National Literatures in Either America: Transfer and Transformation 2. British America and the United States, 1770s–1850s* (2000 – vol. 1:2).
Glasenapp, Jörn. *'Prodigies, anomalies, monsters': Charles Brockden Brown und die Grenzen der Erkenntnis* (2000 – vol. 2).

Publications at Peter Lang GmbH:

Vol.   1   *Do the Americas Have a Common Literary History?* Edited by Barbara Buchenau and Annette Paatz, in cooperation with Rolf Lohse and Marietta Messmer. With an Introduction by Armin Paul Frank. 2002.

Vol.   2   Barbara Buchenau: *Der frühe amerikanische historische Roman im transatlantischen Vergleich.* 2002.

Vol.   3   *Internationality in American Fiction. Henry James. William Dean Howells. William Faulkner. Toni Morrison.* Edited by Armin Paul Frank and Rolf Lohse. 2005.

Vol.   4   Rolf Lohse: *Postkoloniale Traditionsbildung. Der frankokanadische Roman zwischen Autonomie und Bezugnahme auf die Literatur Frankreichs und der USA.* 2005.

Vol.   5   Armin Paul Frank / Christel-Maria Maas: *Transnational Longfellow. A Project of American National Poetry.* 2005

Vol.   6   Kurt Mueller-Vollmer: *Transatlantic Crossings and Transformations. German-American Cultural Transfer from the 18th to the End of the 19th Century.* 2015.

Vol.   7   Marietta Messmer / Armin Paul Frank (eds.): *The International Turn in American Studies.* 2015.

Vol.   8   Gabriele Pisarz-Ramirez / Markus Heide (eds.): *Hemispheric Encounters. The Early United States in a Transnational Perspective.* 2016.

Vol.   9   Jeanette den Toonder / Kim van Dam / Fjære van der Stok (eds.): *Native America. Indigenous Self-Representation in Canada, the U.S. and Mexico.* 2016.

Vol.   10   Elena Furlanetto: *Towards Turkish American Literature. Narratives of Multiculturalism in Post-Imperial Turkey.* 2017.

Vol.   11   Earl E. Fitz: *Inter-American Literary History. Six Critical Periods.* 2017.

Vol.   12   Hans Krabbendam / Derek Rubin (eds.): *American Responses to the Holocaust. Transatlantic Perspectives.* 2017.

www.peterlang.com